THE AIRLINES OF THE UNITED STATES
★ ★ ★

ALASKA AIRLINES, INC.

ALL AMERICAN AVIATION, INC.

AMERICAN AIRLINES, INC.

AMERICAN EXPORT AIRLINES, INC.

BRANIFF AIRWAYS, INC.

CHICAGO AND SOUTHERN AIR LINES, INC.

COLONIAL AIRLINES, INC.

CONTINENTAL AIR LINES, INC.

DELTA AIR LINES

EASTERN AIR LINES, INC.

INLAND AIR LINES, INC.

MID-CONTINENT AIRLINES, INC.

NATIONAL AIRLINES, INC.

NORTHEAST AIRLINES, INC.

NORTHWEST AIRLINES, INC.

PAN AMERICAN AIRWAYS SYSTEM

PAN AMERICAN-GRACE AIRWAYS, INC.

PENNSYLVANIA-CENTRAL AIRLINES CORP.

TRANSCONTINENTAL & WESTERN AIR, INC.

UNITED AIR LINES, INC.

WESTERN AIR LINES, INC.

Modern Art

Monet

Alchemy & Mysticism

Braun/Hogenberg.
Cities of the World

Bourgery. Atlas of
Anatomy & Surgery

D'Hancarville.
Antiquities

Encyclopaedia
Anatomica

Martius.
The Book of Palms

Seba. Cabinet of
Natural Curiosities

The World
of Ornament

Fashion. A History from
18th–20th Century

100 Contemporary
Fashion Designers

Architectural Theory

The Grand Tour

20th Century
Classic Cars

1000 Record Covers

1000 Tattoos

Funk & Soul Covers

Jazz Covers

Mid-Century Ads

Mailer/Stern.
Marilyn Monroe

Erotica Universalis

Tom of Finland.
Complete Kake Comics

1000 Nudes

Stanton.
Dominant Wives

JIM HEIMANN · ALLISON SILVER

20TH CENTURY travel

TASCHEN

Bibliotheca Universalis

"WHEN ONCE YOU HAVE TASTED
FLIGHT, YOU WILL FOREVER
WALK THE EARTH WITH YOUR EYES
TURNED SKYWARD, FOR THERE YOU
HAVE BEEN, AND THERE YOU WILL
ALWAYS LONG TO RETURN."
– LEONARDO DA VINCI

INTROD

«CELUI QUI A VOLÉ
MARCHERA TOUJOURS
SUR LA TERRE AVEC LE
REGARD TOURNÉ VERS
LE CIEL, CAR IL Y A
GOÛTÉ ET VOUDRA TOU-
JOURS Y RETOURNER.»
– LEONARDO DA VINCI

„WER EINMAL DAS FLIEGEN GEKOSTET,
WIRD FÜR IMMER GEN HIMMEL -BLICKEND
AUF ERDEN -WANDELN, DENN DORT
KOMMEN WIR HER, UND DORTHIN
ZURÜCKZUKEHREN WERDEN WIR IMMER
ERSEHNEN."
– LEONARDO DA VINCI

UCTION

THE REPUBLIC OF TRAVEL

American impatience altered the travel metabolism: Faster, better, cheaper were the watchwords throughout the century.

WELL INTO THE 1950S, THE DUKE AND DUCHESS OF WINDSOR, WHITE-HOT STYLE SETTERS, WOULD CROSS THE ATLANTIC BY OCEAN LINER. They always booked the sought-after Duck Suite, three sumptuous upper-deck cabins with a gilded mural of mallards, on their favored liner, the SS *United States*. The Windsors' favorite had been the SS *Queen Mary*, but they jumped ship after the *United States* won the Blue Riband, for the fastest Atlantic crossing, on her maiden voyage, July 11, 1952. That record-breaking journey, still the fastest, took three days, 12 hours, and 12 minutes—ten hours faster than the *Queen Mary*. The Windsors had a staggering array of luggage: 118 trunks made to order from T. Anthony on Park Avenue in New York; numerous pieces from Hermes and La Maison Goyard of Paris. Myriad steamer trunks, shoe trunks, hatboxes, fitted toiletries cases, jewelry cases, document cases, even cocktail cases were par for the course on such a crossing.

The Windsors may have been style arbiters, but their travels were more mid-19th century than mid 20th—a remembrance of the grand ocean liners' potent allure in the heady age of air travel. By the late 1950s, the Jet Set was already at full throttle, taking off to Frank Sinatra's 1957 standard "Come Fly With Me." ("Just say the words, and we'll beat the birds down to Acapulco Bay.") Frank Loesser's 1960 Broadway hit *Guys and Dolls* tells of a big-time New York gambler who thinks nothing of taking a woman to dinner at his favorite restaurant—in Havana. By 1960, air travel was the very essence of glamour, epitomized in the Elizabeth Taylor—Richard Burton movie *The V.I.P.s* (1963), set in the first class lounge of the London Airport.

Prior to the 20th century, leisure travel had been the prerogative of the wealthy, the sort of people who used seasons of the year as verbs. They "summered" in a cottage in Newport, Rhode Island; "wintered" in a villa in the south of France. Only they could afford the complicated logistics of moving the mountains of luggage and armies of domestics required for lengthy stays. In the first half of the century, the very rich, as well as the celebrated, still blazed the trail. But the growing power of the middle class in postwar America changed everything. Once the rich and famous had validated a location as "the place to be," the increasing, and increasingly well-to-do, American middle class was close behind, via ever-expanding means of transportation.

The United States, after all, is a nation fueled by wanderlust. This is at the core of what it means to be an American. The country was built by people who crossed oceans to get there—then crossed the continent once they landed. You could reinvent yourself in new surroundings. Spurred on by the hope that good things awaited—just beyond the next valley or over the next hill—Americans were ever eager to "light out for the territory," as Mark Twain wrote in *Huckleberry Finn* (1844). When the Census Bureau pronounced the frontier officially "closed" in 1890, all this traveling did not stop. In fact, it increased.

Voyages of the next century, however, shifted the focus to leisure travel. American impatience altered the travel metabolism: Faster, better, cheaper were the watchwords throughout the century— as the advertisements for cruise lines, railways, and airlines can attest. Americans demanded the democratization of travel, and by century's end, they got it.

"SPEED IS THE CRY OF OUR ERA," INDUSTRIAL DESIGNER NORMAN BEL GEDDES DECLARED IN 1932, "AND GREATER SPEED, ONE OF THE GOALS OF TOMORROW." Bel Geddes said this at the height of the Machine Age—but it could well apply to any year of the century. In 1900 stagecoaches were still in use; by the century's end, a weekend trip from New York might as likely be to Prague (Czech Republic) as Quogue (Long Island). Speed mattered. In the Gilded Age finely appointed luxury liners like the RMS *Mauretania* vied to break speed records. Soon, trains developed express "flyer" routes; then, in the 1930s, aerodynamically streamlined locomotives, with names like Zephyr and Mercury, roared down the tracks.

1900

1901

1903

Stagecoaches still in use, not fully replaced by motorbus until World War I

Postkutschen bis zum Ersten Weltkrieg noch nicht vollständig durch „Motorbusse" verdrängt

On voyage encore en diligences ; elles ne seront remplacées par les autocars qu'à partir de la Première Guerre mondiale

Visitors astounded as Pan American Exposition in Buffalo, New York, uses electricity generated by Niagara Falls, 25 miles away

Die Pan American Exposition in Buffalo, New York, verwendet von den 40 km entfernten Niagarafällen generierten Strom

La Pan American Exposition de Buffalo, État de New York, est alimentée en électricité par les Chutes du Niagara situées à 40 km

Hawaii Promotion Commission uses exotic images of hula dancers to lure U.S. tourists

Hawaii Promotion Commission verwendet exotische Bilder von Hulatänzerinnen, um US-Touristen anzulocken

La Hawaii Promotion Commission se sert d'images exotiques de danseuses de hula pour attirer les touristes américains

Decade after decade, once-popular means of transportation were discarded when viewed as too slow. Stately ocean liners — even the glamorous French and Cunard lines — could not compete against the speed of air travel. Luxurious long-distance trains fell by the wayside. Most of the mighty railroads declared bankruptcy by the end of the '60s. Amtrak, a government-owned corporation, was cobbled together out of the wreckage in 1971.

Air travel had been bumpy at the start. Early passengers — often celebrities seeking publicity as well as a faster trip — sought speed above all else. Windy cabins lacked temperature controls and made conversation a challenge. But in 1933, the streamlined Boeing 247 introduced soundproofing, heating, and air conditioning — and cut cross-country flights to less than 20 hours. Two years later, the Douglas DC-3 captured the nation's fancy with its shimmering, svelte aluminum body that ferried 28 passengers coast-to-coast in 15 hours.

Yet the élan of elite planes like the Pan Am Clipper did not matter when jetliners, no matter how jam-packed, halved flight time. By 1973, the supersonic Concorde cut transatlantic flights to 3.5 hours — you got there before you took off.

"A BED AND A BATH FOR A BUCK AND A HALF." WHEN IT OPENED IN 1907, HOTEL BUFFALO IN BUFFALO, NEW YORK, (later the Hotel Statler) was the first major urban hotel to offer a private bathroom with every room. Just three years before, John Jacob Astor IV's St. Regis Hotel boasted a telephone in every room, and central heating and air cooling — luxuries the millionaire hotelier and his social set enjoyed at home were now available to middle-class guests for the first time. Just as the public's impatience with the speed of travel had increased, so had its expectations for ease and comfort.

The first fully air-conditioned hotel, the Flamingo in Las Vegas, opened in 1946. Tropical breezes were one thing, but reliable air conditioning made travel to warm climates all the more enjoyable for leisure travelers. Sun-kissed beaches in Hawaii and Cuba may have called to tourists before, but with modern conveniences like air conditioning, travel boomed. By 1961, tourism revenue in Hawaii brought in more money ($161 million) than the island state's two staples — sugar and pineapples.

1904

1905

1907

Travel photographer and lecturer Burton Holmes coins term "travelogue"

Der Reisefotograf und Präsentator Burton Holmes prägt den Begriff „Travelogue"

Le photographe de voyage et conférencier Burton Holmes forge le terme « travelogue »

Las Vegas, Nevada, founded when Union Pacific Railroad officially connects with Central Pacific line

Gründung von Las Vegas (Nevada), als die Union Pacific Railroad offiziell an die Central Pacific angebunden wird

Fondation de Las Vegas, Nevada, quand la compagnie Pacific Railroad assure officiellement la correspondance avec la ligne Central Pacific

After visiting Hawaii, Jack London writes about surfer George Freeth and introduces sport to mainland

Nach einem Hawaiibesuch schreibt Jack London über den Surfer George Freeth und macht das Festland mit diesem Sport bekannt

Après une visite à Hawaï, Jack London écrit sur le surfeur George Freeth et fait connaître ce sport sur le continent

With these innovations, tourism was finally mass-market. The cost of an airline trip had previously been out of reach for the average American, but the prosperous postwar middle class thought the enjoyment and pleasure of travel should be available for everyone. One turning point was in 1968, when the Boeing 737 first flew. The most ordered and most produced jetliner in history, by the end of the century there were roughly 1,250 airborne at any time, with one landing or departing somewhere in the world every five seconds on average. In the 1970s, the Jet Set was no longer limited to the chic elite. It was anyone with an airplane ticket. From exotic panoramas to ancient walled cities, pristine South Sea beaches to stratified European capitals, Americans were traveling, and traveling far and wide.

BUT FOR AMERICANS, "WIDE" COULD MEAN A TRIP ACROSS THE COUNTRY AS WELL AS A TRIP AROUND THE GLOBE. Within the nation's broad expanses, the rapid acceptance of automobiles was testimony to Americans' lust to get up and go, independently. Car sales zoomed to 26.7 million in 1930, from 4,000 units sold domestically in 1900. American travelers were increasingly masters of their own destinies, going where they wanted, when they wanted.

As one of the country's first automobile dealers, Carl G. Fisher, a travel visionary, grasped Americans' love affair with cars. He saw how California, the Golden State at the end of the continent, beckoned. In 1913, Fisher conceived and developed the Lincoln Highway, the first roadway across the country, from New York to San Francisco. The next year, Fisher developed the north-south Dixie Highway, from Indianapolis to Miami. When the U.S. Congress passed the first public highways law in 1916, Fisher had paved the way — literally.

Washington ultimately constructed ribbons of wide roadways — from the creation of Route 66, the "Main Street of America," in 1926, through President Dwight D. Eisenhower's signing of the Interstate Highways Act, the largest public works project the world had ever seen, in 1956. Forget the pyramids! The initial cost estimate for interstate highways was $25 billion over 12 years; actual cost was $114 billion over 35 years. And as these roads were built, Americans filled them. Road trips may well be the national pastime. Young people took off cross-country, in search of themselves. (Consider Jack Kerouac's *On the Road*.) College students on spring break sought romance in sunny climes.

1908

1912

1914

President Theodore Roosevelt declares Grand Canyon U.S. National Monument; will become national park in 1919

Präsident Theodore Roosevelt erklärt den Grand Canyon zum U.S. National Monument (ab 1919 Nationalpark)

Le Président Theodore Roosevelt déclare le Grand Canyon Monument National Américain; il deviendra un parc national en 1919

RMS *Titanic*, queen of White Star Line, hits iceberg and sinks on maiden voyage; 1,517 passengers killed

Die RMS *Titanic*, das Flaggschiff der White Star Line, kollidiert auf ihrer Jungfernfahrt mit einem Eisberg und sinkt; 1517 Tote

Le *Titanic*, fleuron de la compagnie White Star, heurte un iceberg et sombre pendant sa croisière inaugurale ; bilan : 1517 morts

Eiffel Tower, Paris's top tourist attraction, closes with onset of World War I

Der Eiffelturm, die bedeutendste Sehenswürdigkeit von Paris, wird mit Ausbruch des Ersten Weltkriegs geschlossen

La Tour Eiffel, la plus grande attraction touristique de Paris, ferme ses portes quand éclate la Première Guerre mondiale

(Consider Dolores Hart, George Hamilton, and Yvette Mimieux in *Where the Boys Are*.) Families journeyed to sublime destination hotels with stunning natural views. (Consider *The Shining*. Or, maybe not!) Think how American it is to go your own road — and also how incredibly fun. (Consider any Bob Hope–Bing Crosby *Road* picture — especially *Road to Morocco* or *Road to Utopia*.)

But travelers needed a place to stay on these road trips. As part of this democratization, a certain standardized level of hospitality came to be expected. One answer was motel (a combination of "motor" and "hotel") chains. When driving on a family vacation, checking into a Howard Johnson Motor Lodge or Holiday Inn would ensure clean, inexpensive, standardized rooms anywhere in the country. Holiday Inn started in 1952; there were 1,000 franchises by 1968. From Athens, Georgia, to Anaheim, California, the Howard Johnson's restaurant chain featured the same 28 ice cream flavors on every one of its menus across the nation.

While Howard Johnson's would become a reliable stop on the American roadside, more upscale chains like Hilton and Hyatt hotels provided little islands of America in foreign lands. In fact, the hotelier Conrad Hilton said he wanted to display the values that he believed had made America great. During the height of the Cold War, in the 1950s and '60s, Hilton saw his hotels as envoys for American values — and the U.S. government did too. With help from Washington and foreign governments, Hilton placed his hotels in Cold War capitals — where the West confronted the Soviet Bloc.

This was hotel-building with an ideological agenda. Much like the modernist embassies built during the same era, Hilton Hotels were designed to epitomize America. The structures were open and transparent, inviting to all who wanted to enter. Unlike Europe's older grand hotels, where guests walked into ornate, imposing lobbies, Hiltons featured clean lobby spaces with glass curtain-walls that allowed visitors to look through to the view beyond. "We mean these hotels as a challenge," Hilton explained, "not to the people who have so cordially welcomed us into their midst — but to the way of life preached by the Communist world." Hilton viewed his hotels as the vanguard of democracy — of a piece with the nation's desire to democratize travel.

This democratization process continued well after the Cold War ended. With the enactment of the 1978 Airline Deregulation Act, flights became more affordable — and more frequent. Going to the

1916

1917

1919

Nebraskan Joe Saunders loans out Ford Model T to traveling salesmen, starting first car rental business

Joe Saunders aus Nebraska vermietet das Modell T an Geschäftsreisende; der erste Autoverleih ist geboren

Joe Saunders, habitant du Nebraska, loue des Model T aux voyageurs de commerce, lançant la première entreprise de location de voitures

America enters World War I

Eintritt der USA in den Ersten Weltkrieg

Les États-Unis entrent dans la Première Guerre mondiale

At close of World War I, preparation for Treaty of Versailles completed at Trianon Palace Hotel in Versailles

Abschluss der Vorbereitungen des Friedensvertrags von Versailles im Trianon Palace Hotel in Versailles

À la fin de la Première Guerre mondiale, la préparation du Traité de Versailles est finalisée à l'hôtel Trianon Palace de Versailles airport was no longer such a glamorous experience, but more and more people could afford to taxi down the runway. Americans developed this attitude with hotels as well. In the '80s, Ian Schrager, a former nightclub owner, developed the boutique hotel, an intimate hotel where anyone who checked in could feel exclusive. By the end of the '90s, the W chain and the Standard were opened as bigger, more affordable iterations—budget exclusivity.

Americans transformed the notion of travel in the 20th century. They reinvented the form, just as they had reinvented themselves throughout their history. By the century's end, travel was swifter than those present at its start could ever have dreamed. America's vast postwar middle class was peripatetic and unstoppable.

CONSIDER THE DEVELOPMENT OF THE SOUTH OF FRANCE, WHICH MORPHED RADICALLY OVER THE CENTURY—FROM AN EXCLUSIVE WINTER ENCLAVE TO A WIDELY POPULAR SUMMER PLEASURE DOME. In the early 1900s, winters were *the* season. Russian aristocrats would stop at the grand hotels for weeks at a time. The weather might be wet and somewhat chilly, but it was balmy compared to winter in St. Petersburg.

Enter the Jazz Age and a constellation of wealthy Americans who would forever alter the landscape: First, Cole Porter, a rich American songwriter with sophisticated European friends, decided to spend summer at Antibes in 1922. He rented a villa near the Hôtel du Cap, a landmark that closed every summer. Porter invited his close friend, Gerald Murphy, scion of the Mark Cross luggage company, and his family. By the next summer, the Murphys (the basis for Dick and Nicole Diver in F. Scott Fitzgerald's *Tender Is the Night*) convinced the Hôtel du Cap to stay open. They checked in—along with their friend Pablo Picasso and his entire family. Gertrude Stein and Alice B. Toklas stopped by. Summer in the south of France hit the social radar.

This was when suntans became fashionable, and outdoor sports like sailing, tennis, golf, and swimming beckoned women as well as men. Meanwhile, starting in 1922, getting to the south of

1920

1922

1926

Automobile travel miles overtake railroad travel miles in United States

In den USA werden mit dem Auto erstmals mehr Kilometer zurückgelegt als per Bahn

Aux États-Unis, le nombre de kilomètres parcourus en voiture excède celui effectué en train

After the RMS *Titanic* tragedy, ocean liners institute safety drills with designated life boats and life jacket training

Nach der *Titanic*-Tragödie werden auf den Linienschiffen Sicherheitsübungen mit Rettungsbooten und –westen eingeführt

Après la tragédie du *Titanic*, les compagnies transatlantiques introduisent des entraînements au maniement de canots et gilets de sauvetage

Route 66, "The Main Street of America," is created, extending from Chicago to Los Angeles

Entstehung der Chicago und Los Angeles verbindenden Route 66, der „Hauptstraße Amerikas"

Création de la Route 66, « la Grand-rue de l'Amérique », entre Chicago et Los Angeles

France was easier. When the Impressionists had painted there, the area was considered exotic, even by the French. But the Train Bleu, a stylish blue metal train with gold detailing, now traveled from Paris to the Côte d'Azur every night. By 1925, when the Murphys moved into their new home, the Villa America, in Antibes, summer in the south of France was talked of around the globe. It was not only the deep blue of the sea and the sweet perfume of mimosa in the air, the entire Riviera became a vacation spot of choice for so many because it was ever easier to get there. There was a big airport in Nice, less expensive trains, better roads. Not just the rich and famous, but much of the middle class, even pensioners, decided it was worth the trip.

The Cannes Film Festival, which began the year after the end of World War II, only increased the allure. Every spring, Hollywood stars, studio moguls, and assorted beautiful people — usually literally so — jetted to the south of France. Frolicking in the surf could translate into international stardom. In 1953, a young starlet named Brigitte Bardot posed wearing only a bikini — and the world took notice. American movies constantly reminded viewers of the pleasures waiting in the south of France. (Who wouldn't want to film there?) Grace Kelly never looked so creamy or Cary Grant as suave as in Alfred Hitchcock's *To Catch a Thief* (1955). And when Kelly married Prince Rainier III of Monaco, Americans had another reason to check on the Riviera.

By the end of the century, every summer, Riviera beaches were wall-to-wall sunbathers. Travelers flocked from around the globe, whether flying in coach standby or on private jets, taking special trains or mini rental cars, docking on a cruise ship or a huge private yacht. Hotels for all budgets and all attitudes dot the coastline. The grandest hotels were no longer exclusive.

And it was Americans who led the way. This love of travel is one of America's legacies. The American travel plan — faster, easier, and democratized — set the standard for the world.

Page 8 *Lozier*, 1912   ▶▶ SS *Normandie* (Paul Iribe), ca. 1935

1927

1929

1929

Matson Line opens its $4-million "Pink Palace of the Pacific"–The Royal Hawaiian Hotel, built in Spanish-Moorish style

Die Matson Line eröffnet mit dem 4 Mio. $ teuren Royal Hawaiian Hotel den „Pink Palace of the Pacific" im spanisch-maurischen Stil

La Matson Line ouvre son « palais rose du Pacifique », le Royal Hawaiian Hotel, un édifice de 4 millions de dollars

The hotel that defined swank, whether in Harlem or on Park Avenue, is immortalized in Irving Berlin's "Puttin' on the Ritz"

Dieses Hotel, der Inbegriff der Pracht, erlangt durch Irving Berlins Song „Puttin' on the Ritz" Unsterblichkeit

En 1929, l'hôtel parisien symbole de grand luxe selon les Américains est immortalisé par le compositeur Irving Berlin dans « Puttin' on the Ritz »

Worldwide Depression sets in following stock market crash

New Yorker Börsenkrach mündet in eine Weltwirtschaftskrise

La Grande Dépression sévit sur le monde entier après le krach du marché boursier

DIE REISEREPUBLIK

*Die Ungeduld der Amerikaner sorgte
für nachhaltige Veränderung:
Schneller, besser, billiger zieht sich als Parole
durch das gesamte Jahrhundert.*

**DER HERZOG UND DIE HERZOGIN VON WINDSOR, STILIKONEN IHRER ZEIT, WÄHLTEN BIS
WEIT IN DIE 1950ER-JAHRE HINEIN DAS LINIENSCHIFF, UM DEN ATLANTIK ZU ÜBERQUEREN.**
Auf ihrem Lieblingsdampfer, der SS *United States*, buchten sie stets die begehrte Duck Suite – drei
luxuriöse Oberdeckkabinen, benannt nach einem vergoldeten Wandgemälde mit Stockenten. Zuvor
hatten sie die SS *Queen Mary* bevorzugt, dann aber wechselten sie das Schiff, nachdem die *United States*
auf ihrer Jungfernfahrt am 11. Juli 1952 das Blaue Band für die schnellste Atlantiküberquerung gewon-
nen hatte. Die bis heute den Rekord haltende Reise dauerte genau drei Tage, zwölf Stunden und zwölf
Minuten – zehn Stunden weniger als die der *Queen Mary*. Die Windsors reisten mit einer atemberaubenden Menge an Gepäck: allein 118 von T. Anthony von der New Yorker Park Avenue maßgefertigte
Schrankkoffer und zahlreiche Gepäckstücke von Hermès und La Maison Goyard aus Paris. Myriaden
von Überseekoffern, Schuhkisten, Hutschachteln, Toilettengarnituren, Schmuckkästen, Aktenkoffern
und sogar Cocktailsets waren für eine solche Überfahrt nur angemessen.

   Die Windsors mögen Vorreiter in Sachen Stil gewesen sein, doch ihre Reisen erinnern eher an
die Mitte des 19. denn des 20. Jahrhunderts – ein Echo der Verlockungen der Ozeanriesen in einer
temporeichen Ära der Flugreisen. Ende der 1950er-Jahre gab der Jetset bereits Vollgas und nahm
Frank Sinatras Hit „Come Fly With Me" (1957) wörtlich („Just say the words, and we'll beat the birds
down to Acapulco Bay"). Frank Loessers Broadwayhit *Guys and Dolls* (1960) erzählt von einem Kerl,
der in New York illegale Glücksspiele veranstaltet und mal eben eine Frau zum Dinner in sein Lieb-

lingsrestaurant entführt – nach Havanna. Flugreisen waren 1960 der Glamour schlechthin, versinnbildlicht in dem Kinofilm *The V.I.P.s* (*Hotel International*, 1963) mit Elizabeth Taylor und Richard Burton, mit der Erste-Klasse-Lounge des Londoner Flughafens als zentralem Schauplatz.

Vor dem 20. Jahrhundert waren Vergnügungsreisen das Vorrecht der Reichen, von Leuten, die den ganzen Sommer in einem Cottage in Newport auf Rhode Island oder den Winter in einer Villa in Südfrankreich verbrachten. Nur sie konnten sich die komplexe Logistik leisten, die für einen längeren Aufenthalt benötigten Berge von Gepäck und Heerscharen von Dienstboten zu befördern. In der ersten Hälfte des 20. Jahrhunderts gaben die Superreichen wie auch die Berühmten weiterhin den Ton an. Doch im Nachkriegsamerika sollte nun der zunehmende Einfluss der Mittelschicht die Dinge gründlich verändern. Wenn die Reichen und Berühmten einen Ort auserkoren hatten, folgte ihnen die zunehmende und zunehmend gut situierte amerikanische Mittelschicht dicht auf den Fersen, dank stetig verbesserter Transportmöglichkeiten.

Schließlich sind die Vereinigten Staaten eine Nation, die durch Wanderlust angetrieben wird, gleichsam ein Wesenszug des Amerikaners. Das Land wurde von Menschen erschlossen, die Meere überquerten, um dort anzukommen – und nach der Landung überquerten sie noch den Kontinent. Jeder konnte sich in einer neuen Umgebung quasi neu erfinden. Angetrieben von der Hoffnung, dass Gutes auf sie wartete – gleich hinter dem nächsten Tal oder jenseits des nächsten Hügels –, waren die Amerikaner stets darauf erpicht, sich „vor 'n andern [zu] verdünnisieren Richtung Territorium", wie Mark Twain 1884 in *Huckleberry Finn* schrieb. Auch als das Census Bureau das Grenzland 1890 offiziell für „geschlossen" erklärte, blieb nicht jeder an seinem Ort. Im Gegenteil.

Im folgenden Jahrhundert verlagerte sich der Schwerpunkt jedoch auf den Freizeitsektor. Dabei sorgte die Ungeduld der Amerikaner für nachhaltige Veränderungen: Schneller, besser, billiger zieht sich als Parole durch das gesamte Jahrhundert, wie die Anzeigen für Kreuzfahrten, Zug- und Flugreisen bezeugen. Die Amerikaner verlangten die Demokratisierung des Reisens. Ende des 20. Jahrhunderts war diese Forderung erfüllt.

1931

Igor Sikorsky designs and builds first Clipper for Pan American World Airways, more commonly known as Pan Am

Igor Sikorsky entwirft und baut den ersten Clipper für Pan American World Airways, besser bekannt als Pan Am

Igor Sikorsky conçoit et construit le premier Clipper pour Pan American World Airways, plus connue sous le nom de Pan Am

1932

Greta Garbo and all-star cast check into Berlin's *Grand Hotel*, Oscar-winning movie of Vicky Baum's novel

Greta Garbo und weitere Stars steigen in der oscarprämierten Verfilmung von *Menschen im Hotel* von Vicky Baum im Berliner *Grand Hotel* ab

Greta Garbo et une distribution de stars descendent au « Grand Hotel » de Berlin, Oscar du Meilleur Film

1932

Hertz opens first airport-based U.S. car rental franchise, at Chicago's Midway

Hertz eröffnet auf dem Chicagoer Midway Airport die erste Autovermietung an einem Flughafen

À l'aéroport Midway de Chicago, Hertz ouvre la première franchise américaine de location de voitures dans les aéroports

„TEMPO LAUTET DER SCHLACHTRUF UNSERER ZEIT", VERKÜNDETE DER INDUSTRIEDESIGNER NORMAN BEL GEDDES 1932, „UND MEHR TEMPO EINES DER ZIELE VON MORGEN." Bel Geddes sagte diese Worte am Gipfelpunkt des Maschinenzeitalters, doch sie könnten auf jedes Jahr in diesem Jahrhundert zutreffen. Im Jahr 1900 gab es immer noch Postkutschen, während man Ende des Jahrhunderts von New York aus übers Wochenende Quogue auf Long Island, aber auch Prag ansteuern konnte. Tempo war wichtig. Im Gilded Age (Vergoldetes Zeitalter, um 1876–1914) hatten prächtig ausgestattete Luxusliner wie die RMS *Mauretania* um neue Geschwindigkeitsrekorde gewetteifert. Bald darauf entstanden im Zugverkehr spezielle Expressverbindungen, bis in den 1930er-Jahren stromlinienförmige Loks mit Namen wie Zephyr und Mercury vorbeidonnerten.

Jahrzehnt für Jahrzehnt wurden dereinst beliebte Transportmittel wieder verworfen, wenn sie als zu langsam galten. Auch die majestätischen Linienschiffe der renommierten Reedereien French und Cunard konnten mit dem Tempo der Flugreisen einfach nicht konkurrieren. Die luxuriösen Fernzüge blieben ebenfalls auf der Strecke. Das Gros der einst mächtigen Eisenbahngesellschaften war Ende der 1960er-Jahre bankrott. Aus der Konkursmasse ging 1971 die staatseigene Amtrak hervor.

Anfangs waren Flugreisen noch eine recht holprige Angelegenheit. Viele der ersten Passagiere waren Berühmtheiten, die das Rampenlicht wie auch vor allem einen Zeitgewinn anstrebten. Die zugigen Kabinen waren nicht klimatisiert und erschwerten die Konversation. Bis dann 1933 bei der aerodynamischen Boeing 247 Schalldämmung, Heizung und Klimatisierung Einzug hielten – und ein Flug quer über die USA keine 20 Stunden mehr dauerte. Zwei Jahre später begeisterte die Douglas DC-3 mit ihrem glitzernden, grazilen Aluminiumrumpf die Nation und brachte 28 Passagiere in nur 15 Stunden von Küste zu Küste.

Flotte Flugboote wie die Pan Am Clipper spielten keine Rolle mehr, als Linienjets, seien sie auch noch so proppenvoll, die Flugzeit halbierten. Das Überschallflugzeug Concorde reduzierte 1973 einen Transatlantikflug auf dreieinhalb Stunden – man war quasi schon da, bevor man überhaupt abgehoben hatte.

1935

Air travel introduced between Hawaii and mainland

Erste Flugverbindung zwischen Hawaii und dem Festland

Premières liaisons aériennes entre Hawaï et le continent américain

1936

100 small carriers merge to form National Trailways System, second major American bus company to travel coast-to-coast

Union von 100 kleineren Transportunternehmen zu National Trailways System, der zweiten großen US-Busgesellschaft

100 petits transporteurs forment la National Trailways System, deuxième compagnie américaine d'autocars reliant les deux côtes

1938

Industrial designer Henry Dreyfuss reinvents 20th Century Ltd., from locomotive to dinner menus, for N.Y. Central Line

Industriedesigner Henry Dreyfuss überarbeitet den 20th Century Ltd. bis zur Speisekarte für die N.Y. Central Line

Le designer industriel Henry Dreyfuss réinvente le 20th Century Ltd. de la compagnie N.Y. Central Line jusqu'aux menus du restaurant

„BETT UND BAD FÜR ANDERTHALB DOLLAR." DAS 1907 IN BUFFALO, NEW YORK, ERÖFFNETE HOTEL BUFFALO (das spätere Hotel Statler) war das erste große Stadthotel mit einem Bad für jedes Zimmer. Nur drei Jahre zuvor warb das St. Regis Hotel von John Jacob Astor IV. mit einem Telefon auf jedem Zimmer sowie Zentralheizung und Luftkühlung – Annehmlichkeiten, wie sie der Millionär und Hotelier und seinesgleichen daheim genossen, wurden nun erstmals auch den Gästen aus der Mittelschicht geboten. Die Öffentlichkeit erwartete mit wachsender Ungeduld nicht nur verkürzte Reisezeiten, sondern auch immer mehr Behaglichkeit und Komfort.

Das erste voll klimatisierte Hotel ist das 1946 eröffnete Flamingo in Las Vegas. Eine tropische Brise war ja ganz nett, doch eine zuverlässige Klimaanlage machte das Reisen in warme Klimazonen für den Freizeitmenschen doch um einiges angenehmer. Sonnenverwöhnte Strände auf Hawaii oder Kuba, seit jeher nicht ohne Reiz, erlebten dank moderner Annehmlichkeiten wie der Klimaanlage einen Aufschwung. Hawaii erzielte 1961 durch den Tourismus mehr Einnahmen (161 Mio. $) als mit seinen beiden Haupterzeugnissen Zuckerrohr und Ananas.

Dank dieser Neuerungen wurde der Tourismus schließlich zu einem Massenmarkt. Flugreisen waren für den Durchschnittsamerikaner bislang unerschwinglich, doch nachdem Krieg machte sich in der prosperierenden Mittelschicht die Ansicht breit, dieses Reisevergnügen solle niemandem versagt bleiben. Ein Wendepunkt war 1968 der Jungfernflug der Boeing 737. Von dem meistproduzierten Linienjet aller Zeiten befanden sich Ende des Jahrhunderts zu einem beliebigen Zeitpunkt rund 1250 Maschinen in der Luft, und durchschnittlich alle fünf Sekunden landete oder startete eine von ihnen irgendwo auf der Welt. In den 1970er-Jahren gehörte quasi jeder mit einem Flugticket zum Jetset. Von exotischen Panoramen bis zu alten Festungsstädten, von unberührten Südseestränden bis zu den vielschichtigen europäischen Hauptstädten – die Amerikaner reisen, und zwar weit.

DOCH FÜR DIE AMERIKANER KONNTE „WEIT" REISEN EBENSO EINEN TRIP QUER DURCHS LAND BEDEUTEN WIE EINE REISE UM DIE WELT. Angesichts der schieren Größe der Vereinigten Staaten zeugt die rasche Akzeptanz des Automobils von der Lust der Amerikaner, auf eigene Faust aufzubrechen. Der inländische Absatz schnellte von 4000 Autos im Jahr 1900 auf 26,7 Millionen Ein-

1939

New York World's Fair, "The World of Tomorrow," proclaims promise of new technology

Die New Yorker Weltausstellung „Die Welt von morgen" verheißt neue Technologien

L'Exposition Universelle de New York, « Le Monde de Demain », célèbre les promesses des nouvelles technologies

1941

Japanese bomb Pearl Harbor; U.S. enters World War II

Nach dem Angriff Japans auf Pearl Harbor treten die USA in den Zweiten Weltkrieg ein

Les Japonais bombardent Pearl Harbor ; les États-Unis entrent dans la Seconde Guerre mondiale

1943

Washington Statler opens; only modern urban hotel developed and built between start of Depression and end of World War II

Eröffnung des Washington Statler als einziges Stadthotel, das zwischen Wirtschaftskrise und dem Ende des Zweiten Weltkriegs errichtet wurde

Ouverture du Washington Statler, unique hôtel urbain moderne construit entre 1929 et 1945 heiten im Jahr 1930. Und die reisenden Amerikaner nahmen ihr Schicksal zunehmend selbst in die Hand, indem sie Ziel und Zeitpunkt bestimmten.

Als einer der ersten Autohändler im ganzen Land hatte Carl G. Fisher, ein Visionär des Reisens, die Liebesbeziehung der Amerikaner zu ihren Autos erfasst. Er sah, wie sehr Kalifornien, der Golden State am Ende des Kontinents, lockte. Im Jahr 1913 plante und errichtete Fisher mit dem New York und San Francisco verbindenden Lincoln Highway die erste quer durchs Land führende Trasse. Im Jahr darauf schuf er den Dixie Highway, der Indianapolis im Norden mit Miami im Süden verband. Als der U.S. Congress 1916 das erste Gesetz für öffentliche Highways verabschiedete, hatte Fisher buchstäblich den Weg geebnet. Washington sorgte letztlich für ein ganzes Netz aus breiten Trassen – beginnend 1926 mit der Route 66 als „Hauptstraße Amerikas" bis zu Präsident Dwight D. Eisenhowers Unterschrift 1956 unter den Interstate Highways Act als dem weiträumigsten öffentlichen Bauvorhaben, das die Welt je gesehen hat. Was sind dagegen die Pyramiden! Für die Interstate Highways rechnete man anfangs mit Kosten von 25 Mrd. $ über zwölf Jahre, tatsächlich aber wurden es 114 Mrd. $ über 35 Jahre.

Und diese Straßen wurden von den Amerikanern rasch angenommen. Spritztouren entwickelten sich zu *dem* Zeitvertreib. Junge Leute kurvten durchs Land auf der Suche nach sich selbst – siehe Jack Kerouacs *On the Road* (*Unterwegs*). In den Frühjahrsferien suchten Studenten in sonnigen Gefilden nach Romanzen – siehe Dolores Hart, George Hamilton und Yvette Mimieux in *Where the Boys Are* (*Dazu gehören zwei*). Familien fuhren zu erlesenen Landhotels mit faszinierenden Naturpanoramen – siehe *The Shining* (*Shining*), oder vielleicht besser nicht! Wie amerikanisch ist es doch, seinen eigenen Weg zu wählen, und Spaß macht es auch – siehe einen der sieben *Road-to*-Filme mit Bob Hope und Bing Crosby, – speziell *Road to Morocco* (*Der Weg nach Marokko*) oder *Road to Utopia* (*Der Weg nach Utopia*).

Doch auf diesen Autotouren musste man auch irgendwo übernachten können. Immer mehr Menschen konnten verreisen, und zugleich erwartete man einen gewissen Beherbergungsstandard. Eine Antwort war das Motel – ein Kunstwort aus „Motor" und „Hotel". Und wer mit der ganzen Familie in eine der Howard Johnson's Motor Lodges oder ein Holiday Inn eincheckte, konnte überall im

1944

1945

1946

Pan American World Airways, which had resisted using air stewardesses, hires them

Pan American World Airways entscheidet sich nach anfänglichem Zögern für den Einsatz von Stewardessen

La compagnie Pan American World Airways finit par embaucher des hôtesses de l'air

Stan Kenton's hit "Tampico" tells of troubles awaiting unwary tourists in Mexico

Stan Kentons Hit „Tampico" handelt von Problemen, die in Mexiko auf unvorsichtige Touristen warten

Le tube « Tampico » de Stan Kenton évoque les ennuis qui attendent les touristes imprudents au Mexique

Lucky Luciano calls meeting of mobsters at Hotel Nacional in Havana to decide how to divide up Cuba

Auf Betreiben von Lucky Luciano tagen Mafiabosse im Hotel Nacional in Havanna, um Kuba unter sich aufzuteilen

Lucky Luciano organise une réunion de parrains de la mafia à l'Hotel Nacional de La Havane pour décider du « partage » de Cuba

Land mit sauberen, preiswerten und *standardisierten* Zimmern rechnen. Das erste Holiday Inn wurde 1952 eröffnet; 1968 gab es bereits 1000 Franchisenehmer. Und auf jeder Speisekarte bot die Restaurantkette Howard Johnson's die gleichen 28 Eissorten an, sei es in Athens, Georgia, oder in Anaheim, Kalifornien.

Während Howard Johnson's zu einem verlässlichen Haltepunkt wurde, boten gediegenere Hotelketten wie Hilton und Hyatt im Ausland kleine Inseln des Amerikanischen. In der Tat hatte der Hotelier Conrad Hilton den Wunsch ausgesprochen, seine Hotels mögen jene Werte repräsentieren, die seiner Ansicht nach Amerika groß gemacht haben. Auf der Höhe des Kalten Kriegs in den 1950er- und 1960er-Jahren sah Hilton in seinen Hotels Botschafter der amerikanischen Werte – und die US-Regierung auch. Unterstützt durch Washington und ausländische Regierungen, platzierte Hilton seine Hotels in den Kapitalen des Kalten Kriegs – dort, wo der Westen dem Sowjetblock gegenüberstand.

Mit den Hotels verfolgte man eine konkrete Ideologie, denn ganz wie die in der gleichen Zeit entstehenden modernistischen Botschaftsgebäude sollten auch die Hilton-Hotels ein Sinnbild Amerikas verkörpern. Die Gebäude präsentierten sich offen, transparent und einladend. Anders als die älteren Grandhotels in Europa, wo der Gast ein prunkvolles, imposantes Foyer betrat, gab es nun einen aufgeräumten Eingangsbereich hinter gläsernen Vorhangfassaden, die nichts verbargen. „Wir sehen diese Hotels als Herausforderung", erläuterte Hilton, „nicht für die Menschen, die uns in ihrer Mitte so herzlich willkommen geheißen haben, sondern für die von der kommunistischen Welt gepredigte Lebensweise." Hilton betrachtete seine Hotels als Speerspitze der Demokratie – nicht zu trennen von dem Bestreben der Nation, das Reisen zu demokratisieren.

Dieser Demokratisierungsprozess ging weit über das Ende des Kalten Kriegs hinaus. Mit Erlass des Airline Deregulation Act 1978 wurden die Flüge bezahlbarer – und auch häufiger. Die Fahrt zum Flughafen büßte etwas von ihrem einstigen Glamour ein, denn immer mehr Menschen konnten es sich leisten, auch tatsächlich abzuheben. Ähnliches geschah mit den Hotels. In den 1980er-Jahren schuf der einstige Nachtclubbesitzer Ian Schrager mit dem Boutiquehotel ein intimes Hotel, das jedem Gast ein Gefühl der Exklusivität vermittelte. W-Hotels und Standard entstanden Ende der 1990er-Jahre als größere, preiswertere Abwandlungen – exklusiv für den kleinen Geldbeutel.

1947

1949

1950

Production begins on Raymond Loewy designs of Greyhound's Silversides motorcoach; he retools dog logo as well

Produktionsstart von Greyhounds Silversides-Reisebussen nach Raymond Loewys Design, der auch das Logo überarbeitet

Production commence des modèles d'autocars Silversides conçus par Raymond Loewy pour Greyhound; le designer remanie aussi le logo

Under Chinese Communist regime, Shanghai's Palace and Cathay hotels merged into Peace Hotel

Unter der Herrschaft der chinesischen Kommunisten werden das Palace und das Cathay Hotel in Schanghai zum Friedenshotel vereinigt

Sous le régime communiste chinois, les hôtels Shanghai's Palace et Cathay fusionnent pour créer le Peace Hotel

American GIs returning from the Pacific popularize Hawaiian shirts

Die aus dem pazifischen Raum heimkehrenden GIs machen das Hawaiihemd populär

De retour du Pacifique, les G.I. américains popularisent les chemises hawaïennes

Die Amerikaner veränderten die Definition des Reisens im 20. Jahrhundert. Sie erfanden eine neue Form, so wie sie sich während ihrer gesamten Geschichte immer wieder neu erfunden hatten. Gegen Ende des Jahrhunderts reiste man flotter, als man sich um 1900 je erträumt hätte. In der Nachkriegsära zeigte sich die große amerikanische Mittelschicht rastlos und unaufhaltsam.

MAN DENKE ETWA AN DIE TOURISTISCHE ERSCHLIESSUNG DER FRANZÖSISCHEN RIVIERA, DIE SICH IM LAUF DES JAHRHUNDERTS VON EINER EXKLUSIVEN WINTERENKLAVE IN EINEN ÜBERAUS BELIEBTEN SOMMERHIT VERWANDELTE. Anfang des 20. Jahrhunderts war der Winter *die* Saison. Russische Aristokraten quartierten sich gleich für Wochen in den Grandhotels ein. Auch wenn sich das Klima feucht und recht kühl gestaltete, so war das noch heimelig, verglichen mit dem Winter in St. Petersburg.

Vorhang auf für die Ära des Jazz und ein Grüppchen betuchter Amerikaner, die die Szenerie nachhaltig verändern sollten: Cole Porter, ein reicher amerikanischer Komponist und Liedtexter mit erlauchten europäischen Freunden, beschloss 1922, den Sommer in Antibes zu verbringen. Er mietete eine Villa unweit des Hôtel du Cap, ein Wahrzeichen, das jeden Sommer seine Pforten schloss. Porter lud seinen engen Freund Gerald Murphy ein, Spross der Lederwarenkette Mark Cross, nebst Familie. Im nächsten Sommer gelang es den Murphys (die F. Scott Fitzgerald zu Dick und Nicole Diver in *Zärtlich ist die Nacht* inspirierten), dass das Hôtel du Cap offen blieb. Und sie checkten ein – zusammen mit ihrem Freund Pablo Picasso und seiner gesamten Familie. Auch die Schriftstellerin Gertrude Stein und ihre Partnerin Alice B. Toklas schauten vorbei. Ein Sommer in Südfrankreich, das war es doch!

Inzwischen galt Sonnenbräune als schick, und Freiluftaktivitäten wie Segeln, Tennis, Golf und Schwimmen sprachen Frauen wie Männer an. Und ab 1922 konnte man auch immer bequemer nach Südfrankreich gelangen. Als die Impressionisten noch dort gemalt hatten, galt die Region sogar den Franzosen als exotisch. Nun aber gab es Le Train Bleu, einen blauen Luxuszug mit metallenen Schlafwagen und goldener Verzierung, der jede Nacht Paris mit der Côte d'Azur verband. Als die Murphys 1925 ihr neues Heim, die Villa America, in Antibes bezogen, redete man überall auf der Welt von

1951

1954

1957

Travel to desert playground Palm Springs, California, shoots up with air conditioning now ubiquitous

Rasante Zunahme von Reisen in die Wüstenoase Palm Springs, Kalifornien, dank der inzwischen allgegenwärtigen Klimaanlagen

Le tourisme explose à Palm Springs dans le désert de Californie grâce à l'air conditionné, désormais omniprésent

Conrad Hilton buys Statler chain for $111 million, largest price for real-estate venture since Louisiana Purchase

Conrad Hilton erwirbt die Hotelkette Statler für 111 Mio. $ – das teuerste Grundstücksgeschäft seit dem Kauf von Louisiana

Conrad Hilton achète la chaîne d'hôtels Statler pour 111 millions de $, prix le plus élevé pour un projet immobilier depuis la vente de la Louisiane

Publication of *Gidget* and later film and TV show export Southern California surf culture to world

Der Roman *Gidget*, später gefolgt von Spielfilmen, exportiert die Surfkultur Südkaliforniens in die ganze Welt

La publication du livre *Gidget*, suivie d'une adaptation cinématographique, exporte la culture surf californienne dans le monde entier einem Sommer in Südfrankreich. Es waren nicht allein das tiefblaue Meer und der süßliche Duft der Silberakazien, nein, die gesamte Riviera wurde zu einem gefragten Reiseziel, weil man es immer leichter erreichen konnte – es gab einen großen Flughafen in Nizza, preiswertere Züge und bessere Straßen. So machten sich neben den Reichen und Berühmten auch zahlreiche Menschen aus der Mittelschicht auf den Weg, Pensionäre nicht ausgenommen.

Das Filmfestival von Cannes, ein Jahr nach Ende des Zweiten Weltkriegs gestartet, machte die Sache noch reizvoller. Hollywoodstars, Studiobosse und diverse Schönheiten jetteten (meist ist dies wörtlich zu nehmen) jedes Frühjahr nach Südfrankreich. In der Brandung herumzutollen verhieß internationalen Ruhm. Ein Starlet namens Brigitte Bardot posierte 1953 im Bikini – und die Welt nahm Notiz. Amerikanische Kinofilme erinnerten das Publikum immer wieder an die in Südfrankreich wartenden Freuden. Grace Kelly wirkte nie so frisch und Cary Grant nie so weltmännisch wie in Alfred Hitchcocks *To Catch a Thief* (*Über den Dächern von Nizza*, 1955). Und als Kelly Fürst Rainier von Monaco III. heiratete, hatten die Amerikaner noch einen Grund, die Riviera anzusteuern.

Gegen Ende des Jahrhunderts hatten sich die Strände der Riviera im Sommer bis zum Überquellen mit Sonnenanbetern gefüllt. Die Gäste strömten aus der ganzen Welt herbei, sei es per Charterflug oder im Privatjet, mit dem Sonderzug oder im gemieteten Kleinstwagen, auf einem Kreuzfahrtschiff oder an Bord einer riesigen Privatjacht. Hotels für jeden Geldbeutel und Anspruch zieren die Küste. Die besten Hotels waren nicht länger exklusiv.

Und es waren Amerikaner, die vorangingen. Diese Liebe zum Reisen gehört einfach zu ihrem Wesen. Und der amerikanische Fahrplan – schneller, leichter, für alle – wurde weltweit zum Standard.

▶ American Express Travelers Cheques, 1950   ▶▶ American Airlines, 1950

1957

1958

1958

Last gasp of grand cruise ships – Deborah Kerr and Cary Grant fall in love on ocean liner in *An Affair to Remember*

Letzter Seufzer der großen Schiffe: In *Die große Liebe meines Lebens* verlieben sich Deborah Kerr und Cary Grant auf einem Luxusdampfer

Dernier soupir des paquebots de croisière : idylle de Deborah Kerr et Cary Grant à bord d'un paquebot dans *Elle et Lui*

Oscar Niemeyer's Brasilia Palace Hotel one of first structures to open in the stunningly modern Brazilian capital

Oscar Niemeyers Brasilia Palace Hotel als eines der ersten Gebäude in der neuen hypermodernen Hauptstadt Brasiliens eingeweiht

Le Brasilia Palace Hotel d'Oscar Niemeyer est l'un des premiers établissements ouverts dans la nouvelle capitale brésilienne

Mike Todd's star-packed version of the Jules Verne novel *Around the World in 80 Days* soars into movie theaters

Mike Todds hochkarätig besetzte Verfilmung von Jules Vernes Roman *In 80 Tagen um die Welt* lässt die Kinokassen klingeln

La version du roman de Jules Verne *Le Tour du Monde en 80 Jours* produite par Mike Todd déferle dans les salles de cinéma

LA RÉPUBLIQUE DU VOYAGE

*L'impatience américaine modifia le métabolisme
du voyage : plus rapide, plus efficace et moins
cher furent ses mots d'ordre tout au long du siècle.*

**VERS LE MILIEU DES ANNÉES 1950, LE DUC ET LA DUCHESSE DE WINDSOR, LES RÉFÉRENCES
EN MATIÈRE D'ÉLÉGANCE À CETTE ÉPOQUE, TRAVERSAIENT L'ATLANTIQUE EN BATEAU.** Sur
leur paquebot préféré, le SS *United States*, ils réservaient toujours la très convoitée Duck Suite composée de trois somptueuses cabines ornées d'une fresque de canards sauvages dorée à l'or fin. Si leur
bateau de prédilection était auparavant le *Queen Mary*, le *United States* avait gagné leurs faveurs en dé-
crochant le Ruban Bleu le 11 juillet 1952, pendant leur voyage de noces, pour la traversée la plus rapide
de l'Atlantique. Cette transatlantique à vitesse record, encore jamais battue, dura trois jours, 12 heures
et 12 minutes, soit 10 heures de moins que le *Queen Mary*. Les Windsor voyageaient avec un nombre
de bagages impressionnant : 118 malles fabriquées sur commande par la boutique T. Anthony de Park
Avenue à New York, ainsi qu'une multitude de sacs de chez Hermès à Paris et de La Maison Goyard.
Tous ces malles, boîtes à chaussures, cartons à chapeaux, trousses de toilette, coffres à bijoux, porte-
documents et même coffrets à cocktail étaient de mise pour une telle traversée.

Les Windsor dictaient l'élégance du moment, mais leur façon de voyager rappelait plutôt celle du
milieu du XIXᵉ siècle, comme une réminiscence de l'élégance et de la puissance des grands paquebots alors que s'ouvrait l'ère enivrante du voyage aérien. À la fin des années 1950, la jet-set fendait déjà
les cieux à toute allure, décollant au son du standard « Come Fly With Me » (1957) de Frank Sinatra
(« Just say the words, and we'll beat the birds down to Acapulco Bay. »). *Guys and Dolls*, la comédie mu-
sicale à succès de Broadway signée Frank Loesser, mettait en scène un parieur new-yorkais trouvant

parfaitement normal d'emmener une femme à dîner dans son restaurant préféré … à La Havane. En 1960, le voyage en avion représentait l'essence même du glamour, comme l'a incarné le couple Elizabeth Taylor/Richard Burton dans le film *Hôtel International* (1963) qui se déroule dans le salon VIP de l'aéroport de Londres.

Avant le XXᵉ siècle, voyager pour le plaisir était l'apanage des classes aisées, de ceux qui conjuguaient les saisons de l'année comme des verbes. Ils passaient l'été dans un cottage à Newport, dans le Rhode Island, et l'hiver dans une villa du sud de la France. Seuls ces privilégiés pouvaient s'offrir la logistique complexe impliquée par le déplacement des montagnes de bagages et des armées de domestiques nécessaires à ces longs séjours. Pendant la première moitié du siècle, les riches et les célébrités avaient ouvert la voie, mais dans l'Amérique d'après-guerre, le pouvoir croissant de la classe moyenne fit tout changer. Dès que les plus privilégiés avaient validé tel ou tel endroit comme « the place to be », la classe moyenne américaine, toujours plus nombreuse et plus aisée, les suivait de près grâce à des moyens de transport en constant développement.

Après tout, les États-Unis sont nés du désir de découvrir le monde. Ce désir se trouve au cœur de la définition de l'Américain. Le pays a été construit par des gens qui ont traversé des océans pour l'atteindre, puis tout un continent après avoir débarqué. Dans un nouvel environnement, il était possible de se réinventer. Motivés par l'espoir que, juste après la prochaine vallée ou derrière la prochaine colline, de bonnes choses les attendaient, les Américains étaient toujours plus impatients « d'éclairer le territoire », comme l'a écrit Mark Twain dans *Les Aventures de Huckleberry Finn* (1884). Le Bureau du Recensement eut beau déclarer la frontière officiellement « fermée » en 1890, cela n'éteignit en rien cette passion du voyage. En fait, cela ne fit que l'attiser.

Les voyages du XXᵉ siècle s'orientèrent toutefois davantage vers le loisir. L'impatience américaine modifia le métabolisme du voyage : plus rapide, plus efficace et moins cher furent ses mots d'ordre tout au long du siècle, comme en témoignent les publicités des compagnies de croisières, ferroviaires et aériennes. Les Américains exigeaient la démocratisation du voyage, et obtinrent gain de cause à la fin du siècle.

1959

1960

1961

Hotel del Coronado in San Diego, California, stands in for Florida resort in *Some Like It Hot*

Das Hotel del Coronado im kalifornischen San Diego fungiert in *Manche mögen's heiß* als Florida-Resort

Censé se dérouler en Floride, le film *Certains l'Aiment Chaud* est en fait tourné à l'Hôtel del Coronado de San Diego, en Californie

First year that Hawaiian tourism brings in more money than pineapples or sugar— $161 million

Der Tourismus bringt Hawaii mit 161 Mio. $ erstmals mehr Geld ein als Ananas oder Zuckerrohr

Première année où le tourisme rapporte plus à Hawaï que les ananas et le sucre : 161 millions de dollars

Rat Pack hits Las Vegas—Frank Sinatra, Dean Martin, and Sammy Davis Jr. film *Ocean's 11* at the Sahara Hotel

Das Rat Pack landet in Las Vegas: Frank Sinatra, Dean Martin und Sammy Davis Jr. drehen im Sahara Hotel

Le Rat Pack se produit à Las Vegas : Frank Sinatra, Dean Martin et Sammy Davis Jr. tournent dans *L'Inconnu de Las Vegas* à l'hôtel Sahara

« LA VITESSE EST LE MOT D'ORDRE D'AUJOURD'HUI », DÉCLARA LE DESIGNER INDUSTRIEL NORMAN BEL GEDDES EN 1932, « ET PLUS DE VITESSE, L'UN DES OBJECTIFS DE DEMAIN ». L'ère des machines vivait alors son apogée, mais une telle affirmation pourrait s'appliquer à n'importe quelle année du siècle. En 1900, on voyageait encore en diligence ; à la fin du siècle, on quittait New York en avion pour un week-end à Prague (République Tchèque) ou Quogue (Long Island). La vitesse avait son importance. Pendant la seconde moitié du XIXe siècle, les paquebots de luxe aménagés avec raffinement comme le RMS *Mauretania* rivalisaient pour battre des records de vitesse. Les chemins de fer ne tardèrent pas à créer des itinéraires « express ». Dans les années 1930, des locomotives aérodynamiques baptisées Zephyr ou Mercury filaient à toute allure sur les rails.

D'une décennie à l'autre, les moyens de transport les plus populaires étaient ensuite délaissés dès qu'ils paraissaient trop lents. Les majestueux transatlantiques, même les paquebots français si glamour et ceux de la compagnie Cunard, ne pouvaient pas lutter face à la vitesse des voyages en avion. Les trains de luxe empruntés pour parcourir de longues distances restèrent au bord du chemin. La plupart des puissantes compagnies ferroviaires se déclarèrent en faillite à la fin des années 1960. Amtrak, entreprise appartenant à l'État, fut sauvée de justesse de la banqueroute en 1971.

Au début, les vols en avion étaient très chahutés. Les premiers passagers aériens – souvent des célébrités en quête de publicité et de rapidité – recherchaient avant tout la vitesse. Balayées de courants d'air, les cabines ne possédaient pas de système de régulation thermique et rendaient difficile toute conversation. En 1933, les voyageurs découvrirent le Boeing 247 aux lignes fuselées et équipé d'une isolation phonique, du chauffage et de l'air conditionné. Il réduisit les vols d'un bout à l'autre du pays à une durée inférieure à 20 heures. Deux ans plus tard, le Douglas DC-3 enflamma l'imagination des Américains grâce à son fuselage élancé et scintillant d'aluminium, d'autant plus qu'il était capable de transporter 28 passagers d'une côte à l'autre en 15 heures. Néanmoins, la fougue des avions d'élite comme le Pan Am Clipper fit pâle figure quand les avions courrier à réaction, même pleins à craquer, divisèrent par deux le temps de vol. En 1973, le Concorde supersonique réduisit les vols transatlantiques à une durée de 3h30 : on arrivait à destination avant même d'avoir décollé.

1961

1962

1964

Cold War divide in Europe deepens; border between East and West Berlin closes with construction of Berlin Wall

Der Bau der Berliner Mauer vertieft die mit dem Kalten Krieg einhergehende Teilung Europas

Renforcement du rideau de fer en Europe ; la frontière entre Berlin-Est et Berlin-Ouest est matérialisée par la construction du Mur

Eero Saarinen designs swooping TWA Terminal at New York's Idlewild Airport

Eero Saarinen kreiert den geschwungenen TWA-Terminal für den New Yorker Idlewild Airport

Eero Saarinen conçoit le terminal futuriste de la TWA à l'aéroport Idlewild de New York

Gio Ponti designs Parco dei Principi Hotel, in shades of green and white, in Rome

Gio Ponti entwirft das ganz in Grün und Weiß gehaltene römische Hotel Parco dei Principi

À Rome, Gio Ponti conçoit le Parco dei Principi Hotel dans des tons de vert et de blanc

« A BED AND A BATH FOR A BUCK AND A HALF.» LORS DE SON OUVERTURE EN 1907, L'HÔTEL BUFFALO (rebaptisé plus tard l'Hôtel Statler) **DE BUFFALO, ÉTAT DE NEW YORK,** fut le premier grand hôtel urbain à proposer une salle de bains séparée dans chaque chambre. À peine trois ans plus tôt, le St. Regis Hotel de John Jacob Astor IV se targuait d'offrir un téléphone dans toutes les chambres, ainsi que le chauffage central et la climatisation : les luxes dont l'hôtelier millionnaire et ses pairs de la haute société profitaient chez eux étaient désormais mis pour la première fois à la disposition des clients de la classe moyenne. L'impatience du public concernant la vitesse du voyage avait grandi de pair avec ses attentes en termes de bien-être et de confort.

Le Flamingo de Las Vegas, premier hôtel entièrement climatisé, ouvrit ses portes en 1946. Certes, les voyageurs de loisirs appréciaient les brises tropicales, mais un système d'air conditionné fiable rendait les destinations au climat chaud d'autant plus attrayantes. Si les plages ensoleillées de Hawaï et de Cuba attiraient déjà les touristes, le confort moderne offert par la climatisation fit exploser l'industrie du voyage. En 1961, les revenus du tourisme (161 millions de dollars) rapportèrent plus à Hawaï que le sucre et les ananas, les deux principales ressources de l'État insulaire.

Grâce à de telles innovations, le tourisme devint enfin un marché de masse. Avant, l'Américain lambda ne pouvait pas se permettre de voyager en avion, mais la classe moyenne prospère de l'après-guerre estimait que le divertissement et le plaisir du voyage devaient être accessibles à tous. Le premier vol du Boeing 737 en 1968 marqua un grand tournant. C'est l'avion de ligne le plus commandé et le plus produit de l'histoire aéronautique.

À la fin du siècle, on comptait environ 1250 Boeing 737 en vol simultanément, avec en moyenne un décollage ou un atterrissage toutes les cinq secondes dans le monde. Dans les années 1970, le club des voyageurs aériens n'était plus réservé à l'élite. Il accueillait parmi ses membres toute personne munie d'un billet d'avion. Des panoramas exotiques aux anciennes cités fortifiées, des plages vierges des mers du Sud aux villes européennes chargées d'histoire, les Américains voyageaient, toujours plus loin et dans le monde entier.

1964

1965

1966

New York World's Fair proves "It's a Small World after All"

Die New Yorker Weltausstellung bestätigt ihr Motto „Eigentlich ist die Welt doch klein"

« Le Monde est petit », proclame la Foire Internationale de New York

Laurance Rockefeller opens luxe Mauna Kea Beach Hotel on Hawaii's Kona-Kohala Coast

Laurance Rockefeller eröffnet das luxuriöse Mauna Kea Beach Hotel an Hawaiis Kona-Kohala-Küste

Laurance Rockefeller ouvre le luxueux Mauna Kea Beach Hotel sur la côte Kona-Kohala de Hawaï

Howard Hughes moves into Wilbur Clark's Desert Inn in Las Vegas, which he buys, with four other casinos

Howard Hughes zieht in das Wilbur Clarks Desert Inn in Las Vegas, das er zusammen mit vier weiteren Kasinos aufkauft

Howard Hughes s'installe à Las Vegas dans l'hôtel Desert Inn de Wilbur Clark. Il finit par le racheter, ainsi que quatre autres casinos

QU'IL S'AGISSE DE VOYAGER À L'AUTRE BOUT DU PAYS OU L'AUTRE BOUT DU MONDE, LE MOT «LOIN» REVÊT DIVERSES SIGNIFICATIONS POUR LES AMÉRICAINS. Sur l'immense territoire national, l'adoption rapide de l'automobile refléta le désir de partir à l'aventure en toute liberté. En 1930, les ventes de voitures atteignirent 26,7 millions d'unités, contre seulement 4000 en 1900. Les voyageurs américains étaient toujours plus maîtres de leur destin. Ils allaient où ils voulaient, quand ils voulaient.

Figurant parmi les premiers concessionnaires automobiles du pays, le visionnaire du voyage Carl G. Fisher misa sur l'histoire d'amour des Américains avec leurs voitures. Il comprit tout le pouvoir d'attraction de la Californie, ce «Golden State» aux confins du continent. En 1913, Fisher conçut et fit construire le Lincoln Highway, première route transcontinentale reliant New York à San Francisco. L'année suivante, il lança les travaux du Dixie Highway nord-sud entre Indianapolis et Miami. Quand le Congrès américain vota les premières lois sur les autoroutes publiques en 1916, Fisher avait déjà – littéralement – ouvert la voie. Washington finit par faire construire de nombreuses et larges routes, de la Route 66, «Grand-rue de l'Amérique», en 1926, à la signature par le Président Eisenhower de l'Interstate Highways Act en 1956, le plus grand projet de travaux publics que le monde eût jamais connu. Oubliez les pyramides! Le devis initial pour ces autoroutes inter-États s'élevait à 25 milliards de dollars sur 12 ans; en fin de compte, les travaux coûtèrent 114 milliards de dollars sur 35 ans. Les Américains investirent ces routes au fur et à mesure de leur construction. D'ailleurs, le voyage en voiture constitue sans doute leur passe-temps préféré. Les jeunes traversaient le pays à la recherche d'eux-mêmes (comme en parle Jack Kerouac dans *Sur la Route*). Les étudiants en quête de romance passaient les vacances de Pâques au soleil (comme dans le film *Where the Boys Are* avec Dolores Hart, George Hamilton et Yvette Mimieux). Les familles voyageaient vers de sublimes destinations touristiques et séjournaient dans des hôtels offrant des vues spectaculaires sur la nature (comme dans *Shining* ... ou peut-être pas!). Imaginez comme il est typiquement américain de suivre son propre chemin, et si amusant aussi (comme dans n'importe quel film de la saga *En Route* avec Bob Hope et Bing Crosby, notamment *En Route pour le Maroc* ou *En Route pour l'Alaska*).

1967

1968

1969

Latin American carrier Panagra merges with Braniff

Die lateinamerikanische Fluggesellschaft Panagra fusioniert mit Braniff

La compagnie aérienne sud-américaine Panagra fusionne avec Braniff

American Airlines introduces curbside baggage check

American Airlines führt die Gepäckaufgabe am Straßenrand ein

American Airlines introduit les comptoirs d'enregistrement de bagages

Neil Armstrong and Buzz Aldrin first humans to walk on Moon

Neil Armstrong und Buzz Aldrin betreten als erste Menschen den Mond

Neil Armstrong et Buzz Aldrin sont les premiers hommes à marcher sur la Lune

Ces voyageurs automobiles avaient cependant besoin d'endroits où dormir. Dans le cadre de cette démocratisation, on en vint à attendre un certain standard d'hospitalité. L'une des réponses fut apportée par les chaînes de motels (la contraction de « moteur » et de « hôtel »). Quand une famille voyageait en voiture, descendre dans un Howard Johnson's Motor Lodge ou un Holiday Inn lui assurait des chambres propres, bon marché et *standardisées* partout à travers le pays. Fondée en 1952, la chaîne Holiday Inn comptait déjà 1 000 enseignes en 1968. D'Athens, Géorgie, à Anaheim, Californie, la chaîne de restaurants Howard Johnson's proposait les mêmes 28 parfums de glace d'une carte de restaurant à l'autre.

Alors qu'Howard Johnson's allait devenir une enseigne digne de confiance le long des routes américaines, des chaînes plus haut de gamme comme les hôtels Hilton et Hyatt reproduisirent de petits îlots d'Amérique dans les pays étrangers. En fait, l'hôtelier Conrad Hilton affirma que ses hôtels devaient refléter les valeurs qui, selon lui, avaient fait la grandeur de l'Amérique. En pleine Guerre Froide, dans les années 1950 et 1960, Hilton considérait ses hôtels comme autant d'ambassadeurs des valeurs américaines – et le gouvernement américain le pensait aussi. Avec l'aide de Washington et des gouvernements étrangers, Hilton installa ses hôtels dans les capitales de la Guerre Froide, là où l'Occident affrontait le Bloc soviétique.

Ces projets hôteliers visaient un but idéologique. Comme les ambassades modernistes construites à la même époque, les hôtels Hilton étaient conçus pour symboliser l'Amérique. Leurs structures étaient ouvertes, transparentes et accueillantes pour tous ceux qui souhaitaient y entrer. Contrairement aux grands hôtels européens plus anciens, où les clients pénétraient dans des halls imposants et richement décorés, ils se distinguaient par des volumes épurés et des parois en verre permettant aux visiteurs de regarder à travers. « Pour nous, ces hôtels sont un défi », expliquait Hilton. « Non pas envers ceux qui nous ont si cordialement accueillis sur leur territoire, mais envers le mode de vie prêché par le monde communiste ». Hilton considérait ses hôtels comme l'avant-garde de la démocratie, des pions placés par son pays pour démocratiser le voyage.

Ce processus de démocratisation se poursuivit bien après la fin de la Guerre Froide. Avec le vote de l'Airline Deregulation Act en 1978, les voyages en avion devinrent plus abordables, et plus

1970

1970

1971

After President Richard M. Nixon hosts Apollo 11 astronauts, Century Plaza Hotel nicknamed "West Coast White House"

Präsident Richard M. Nixon empfängt die Astronauten von Apollo 11 im Century Plaza Hotel, Spitzname „Weißes Haus der Westküste"

Nixon y ayant reçu les astronautes d'Apollo 11, le Century Plaza Hotel est surnommé « la Maison Blanche de la Côte Ouest »

First commercial flight of Boeing 747 jumbo jet, which holds passenger capacity record for rest of century

Erster kommerzieller Flug der Boeing 747 (Jumbojet), die den Sitzplatzrekord für den Rest des Jahrhunderts verteidigen kann

Premier vol commercial du « jumbo jet » Boeing 747, qui conserve le record de capacité d'accueil de passagers jusqu'à la fin du siècle

First-class airline lounges go disco

Discofeeling nun auch in der ersten Klasse

Dans les aéroports, les salons de première classe se mettent à la mode disco fréquents. Si se rendre à l'aéroport n'avait plus rien de glamour, un nombre croissant de personnes pouvait se permettre de rouler sur le tarmac. Les Américains développèrent la même attitude envers l'hôtellerie. Dans les années 1980, Ian Schrager, ancien propriétaire de boîtes de nuit, inventa le concept de « boutique hotel », un hôtel à l'ambiance feutrée où chaque client a l'impression de bénéficier d'un traitement exclusif. À la fin des années 1990, la chaîne W et le Standard ouvrirent leurs portes sous forme de copies plus grandes et plus abordables : le luxe version économique.

Au XXᵉ siècle, les Américains ont transformé l'idée du voyage. Ils en ont réinventé la forme, tout comme ils n'ont cessé de se réinventer eux-mêmes au cours de leur histoire. À la fin du siècle, le voyage était devenu plus rapide que ce dont ses pionniers n'auraient jamais rêvé. La vaste classe moyenne de l'Amérique d'après-guerre était nomade et intrépide.

LE SUD DE LA FRANCE OFFRE UN BON EXEMPLE D'UN TEL DÉVELOPPEMENT. CETTE ANCIENNE ENCLAVE HIVERNALE DE LUXE S'EST RADICALEMENT MÉTAMORPHOSÉE AU COURS DU SIÈCLE, AU POINT DE DEVENIR UN PARADIS ESTIVAL EXTRÊMEMENT POPULAIRE. Au début des années 1900, l'hiver était *la saison*. Les aristocrates russes séjournaient plusieurs semaines d'affilée dans les grands hôtels. Même s'il pleuvait et faisait un peu froid, le climat leur semblait doux par rapport aux rigueurs de l'hiver russe.

Pendant les Années Folles, une myriade d'Américains fortunés devait à jamais transformer le paysage : en 1922, Cole Porter, riche compositeur américain aux amis européens sophistiqués, décida de passer l'été à Antibes. Il loua une villa près de l'Hôtel du Cap, une adresse de référence qui fermait chaque été. Porter invita son ami proche Gerald Murphy, héritier du bagagier Mark Cross, avec sa famille. L'été suivant, les Murphy, le couple qui inspira les personnages de Dick et Nicole Diver à F. Scott Fitzgerald dans *Tendre est la Nuit*, persuadèrent l'Hôtel du Cap de rester ouvert. Ils s'y installèrent avec leur ami Pablo Picasso et tous les siens. Gertrude Stein et Alice B. Toklas y descendirent aussi. Les vacances d'été dans le sud de la France venaient d'apparaître sur le radar de la jet-set.

C'est à cette époque que les bains de soleil devinrent à la mode et que la voile, le tennis, le golf et la natation séduisirent les femmes comme les hommes. Dès 1922, il était plus facile de rejoindre le

1973

1973

1982

Braniff hires artist Alexander Calder to paint Douglas DC-8 jet, dubbed "Flying Colors"

Alexander Calder taucht die Douglas DC-8 für Braniff in neue Farben („Flying Colors")

La compagnie Braniff demande à Alexander Calder de peindre son Douglas DC-8, surnommé « Flying Colors »

Energy shortage leads to gasoline lines and skyrocketing airfares

Die Energiekrise führt zu Schlangen an den Tankstellen und lässt die Preise für Flugtickets in die Höhe schnellen

La crise pétrolière provoque de longues files d'attente devant les stations essence et voit monter en flèche le prix des billets d'avion

Enactment of 1978 Airline Deregulation Act sends industry into tailspin, more than 100 small carriers go out of business

Der Airline Deregulation Act von 1978 bringt die gesamte Branche ins Trudeln und kostet über 100 Fluglinien die Existenz

Avec l'entrée en vigueur de l'Airline Deregulation Act voté en 1978, plus de 100 compagnies aériennes déposent le bilan sud de la France. Quand les Impressionnistes venaient y peindre, même les Français considéraient cette région comme « exotique », mais l'élégant Train Bleu effectuait désormais chaque nuit la liaison Paris/Côte d'Azur. En 1925, quand les Murphy s'installèrent dans la Villa America, leur nouvelle maison à Antibes, le monde entier ne parlait plus que des étés dans le sud de la France. Ce n'était pas que le bleu profond de la mer et le doux parfum du mimosa. Toute la Côte d'Azur devint une destination de prédilection pour de très nombreuses personnes car il était de plus en plus facile de s'y rendre. Il y avait un grand aéroport à Nice, des trains moins chers, de meilleures routes. Tout le monde décida que ça valait le déplacement, non seulement les riches et les célébrités, mais aussi une bonne partie de la classe moyenne, même les retraités.

Le Festival du Film de Cannes, créé un an après la fin de la Seconde Guerre mondiale, ne fit qu'augmenter l'attrait de la région. Chaque printemps, les stars d'Hollywood, les patrons des studios et tout un assortiment de « beautiful people » – généralement au sens propre du terme – s'envolaient pour le sud de la France. On pouvait devenir une vedette internationale simplement en folâtrant dans les vagues. En 1953, une jeune starlette nommée Brigitte Bardot posa en bikini devant les photographes, et son nom fit le tour du monde. Les films américains ne cessaient de rappeler aux spectateurs les plaisirs qui les attendaient dans le sud de la France (qui n'aurait pas envie de tourner un film là-bas ?). Grace Kelly ne fut jamais plus délicieuse et Cary Grant plus suave que dans *La Main au Collet* d'Alfred Hitchcock (1955). Et quand Grace Kelly épousa le Prince Rainier III de Monaco, les Américains eurent une autre bonne raison d'aller visiter la Riviera.

À la fin du siècle, les plages de la Côte d'Azur étaient bondées d'estivants serrés comme des sardines. Les voyageurs arrivaient des quatre coins du globe, qu'ils volent en classe éco ou à bord de jets privés, roulent dans des trains supplémentaires ou de minuscules voitures de location, fassent une escale pendant une croisière ou débarquent d'un énorme yacht. La côte fourmille d'hôtels adaptés à tous les budgets et tous les styles. Les meilleurs hôtels ne sont plus réservés à l'élite.

Et ce, grâce aux Américains. Accélérer, simplifier et démocratiser le voyage : l'objectif américain a défini la norme mondiale.

▶ United States Virgin Islands Division of Tourism, 1981

1984

1986

1988

With inexpensive screen printing widely available, T-shirts becoming popular tourist souvenir

Die weite Verbreitung des preiswerten Siebdruckverfahrens macht das bedruckte T-Shirt zu einem beliebten Souvenir

Les impressions bon marché par sérigraphie font le succès du « T-shirt souvenir » auprès des touristes

The Love Boat TV series docks after nine years at sea, but Princess Cruises more popular than ever

Die Fernsehserie *The Love Boat* wird nach neun Jahren eingestellt, doch Princess Cruises ist beliebter denn je

Si la série télé *La Croisière s'amuse* est arrêtée au bout de neuf ans, la compagnie Princess Cruises n'a jamais eu autant de succès

Amanpuri, flagship of Aman Resorts, small luxury hotels emphasizing natural surroundings, opens in Phuket, Thailand

Die Aman Resorts sind um natürliche Umgebung bemühte Luxushotels. Ihr Flaggschiff, das Amanpuri, öffnet in Phuket seine Pforten

Ouverture de l'Amanpuri – fleuron d'Aman Resorts, petits hôtels de luxe dans de superbes cadres naturels – à Phuket en Thaïlande

"TRAVEL IS FATAL TO
PREJUDICE, BIGOTRY, AND
NARROW-MINDEDNESS."
–MARK TWAIN

„REISEN IST TÖDLICH
FÜR VORURTEILE,
BIGOTTERIE UND
ENGSTIRNIGKEIT."
–MARK TWAIN

1900

« LE VOYAGE EST FATAL AUX PRÉJUGÉS, AU FANATISME ET À L'ÉTROITESSE D'ESPRIT. »
– MARK TWAIN

1919

CHECKING IN

When guests walked into a palatial hotel in
Paris… they stayed the season, not the week.

AT THE TURN OF THE CENTURY, LEISURE TRAVEL WAS A LUXURY, THE RECREATION OF CHOICE FOR THE VERY RICH. JOURNEYS COULD BE FASHIONABLY EDUCATIONAL, LIKE A GRAND TOUR OF EUROPE, or exotically sybaritic, like a stay in a North African casbah. In the first decade of the new century, a grand procession of Beaux Arts hotels opened around the globe. When guests checked in to a palatial hotel in Paris or a vast Victorian Saracenic pile in Cairo, they entered a world of opulence. They stayed the season, not the week.

These stately hotels sought to outshine each other. The Hôtel des Bains, a monumental resort that helped make sunbathing acceptable, opened on the Venice Lido in 1900. In 1903, the massive Taj Mahal Hotel opened in Bombay. The next year, John Jacob Astor IV built the $5.5-million St. Regis in New York. Soon, the Palace Hotel debuted on the Bund in Shanghai, the Ritz in London, the Adlon in Berlin, the Plaza Hotel in New York, and the Hotel Excelsior in Rome. Each staked its claim as "greatest hotel in the world."

Out West, Americans built their own version of a grand hotel — sprawling rustic lodges made of natural, local materials, developed by public and private interests. President Theodore Roosevelt, an ardent conservationist, pushed the federal government to create national parks, including the Grand Canyon. Yet it was Western railroads, eager for passengers, that built the picturesque destination hotels. The influential 1904 Old Faithful Inn, built by the Northern Pacific Railroad in Yellowstone National Park, featured a vast seven-story lobby made entirely of logs. The next year, the Atchison, Topeka and Santa Fe Railway opened El Tovar, a grand lodge at the southern rim of the Grand Canyon.

It was owned and run by Fred Harvey, who built the Harvey House restaurants into the first national chain and brought the same meticulous service to the hotel. It did what it was designed to do: dramatically increase tourism in the area.

When Europe beckoned, Gilded Age travelers embarked on grand ships. The Hamburg-American Line was most popular, and its *Deutschland* won the Blue Riband in 1900 for the fastest voyage across the Atlantic — five days, 15 hours, five minutes. Travel to Hawaii blossomed as well. In 1902, the Matson Navigation Company, which steamed between Hawaii and the mainland, opened the Moana, the first hotel on Waikiki Beach. Jack London's 1907 magazine article about the Hawaiian surfer George Freeth introduced that sport to the mainland. By 1908, William Matson had built the steamship *Lurline*, named for his daughter, to carry freight and 51 passengers. Hawaii was on its way to becoming a major travel destination.

Yet, one of the decade's biggest attractions was not an exotic locale, but the 1904 St. Louis World's Fair. More than 20 million visitors from around the globe saw the Louisiana Purchase Exposition. The newfangled ice cream cone was a crowd favorite. This large turnout signaled that U.S. travel destinations appealed to the growing middle class. Democratization of travel had begun.

ONCE HENRY FORD STARTED SELLING HIS MODEL T IN 1908, IT REVOLUTIONIZED THE WAY AMERICANS APPROACHED TRAVEL. At the dawn of the 1910s, trains provided 95% of all intercity transportation in the United States. By the decade's close, automobile travel miles surpassed railroad miles.

Yet throughout the 1910s, trains seemed in a golden era, moving ever faster and more comfortably. The California land boom, for one, created huge demand. Cited for its cheap land and endless sunshine, California was also considered exotic and fascinating by Easterners. In 1912, a leading Hawaiian surfer, Duke Kahanamoku, emerged as the worldwide envoy for the sport, giving demonstrations on Southern California beaches. The fact that the young movie industry settled there was also alluring.

1900

Hôtel des Bains opens; Thomas Mann writes *Death in Venice* after 1911 stay there

Eröffnung des Hôtel des Bains; Thomas Mann verfasst *Der Tod in Venedig*, nachdem er 1911 dort abgestiegen war

Ouverture de l'Hôtel des Bains ; Thomas Mann écrira *La Mort à Venise* après y avoir séjourné en 1911

1901

Louis Vuitton introduces steamer bag, designed to fit inside larger trunks

Louis Vuitton präsentiert die in größere Koffer passende Dampfer-Tasche

Louis Vuitton lance le « steamer bag », un sac conçu pour tenir à l'intérieur des grandes malles

1901

New York Central debuts overnight 20th Century Limited train from New York to Chicago

New York Central führt mit dem Zug 20th Century Limited die erste Nachtstrecke zwischen New York und Chicago ein

La compagnie New York Central lance le train de nuit « 20th Century Limited » qui relie New York à Chicago

Travelers flocked to the Golden State. The Atchison, Topeka and Santa Fe responded, in 1911, with Santa Fe de-Lux service. Flyers roared express to California, for $25 more than the standard ticket price. Two years later, the Sante Fe Line tried a new form of advertising—billboards. Demand only increased.

But there was an enticing alternative: the automobile. And when it comes to car travel, all roads lead to Carl G. Fisher, an entrepreneur infatuated by automobiles, auto racing, and land development. Later in the century, Fisher would dream of dazzling resorts in Miami Beach, Florida, and Montauk, New York, but he was practical enough to realize you first needed roads to get there. So, in 1913, he developed the first cross-country roadway, the Lincoln Highway, beating the U.S. Congress's first public highways legislation by three years.

While land travel was on the rise, ocean travel faced rocky shoals. Ocean liners had grown ever more glorious each passing year. But on April 14, 1912, the RMS *Titanic*, queen of the White Star Line and the largest passenger steamship, hit an iceberg and sank on its maiden voyage. It was one of the deadliest peacetime maritime disasters—1,517 passengers were killed (including hotelier John Jacob Astor IV), and only 706 survived. Then, with the onset of World War I in 1914, passenger travel plummeted. Many sumptuous liners, like the Hamburg-American Line's *Vaterland*, the largest ship afloat, were refitted as troop ships. Passenger travel slumped even more after the RMS *Lusitania*, part of the Cunard Line, was torpedoed by a German U-boat in 1915. It sank in 18 minutes, and of the 1,959 people aboard, 1,198 died.

Yet ocean travel did see advances when the Panama Canal, dubbed "the 13th labor of Hercules," opened in 1914. Travel by ship between New York and San Francisco was cut by more than half—to 11,000 km (6,000 miles), from 25,900 km (14,000 miles). The new canal was celebrated with the Panama-Pacific International Exposition in San Francisco in 1915. This world's fair signaled the host city's rebirth after the devastating 1906 earthquake. One exhibit, built by Henry Ford, featured an assembly line. It produced cars three hours a day, six days a week. This was so popular that the line of visitors waiting to see it never seemed to shorten.

Page 38 Hotel St. Francis, 1904　▶▶ Hamburg-American Line, 1914

1902

First science fiction film, and one of earliest movies, *A Trip to the Moon* imagines flight beyond Earth

Die Reise zum Mond, der erste Science-Fiction-Film und einer der frühesten Filme überhaupt, träumt von einem Vorstoß ins All

Le Voyage dans la Lune, l'un des premiers films et le premier de science-fiction met en scène une expédition spatiale

1903

Wright Brothers' first flight at Kitty Hawk, North Carolina

Erster Flug der Gebrüder Wright in Kitty Hawk, North Carolina

Premier vol des frères Wright à Kitty Hawk, Caroline du Nord

1903

Horatio Nelson Jackson and dog Bud make first transcontinental car journey

Horatio Nelson Jackson unternimmt mit seinem Hund Bud die erste transkontinentale Autoreise

Horatio Nelson Jackson et le chien Bud effectuent le premier voyage transcontinental en voiture

EINCHECKEN

*Wenn ein Gast ein feudales Pariser Hotel
betrat, dann blieb er nicht eine Woche,
sondern die ganze Saison.*

VERGNÜGUNGSREISEN WAREN UM 1900 PURER LUXUS, DIE VON DEN WIRKLICH REICHEN BEVORZUGTE ART DER ERHOLUNG. DIE REISEN KONNTEN, WIE ES DAMALS SCHICK WAR, PÄDAGOGISCH WERTVOLL SEIN WIE EINE BILDUNGSREISE DURCH EUROPA oder aber in Exotik schwelgen wie der Aufenthalt in einer nordafrikanischen Kasba. In der ersten Dekade des neuen Jahrhunderts entstanden überall auf der Welt zahlreiche „Beaux Arts"-Hotels. Wer in ein feudales Hotel in Paris oder einen viktorianisch-sarazenischen Prachtbau in Kairo eincheckte, betrat eine opulente Welt. Und er blieb nicht eine Woche, sondern die ganze Saison.

Jedes dieser Prachthotels wollte das Beste sein. Das Hôtel des Bains, eine monumentale Anlage, die das Sonnenbaden salonfähig machte, öffnete im Jahr 1900 seine Pforten auf dem Lido von Venedig, 1903 folgte das wuchtige Taj Mahal Hotel in Bombay. Im Jahr darauf baute John Jacob Astor IV. für 5,5 Mio. $ das St. Regis in New York. Kurz danach kamen das Palace Hotel auf dem Bund in Schanghai, das Ritz in London, das Adlon in Berlin, das Plaza Hotel in New York und das Hotel Excelsior in Rom. Jedes von ihnen beanspruchte eine weltweite Spitzenstellung.

Weit im Westen schufen die Amerikaner ihre eigene Version eines „Grandhotels" – ausufernde rustikale Lodges aus natürlichen, lokalen Materialien, finanziert mit öffentlichen und privaten Mitteln. Präsident Theodore Roosevelt, ein leidenschaftlicher Naturschützer, drängte die nationale Regierung zur Einrichtung von Nationalparks, darunter auch der Grand Canyon. Die pittoresken Landhotels verdanken sich indes der auf mehr Fahrgäste bedachten Eisenbahngesellschaft Western Railroads. Das stilbildende, 1904 von der Northern Pacific Railroad im Yellowstone National Park er-

Southern Pacific, 1907

richtete Old Faithful Inn bestach mit einer gewaltigen siebenstöckigen Lobby in Blockbauweise. Im Jahr darauf eröffnete die Atchison, Topeka and Santa Fe Railway das El Tovar, eine große Lodge am Südrand des Grand Canyon. Eigentümer und Betreiber war Fred Harvey, der die Harvey House Restaurants zur ersten landesweiten Restaurantkette ausgebaut hatte und deren untadeligen Service nun auf den Hotelsektor übertrug. Der Plan ging auf, denn die regionalen Besucherzahlen schnellten in die Höhe.

Amerikaner, die sich im Gilded Age von Europa angelockt fühlten, gingen an Bord eines der großen Dampfer. Am beliebtesten war die Hamburg-Amerika-Linie (HAPAG), deren *Deutschland* 1900 das Blaue Band für die schnellste Atlantiküberquerung gewann – fünf Tage, 15 Stunden und fünf Minuten. Reisen nach Hawaii waren ebenfalls gefragt. Zwischen Hawaii und dem Festland verkehrend, eröffnete die Matson Navigation Company 1902 mit dem Moana das erste Hotel von Waikiki Beach. Jack Londons 1907 erschienener Zeitschriftenartikel über den hawaiianischen Surfer George Freeth machte auch die Landratten mit diesem Sport bekannt. Und 1908 lief William Matsons nach seiner Tochter benanntes Dampfschiff *Lurline* vom Stapel, das Fracht plus 51 Passagiere beförderte. Hawaii war auf dem besten Weg, ein gefragtes Reiseziel zu werden.

Doch zu den größten Attraktionen dieser Dekade zählte nicht ein exotischer Schauplatz, son-

1904

Hotel St. Francis opens in San Francisco, but soon destroyed in 1906 earthquake

Eröffnung des Hotel St. Francis in San Francisco, das jedoch durch das Erdbeben von 1906 zerstört wird

L'Hotel St. Francis ouvre à San Francisco, avant d'être détruit par le tremblement de terre de 1906

1904

Old Faithful Inn opens in Yellowstone National Park, influences all rustic grand hotels

Eröffnung des Old Faithful Inn im Yellowstone National Park als wegweisendes Beispiel für ein rustikales Grandhotel

Ouverture de l'Old Faithful Inn dans le Parc National de Yellowstone, hôtel qui influencera la conception de tous les grands pavillons hôteliers rustiques

1905

El Tovar, grand resort lodge at south rim of Grand Canyon, opens, dramatically increasing tourism to area

Die Eröffnung des El Tovar, einer großen resortartigen Lodge am Grand Canyon, führt zu einem Anstieg des Tourismus in der Region

Avec l'ouverture d'El Tovar, grand pavillon hôtelier sur la bordure sud du Grand Canyon, le tourisme explose dans la région dern die Weltausstellung von 1904 in St. Louis. Mehr als 20 Millionen Menschen aus aller Welt besuchten die Louisiana Purchase Exposition. Das neumodische Eishörnchen entwickelte sich zum Publikumsmagneten. Die wachsende Mittelschicht fand an inländischen Reisezielen Gefallen. Die Demokratisierung des Reisens hatte begonnen.

SOBALD HENRY FORD 1908 SEIN MODELL T ANGEBOTEN HATTE, VERWANDELTE SICH DIE AUFFASSUNG DER AMERIKANER VOM REISEN GRUNDLEGEND. Um 1910 sorgten Züge noch für 95 % aller Transporte zwischen den Städten. Gegen Ende des Jahrzehnts wurden die Eisenbahnkilometer indes von den Autokilometern übertroffen.

Dennoch war dieses Jahrzehnt eine Blütezeit der Eisenbahn. Eine immense Nachfrage entstand etwa durch den Bauboom in Kalifornien. Das wegen seiner niedrigen Grundstückspreise und des endlosen Sonnenscheins gerühmte Kalifornien wirkte auf die Menschen im Osten zudem exotisch und faszinierend. Duke Kahanamoku, einer der besten Surfer von Hawaii, trat 1912 als weltweiter Botschafter seines Sports auf und gab Kostproben an den Stränden von Südkalifornien. Verlockend war auch, dass sich die noch junge Filmindustrie hier niedergelassen hatte.

Die Reisenden strömten in den Golden State. Bereits 1911 reagierte die Bahngesellschaft Atchison, Topeka and Santa Fe mit dem „Santa Fe de Lux"-Service. Für einen Zuschlag von nur 25 $ donnerten Schnellzüge nach Kalifornien. Zwei Jahre darauf versuchte es die Santa Fe mit einer neuen Art der Werbung: Reklametafeln.

Es gab jedoch eine verführerische Alternative: das Auto. Und beim Thema Autoreisen führen gleichsam alle Straßen zu Carl G. Fisher, einem Unternehmer mit einem Faible für Autorennen und Landerschließung. Später würde Fisher von prächtigen Resorts in Miami Beach und Montauk, New York, träumen, doch ihm war klar, dass man zunächst einmal Straßen brauchte, um dorthin zu gelangen. Mit dem Lincoln Highway entwickelte er 1913 die erste Überlandtrasse und kam damit den ersten Gesetzen für öffentliche Highways um drei Jahre zuvor.

Während das Reisen zu Lande einen Aufschwung nahm, hatten die Reedereien schwer zu kämpfen. Bisher waren jedes Jahr immer prachtvollere Linienschiffe vom Stapel gelaufen. Dann aber kam

1907

1908

1908

Hotel Buffalo debuts as first major urban hotel with bath in each room

Hotel Buffalo als erstes großes Stadthotel mit Bad für jedes Zimmer

Ouverture de l'Hotel Buffalo, le premier grand hôtel urbain avec salle de bains dans chaque chambre

Cunard's Mauretania wins Blue Riband for fastest Atlantic crossing and holds it for 22 years

Cunards *Mauretania* gewinnt das Blaue Band für die schnellste Atlantiküberquerung und kann es 22 Jahre verteidigen

Le *Mauretania* de la compagnie Cunard remporte le Ruban Bleu pour la traversée la plus rapide de l'Atlantique et le conserve pendant 22 ans

Henry Ford's new Model T democratizes road travel in America

Henry Fords neues Model T demokratisiert das Reisen mit dem Auto in den USA

La nouvelle Model T d'Henry Ford démocratise le voyage en voiture aux États-Unis

Panama-Pacific International Exposition, 1915

der 14. April 1912: Die RMS *Titanic*, Flaggschiff der White Star Line und größtes Passagierschiff der Welt, kollidiert auf ihrer Jungfernfahrt mit einem Eisberg und geht unter. Dies war eines der verheerendsten Seeunglücke in Friedenszeiten – 1517 Passagiere und Besatzungsmitglieder kamen um, und nur 706 überlebten. Als 1914 der Erste Weltkrieg ausbrach, gingen die Passagierzahlen in den Keller. Viele Luxusliner wie HAPAGs *Vaterland*, das größte Schiff der Meere, wurden für den Truppentransport umgerüstet. Das Passagieraufkommen ging noch stärker zurück, nachdem die RMS *Lusitania* der Cunard Line 1915 von einem deutschen U-Boot torpediert worden war.

Positiv war indessen die Eröffnung des Panamakanals im Jahr 1914. Eine Schiffsreise von New York nach San Francisco verkürzte sich fortan um mehr als die Hälfte – von 25 900 auf 11 000 Kilometer. Den neuen Kanal feierte man 1915 mit der Panama-Pacific International Exposition in San Francisco. Diese Weltausstellung kündete von der Wiedergeburt der gastgebenden Stadt nach dem verheerenden Erdbeben von 1906. Ausgestellt wurde auch ein von Henry Ford stammendes Montageband, das drei Stunden täglich und sechs Tage pro Woche Autos ausspuckte und derart populär war, dass die Schlange der Besucher niemals kürzer zu werden schien.

► Hamburg-American Line, 1911   ►► Austrian Lloyd, 1912

1909

1910

1912

With travel becoming more accessible to the middle class, luggage begins to lighten up

Reisen werden auch für die Mittelschicht erschwinglich, und das Gepäck wird allmählich leichter

Alors que le nouveau siècle bat son plein et que le voyage devient plus accessible à la classe moyenne, les bagages commencent à s'alléger

Kaiser Wilhelm II stays at Zurich, Switzerland's Baur au Lac, built facing lake rather than town—new idea for hotels at the time

Aufenthalt von Kaiser Wilhelm II. im Zürcher Hotel Baur au Lac, das – damals ungewöhnlich – dem See zugewandt ist

L'Empereur Guillaume II séjourne à l'hôtel Baur au Lac de Zurich en Suisse, un établissement construit face au lac et non face à la ville

1,517 passengers killed when RMS *Titanic* sinks — including John Jacob Astor IV, hotelier; only 706 survive

Untergang der RMS *Titanic*; 1517 Passagiere kommen ums Leben, darunter der Hotelier John Jacob Astor IV.; nur 706 überleben

1517 passagers meurent dans le naufrage du *Titanic*, dont l'hôtelier John Jacob Astor IV ; seules 706 personnes survivent

HAMBURG-AMERICAN LIN

LA VIE DE PALACE

Quand les clients descendaient dans un palace parisien … ils n'y passaient pas qu'une semaine, mais toute une saison.

AU DÉBUT DU SIÈCLE DERNIER, VOYAGER POUR LE PLAISIR ÉTAIT UN LUXE. LES VOYAGES POUVAIENT ÊTRE À LA FOIS INSTRUCTIFS ET TRÈS À LA MODE, COMME LE GRAND TOUR D'EUROPE, ou d'un exotisme sybaritique, tel un séjour dans une casbah d'Afrique du Nord. Pendant la première décennie du nouveau siècle, un grand nombre d'hôtels style Beaux-arts ouvrit ses portes à travers le monde entier. Quand les clients descendaient dans un palace parisien ou un immense hôtel de style victorien et mauresque au Caire, ils pénétraient dans un univers d'opulence. Ils n'y passaient pas qu'une semaine, mais toute une saison.

Ces splendides hôtels cherchaient tous à s'éclipser les uns les autres. L'Hôtel des Bains, un édifice monumental qui contribua à rendre les bains de soleil acceptables, ouvrit sur le Lido de Venise en 1900. En 1903, l'impressionnant Taj Mahal Hotel était inauguré à Bombay. L'année suivante, John Jacob Astor IV fit construire le St. Regis à New York pour un montant de 5,5 millions de dollars. Tous furent rapidement suivis par le Palace Hotel du Bund de Shanghai, le Ritz à Londres, l'Adlon à Berlin, le Plaza Hotel à New York et l'Excelsior à Rome. Chacun se targuait d'être « le meilleur hôtel du monde ».

Outre-atlantique, les Américains inventèrent leur propre version du grand hôtel : des complexes tentaculaires composés de pavillons rustiques construits dans des matériaux naturels locaux à l'aide de participations publiques et privées. Le Président Theodore Roosevelt incita le gouvernement fédéral à créer des parcs nationaux, notamment celui du Grand Canyon. Ce furent néanmoins les compagnies de chemins de fer de l'Ouest, avides de passagers, qui construisirent ces pittoresques

Pacific Mail, ca. 1916

hôtels. Bâti par la Northern Pacific Railroad dans le Parc National de Yellowstone, l'influent Old Faithful Inn de 1904 comprenait un vaste hall de sept étages entièrement construit de rondins de bois. L'année suivante, la compagnie ferroviaire Atchison, Topeka and Santa Fe Railway inaugura El Tovar, un grand pavillon situé sur la bordure sud du Grand Canyon. Il appartenait à Fred Harvey, qui fit de ses restaurants Harvey House la toute première chaîne nationale et soigna les prestations hôtelières, avec l'effet escompté : l'essor de tourisme dans la région.

Pour se rendre en Europe, les voyageurs du « Gilded Age » embarquaient à bord de navires grandioses. Le paquebot *Deutschland* de la Hamburg-American Line remporta le Ruban Bleu en 1900 pour la traversée la plus rapide de l'Atlantique en cinq jours, 15 heures, cinq minutes. Le tourisme à Hawaï prospérait aussi. En 1902, la Matson Navigation Company qui effectuait la liaison entre Hawaï et le continent ouvrit le Moana, le premier hôtel de Waikiki Beach. Les Américains découvrirent le surf dans l'article de Jack London paru en 1907 sur le surfeur hawaïen George Freeth. En 1908, William Matson fit construire son bateau vapeur *Lurline*, ainsi baptisé en hommage à sa fille, pour transporter du fret et 51 passagers. Hawaï allait s'imposer comme une grande destination touristique.

L'une des plus grandes attractions de la décennie ne fut toutefois pas un lieu exotique, mais l'Exposition Universelle de 1904 à Saint-Louis qui accueillit plus de 20 millions de visiteurs venus du monde entier. Les tout nouveaux cônes gaufrés utilisés pour la dégustation des crèmes glacées firent

1912

1912

1913

Women begin to do more than just go for a dip in the ocean; they go swimming with men

Die ersten Frauen mischen sich unter die männlichen Schwimmer, anstatt wie bisher nur im seichten Wasser zu planschen

Au bord de la mer, les femmes ne se contentent plus de timides bains de pieds ; elles se mettent à nager, comme les hommes

Hawaiian Duke Kahanamoku acts as surfing ambassador, giving demonstrations in California before swimming in Olympics

Duke Kahanamoku wirbt für das Surfen und demonstriert vor seiner Olympiateilnahme als Schwimmer sein Können

En surfant en Californie avant de nager aux Jeux Olympiques, le Hawaïen Duke Kahanamoku devient l'ambassadeur de son sport

Great White Fleet of United Fruit Company grows to meet to U.S. demand for travel to Latin America

Die „Große Weiße Flotte" der United Fruit Company reagiert auf die US-Nachfrage nach Reisen nach Mittelamerika

Le Great White Fleet de la United Fruit Company répond à la demande en voyages aux Caraïbes et en Amérique Centrale fureur auprès du public. Les destinations touristiques américaines attiraient la classe moyenne en plein essor. La démocratisation du voyage venait de commencer.

LORSQUE HENRY FORD LANÇA LA MODEL T EN 1908, LA FAÇON DE VOYAGER DES AMÉRICAINS CHANGEA. À l'aube des années 1910, le train représentait 95 % de la totalité du trafic interurbain aux États-Unis. Dix ans plus tard, on voyageait davantage par la route que par le rail.

Toujours plus rapides et plus confortables, les trains connurent leur âge d'or de 1910 à 1920. La ruée vers la Californie, entre autres, contribua au boom des voyages ferroviaires. Recherchée pour ses terres bon marché et son soleil éternel, la Californie fascinait les habitants de l'Est. En 1912, le grand surfeur hawaïen Duke Kahanamoku devint l'ambassa

La Reserve de Nice, ca. 1910

deur mondial de son sport en s'y adonnant sur les plages de Californie du Sud. L'installation de la jeune industrie du cinéma en Californie rendit cet État d'autant plus attirant.

Les voyageurs se précipitèrent vers le « Golden State ». La compagnie de chemins de fer Atchison, Topeka and Santa Fe réagit dès 1911 en introduisant le service Santa Fe de Lux : pour seulement 25 dollars de plus que le prix d'un billet standard, on pouvait rejoindre la Californie par voie « express ». Deux ans plus tard, la ligne de Sante Fe testa une nouvelle forme de publicité : les panneaux d'affichage. La demande ne fit qu'augmenter.

La voiture restait toutefois séduisante. Et en matière de voyage automobile, toutes les routes mènent à Carl G. Fisher, homme d'affaires passionné de voitures et d'aménagement foncier. Fisher

1913

Gustave Eiffel devises metal framing for the large dome of Hôtel Negresco in Nice, France

Gustave Eiffel entwirft das Metallgerüst für die große Kuppel des Hôtel Negresco in Nizza

Gustave Eiffel invente la structure en métal du grand dôme de l'Hôtel Negresco de Nice

1914

Opening of Panama Canal; cuts voyage between New York and California by more than half

Eröffnung des Panamakanals, der die Reise von New York nach Kalifornien um mehr als die Hälfte verkürzt

Ouverture du Canal de Panama, qui réduit de moitié le trajet par bateau entre New York et la Californie

1915

Cunard's RMS *Lusitania* torpedoed by German U-boat and sinks in 18 minutes; of 1,959 people aboard, 1,198 die

Cunards RMS *Lusitania* wird durch ein deutsches U-Boot torpediert und sinkt innerhalb von 18 Minuten; 1198 von 1959 Menschen sterben

Torpillé par un U-boat allemand, le *Lusitania* de la Cunard sombre en 18 minutes ; sur les 1959 personnes à bord, 1198 périssent imaginera des hôtels éblouissants à Miami Beach en Floride et à Montauk dans l'État de New York, mais il possédait suffisamment de bon sens pour savoir qu'il fallait d'abord des routes. En 1913, il fit donc construire la première route transcontinentale du pays, le Lincoln Highway, avec trois ans d'avance sur les premières lois sur les autoroutes publiques des États-Unis.

Alors que le voyage terrestre se développait, les compagnies maritimes naviguaient en eaux troubles. Le 14 avril 1912, le *Titanic*, fleuron de la White Star et plus grand bateau vapeur destiné au transport de passagers, heurta un iceberg et sombra pendant sa croisière inaugurale. Ce fut l'une des catastrophes maritimes les plus mortelles jamais connues en temps de paix : 1517 morts (dont l'hôtelier John Jacob Astor IV) pour seulement 706 survivants. Avec le début de la Première Guerre mondiale en 1914, le trafic de voyageurs continua de chuter. De nombreux paquebots somptueux, comme le *Vaterland* de la Hamburg-American Line, plus grand navire à flot, furent reconvertis pour le transport de troupes. Le trafic de passagers toucha le fond quand le *Lusitania,* membre de la Cunard Line, fut torpillé par un U-boat allemand en 1915. Il coula en 18 minutes, et sur les 1959 personnes à bord, 1198 périrent.

Les voyages en paquebot connurent pourtant une embellie quand le Canal de Panama, surnommé « le 13ᵉ travail d'Hercule », fut inauguré en 1914. La durée de la traversée de New York à San Francisco fut ainsi plus que divisée par deux, passant de 11 000 à 5900 kilomètres. Le nouveau canal fut célébré à l'occasion de l'Exposition internationale Panama-Pacific de San Francisco en 1915, qui annonçait la renaissance de sa ville hôte après le terrible tremblement de terre de 1906. L'un des stands, construit par Henry Ford, présentait une ligne de montage qui produisait des voitures trois heures par jour, six jours par semaine. Elle remporta un tel succès que la file d'attente de visiteurs ne désemplit pas.

► North German Lloyd, 1909

1917

1918

1919

King Constantine I. of Greece and family move into Grand Hotel National, in Lucerne, Switzerland, for two years

Der griechische König Konstantin I. zieht mitsamt Familie für zwei Jahre ins Luzerner Grand Hotel National

Le Roi Constantin de Grèce et sa famille s'installent pendant deux ans au Grand Hotel National de Lucerne en Suisse

Grand dame Art Nouveau hotel Gellert Spa and Bath opens in Budapest, Hungary

Eröffnung des im Sezessionsstil errichteten Gellert Hotel und Bad in Budapest

L'hôtel Gellert, la « grande dame » de l'architecture Art Nouveau, ouvre avec thermes et bains à Budapest en Hongrie

Lufthansa predecessor Deutsche Luft Reederei adopts flying crane symbol; first airline to have logo

Die Deutsche Luft-Reederei, Vorläuferin der Lufthansa, präsentiert einen fliegenden Kranich; erste Airline mit Logo

La Deutsche Luft Reederei, prédécesseur de la Lufthansa, adopte le logo de la grue en vol ; première compagnie aérienne à se doter d'un logo

NEW YORK
NEW ORLEANS
BY
WATER
For HEALTH or PLEASURE

The Southern Pacific Morgan line
steamers "Proteus," "Comus" and
"Excelsior" sail regularly between
New York and New Orleans, leaving
New York on Saturdays and New
Orleans on Wednesdays, making
the trip in five days without stops

FOLLOW THE COURSE
OF THE GULF STREAM

Information at all offices of the
SOUTHERN PACIFIC COMPANY

◄ Southern Pacific, 1903

Cunard, 1911

In addition to transatlantic voyages, Cunard Lines offered Mediterranean cruises and voyages on the Adriatic. These ships often had a different configuration, with fewer first-class accommodations than those used for ocean journeys.

Neben transatlantischen Reisen offerierte Cunard Lines Mittelmeerkreuzfahrten und Adriatouren. Diese Schiffe waren oft anders aufgeteilt und besaßen weniger Erste-Klasse-Kabinen als die Ozeandampfer.

Outre les voyages transatlantiques, la compagnie Cunard proposait des croisières en Méditerranée et dans l'Adriatique sur des bateaux présentant une configuration différente et moins de cabines de première classe, contrairement aux navires dédiés aux transatlantiques.

CUNARD LINE

MEDITERRANEAN ~ EGYPTIAN ~ ADRIATIC CRUISES

NIAGARA

SAILING BETWEEN

LEWISTON, QU

AND TOR

◀ ◀ Niagara River Steamship Line, ca. 1904

Cunard, ca. 1914

The Cunard Line aimed for speed, leaving luxury to White Star. But the SS *Aquitania* was the "White Star Cunarder," nicknamed "Ship Beautiful." She was sister to the ill-fated *Lusitania* and the *Mauretania*, which won the Blue Riband for fastest Atlantic crossing in 1906 and held it 22 years.

Der Cunard Line ging es ums Tempo. Den Luxus überließ man der Reederei White Star. Doch die SS *Aquitania* war der „White Star von Cunard" alias „Ship Beautiful". Sie war das Schwesterschiff der unglückseligen *Lusitania* und der *Mauretania*, die 1906 das Blaue Band für die schnellste Atlantiküberquerung gewann und 22 Jahre lang verteidigte.

Laissant le luxe à la White Star, la compagnie Cunard faisait de la vitesse sa priorité. Son paquebot *Aquitania*, surnommé « le beau bateau », n'avait pourtant rien à envier à ceux de la White Star. C'était l'un des navires jumeaux de l'infortuné *Lusitania* et du *Mauretania*, qui remporta le Ruban Bleu pour la traversée la plus rapide de l'Atlantique en 1906, un titre qu'il conserva pendant 22 ans.

▶ White Star Line, 1913

The
Mediterranean
by the
WHITE STAR LINE

VENICE

White Star Line, 1914   ▸ Southern Pacific, 1907

California

THE OLD AND THE NEW WAY

The NEW way is by the SOUTHERN PACIFIC, Sunset Route Express Trains, equipped with latest Pullman Drawing-Room Sleepers, Combination Library, Observation and Buffet Cars, Dining and Chair Cars, a veritable "Hotel on Wheels" with clean Motive Power, Oil-Burning Locomotives, no dirt, dust or cinders, traversing the sugar plantations and rice fields of quaint Louisiana, the historic cities of the great State of Texas, through the interesting states of Arizona and New Mexico, on to the "Road of a Thousand Wonders," to the Garden of the World, the "Italy of America," CALIFORNIA. Connections made at San Francisco with magnificent new steamers of the Pacific Mail Steamship Company for Honolulu, China, Japan, Philippines and Round the World. For all information apply to any agent of

Southern Pacific

NEW YORK, N. Y.	BALTIMORE, MD.
349 Broadway	Baltimore, and Hanover Sts.
1 Broadway	
CHICAGO, ILL.	LOS ANGELES, CAL.
120 Jackson Boulevard	600 South Spring St.
ATLANTA, GA.	NEW ORLEANS, LA.
12½ Peachtree St.	Magazine and Natchez Sts.
BOSTON, MASS.	PHILADELPHIA, PA.
170 Washington St.	632 Chestnut St.
CINCINNATI, OHIO	SAN FRANCISCO, CAL
53 East Fourth St.	Ferry Building
HOUSTON, TEXAS	SYRACUSE, N. Y.
Main and Franklin Sts.	212 West Washington St.
HAMBURG, GERMANY	
"Amerikahaus," Ferdinand Strasse	

The Rock Island Lines
8000 Miles of Modern Railroad

Winter is Only a Name in Golden California

—only a word used to designate a season of the year.

Don't risk the cold weather with its dangers and discomforts.

Take the most enjoyable vacation of your whole life and escape the blizzards and the cold.

Take the "GOLDEN STATE LIMITED" to the balmy land of sea and sunshine—where mountains merge with meadows—where lakes and lagoons lie sparkling under sapphire skies—where springs flow their crystal waters into splendid streams—where fruits and flowers are abundant the whole year through—and where health and happiness await you with a warm welcom .

This semi-tropic land is less than three days from Chicago and St. Louis by the magnificent

"GOLDEN STATE LIMITED"
VIA ROCK ISLAND LINES

New all-steel Pu'lman equipment—entire train, baggage to observation car, through between Chicago and Los Angeles without change—every luxury of modern travel—for first-class passengers exclusively.

Leaves Chicago 9:00 p. m.
"   St. Louis 10:30 p. m. } *Kansas City 11:05 a. m. Arrives Los Angeles 3:30 p. m. third day.*

THE DIRECT ROUTE OF LOWEST ALTITUDES

The most comfortable and interesting route to California.

The Californian—a second transcontinental train via the *Golden State Route*—modern equipment—excellent service. Reservations, tickets and descriptive booklets about the "Golden State Limited" and "The Californian" from

L. M. ALLEN, Passenger Traffic Manager
Room 278, La Salle Station, Chicago

Rock Island

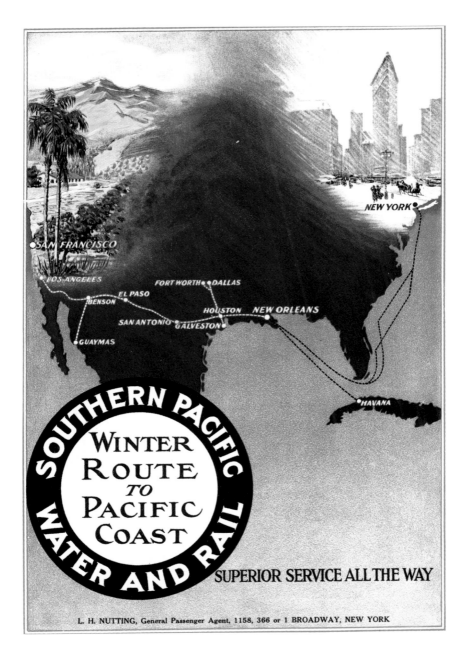

SOUTHERN PACIFIC
WATER AND RAIL

WINTER ROUTE TO PACIFIC COAST

SUPERIOR SERVICE ALL THE WAY

L. H. NUTTING, General Passenger Agent, 1158, 366 or 1 BROADWAY, NEW YORK

◄ The Rock Island Lines, 1915   Southern Pacific, 1910

SOUTH AMERICA

NEW YORK

BARBADOS
TRINIDAD

COLON
PANAMA

GUAYAQUIL

PERNAMBUCO

CALLAO

BAHIA

MOLLENDO

RIO DE JANEIRO
SANTOS

VALPARAISO

MONTEVIDEO
BUENOS AYRES

PUNTA ARENAS

LAMPORT & HOLT LINE

◄ Lamport & Holt Line, ca. 1912

Santa Fe Railway, 1916

The Sante Fe Railway created a series of
influential campaigns that adroitly blended
its corporate image with the routes traveled.
Artists captured the romance of the Southwest,
blending the Indian and Spanish heritage into
an alluring ad. Even before the Indian chief logo
was devised, there was an identifiable brand.

Santa Fe Railway schuf eine Reihe einflussreicher Werbekampagnen, die das eigene Image
mit den bedienten Routen geschickt vermeng-
ten. Künstler fingen die Romantik des Südwes-
tens ein und vereinigten das indianische mit
dem spanischen Erbe in einer verlockenden
Anzeige. Noch bevor man das Logo mit dem
Indianerhäuptling erfand, war dies bereits eine
unverwechselbare Marke.

La compagnie Sante Fe Railway lança une série
de campagnes marquantes qui mêlaient adroi-
tement son image institutionnelle avec son offre
d'itinéraires. Des artistes saisirent le roman-
tisme du sud-ouest américain en fusionnant son
héritage indien et espagnol dans une publicité
très attrayante. Bien avant la création du logo de
chef indien, la marque était déjà reconnaissable.

See the Apache Trail
En route to or from
CALIFORNIA

This marvelous motor side trip which has just been opened through Arizona's National Reserve is possible only if you choose the

Southern Pacific—Sunset Route

New Orleans   Los Angeles   San Diego   San Francisco

Eight magic hours of sightseeing in Oldest America—stupendous canyons, ancient cliff dwellings, picturesque copper camps and the famous Roosevelt Dam.

The Sunset Limited and other splendid trains afford daily service at **No Extra Fare**. Read the story of the Apache Trail in this issue of TRAVEL.

GENERAL OFFICES:

New York City   San Francisco   New Orleans   Houston
366 Broadway   Flood Building   Metropolitan Bank Building   Southern Pacific Building

◄ Southern Pacific, 1910   Southern Pacific, 1916

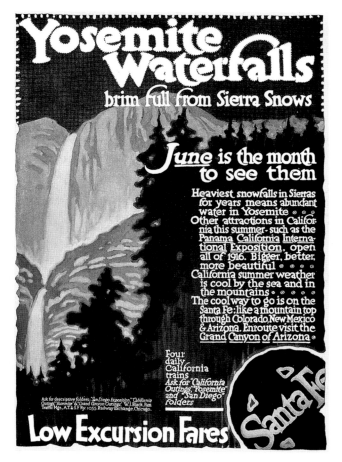

Great Northern Pacific S. S. Company, 1916

The Hawaii Promotion Committee was started in 1903 to help entice tourists to the tropical isles. By the teens, surfing was one of its most successful exports, largely popularized by Hawaiian swimming champion Duke Kahanamoku. While en route to the 1912 Olympics, Duke brought the island sport to America by giving surfing demonstrations as well as swimming demonstrations on Southern California beaches. He won multiple medals in swimming, but his surfing élan captured America's attention.

Das 1903 gegründete Hawaii Promotion Committee diente dem Zweck, mehr Touristen auf die tropischen Inseln zu locken. Schon 1910 zu einem der Exportschlager geworden, hatte der hawaiianische Schwimm-Champion Duke Kahanamoku das Surfen sehr populär gemacht. Auf dem Weg zur Olympiade 1912 brachte Duke den bisher auf Hawaii beschränkten Sport in die USA, indem er an den Stränden Südkaliforniens Kostproben seiner Surf- und auch Schwimmkünste gab. Als Schwimmer gewann er zahlreiche Medaillen, doch es war sein Surfstil, der die Menschen in den Bann zog.

Le Hawaii Promotion Committee fut créé en 1903 pour faire venir les touristes dans l'archipel tropical. Auprès des adolescents, l'une de ses exportations les plus plébiscitées fut le surf, popularisé par le champion de natation hawaïen Duke Kahanamoku. En route pour les Jeux Olympiques de 1912, Kahanamoku importa ce sport insulaire en Amérique en donnant des démonstrations de surf et de natation sur les plages de Californie du Sud. Il a remporté de nombreuses médailles de natation, mais l'Amérique se souvient surtout de ses prouesses de surfeur.

◄ Santa Fe Railway, 1916

HAWAII
PLEASURELAND
For The TOURIST

A Trip Exceeding All Anticipation

Y OUR enjoyment of fascinating Honolulu and the "Isles of Peace" depends largely upon **the route you travel.**

For the traveler who desires a fast, safe trip—with every comfort and luxury—the new de luxe service offered by the floating

"Palace of the Pacific"—S. S. GREAT NORTHERN

should prove attractive.

This trip will prove a realization of your fondest travel dreams— the delightful ocean voyage on this $3,000,000 triple turbiner—the tropical climate, picturesque scenery, and natural wonders all combining to make it a trip never to be forgotten.

VOLCANO KILAUEA—"HOME OF ETERNAL FIRE"

Stop is made at Hilo, affording passengers opportunity of seeing the world-famous Volcano Kilauea both by day and by night.

Mail the coupon below and let us give you full details of a trip to the "Paradise of the Pacific" via the "Palace of the Pacific."

H. A. JACKSON, General Traffic Manager, SAN FRANCISCO

- -

H. A. JACKSON, General Traffic Manager,
    Great Northern Pacific S. S. Co., San Francisco.

Please send me your free information and descriptive literature on the Hawaiian Islands.

Name..

Address..

City...State........................

- -

SAILINGS
From San Francisco
Nov. 7, 27; Dec. 15; Jan.
4, 23; Feb. 12; Mar. 5, 23.
From Los Angeles
One Day Later.

Fares on Application
————
Only Four Days
From The Mainland

GREAT NORTHERN PACIFIC
STEAMSHIP CO.

THE GREAT WHITE FLEET

"—there she lies

white as a swan—
our home for two weeks"

—and such a home; all the staterooms ar
outside rooms, de luxe and en suite; ther
are baths in plenty; spacious decks; mea
that tempt the appetite. Courteous service
restful ease.

Havana, the beautiful; Jamaica, "Land o
Smiling Summer;" the Panama Canal; th
romantic byways of the Spanish Main—yo
can enjoy them all in the wonderful ships o
the GREAT WHITE FLEET, built es
pecially for tropical travel.

Sailings of GREAT WHITE FLEET
Ships from New York and New Orlean
every Wednesday, Thursday and Saturday

Cruises from 17 to 22 days to

CUBA, JAMAICA, PANAMA CANAL COLOMBIAN PORTS, CENTRAL and SOUTH AMERICA

Liberal stopover privileges granted.

Ships sailing from New York on Wednesdays
and on all days from New Orleans are Ameri-
can-plan service; fare includes meals and
berth. Cruises de luxe from New York,
sailings every Saturday on the palatial new
steamers, Pastores, Tenadores and Calamares.
A la carte service on these ships only. Pay
for what you eat.

OFFICES FOR INFORMATION

Long Wharf, Boston; 630 Common Street, New Or
leans; 1955 Continental and Commercial Bank Build
ing, Chicago, or any ticket or tourist agent; or wri

PASSENGER DEPARTMENT
UNITED FRUIT COMPANY STEAMSHIP SERVIC
17 Battery Place, New York
for folders, sailing list and full information.

Write
for our
new book
—edition de
luxe—

The Story of a la Carte

A historic gem, in which is
related in Ancient Medieval
and Modern times what people ate at Sea—and how.
A story of sea dining from
4,500 B.C. to date.

SAILING UNDER THE AMERICAN FLAG

UNITED FRUIT COMPANY STEAMSHIP SERVIC

◄ United Fruit Company Steamship Service, 1914

United Fruit Company Steamship Service, 1916

The United Fruit Company began taking passengers with cargos of bananas in Latin America in 1907. It increased passenger counts, and ships, throughout the 1910s. The ships were dubbed the Great White Fleet, after the white armada that President Theodore Roosevelt sent around the globe to display U.S. sea power.

Die United Fruit Company begann 1907, im Verkehr nach Lateinamerika neben Bananen auch Passagiere zu befördern. Die Anzahl der Passagiere wie auch der Schiffe nahm in dem Jahrzehnt stetig zu. Dies war die „Große Weiße Flotte", benannt nach der „weißen Armada", die Präsident Theodore Roosevelt als Zeichen der Seemacht USA rund um den Globus entsandt hatte.

En 1907, la United Fruit Company commença à transporter des passagers en Amérique Latine avec ses cargos de bananes. Le nombre de passagers et de navires augmenta tout au long des années 1910. Sa flotte fut surnommée la « Great White Fleet » après que le Président Theodore Roosevelt a eu envoyé son armada blanche faire le tour du monde pour afficher la puissance de la marine américaine.

THE **GREAT WHITE FLEET**

The Call of the Caribbean

South with the birds; cruising over calm seas, blue as sapphire, where winter never comes and where the soft trade winds bring renewed health

—with all the comforts and all the luxuries of life you enjoy aboard the palatial ships of the GREAT WHITE FLEET.

Delicious meals a la carte—included in price of ticket; prompt and efficient service. Dainty staterooms, perfectly ventilated, commanding a view of sea and sky; wide decks for playing games

—every facility for the enjoyment of a glorious out-of-door rest and vacation, amid the scenes of romance and history in the Caribbean.

And with it the opportunity to win for yourself a treasure of health and happiness, of greater benefit than the fabled fountain of youth, sought by adventurers in the tropic isles of the Spanish Main.

Cruises from 16 to 24 Days to
CUBA, JAMAICA, PANAMA CANAL, CENTRAL and SOUTH AMERICA

Sailing of GREAT WHITE FLEET Ships from New York every Wednesday and Saturday and fortnightly on Fridays. Sailing from New Orleans every Wednesday, Thursday and Saturday. Write for literature to :

Passenger Department
UNITED FRUIT COMPANY STEAMSHIP SERVICE
17 Battery Place   New York

"Long Sunny Days on Magic Seas That Welcome You With Health"

Hôtel Riviera, 1912   ▶ United Fruit Company Steamship Service, 1912   ▶▶ Panama California San Diego Exposition, 1915

UNITED FRUIT COMPANY
STEAMSHIP SERVICE
SAILINGS OF
THE GREAT WHITE FLEET

BETWEEN
NEW YORK,
BOSTON,
PHILADELPHIA,
BALTIMORE,
NEW ORLEANS
— AND —
JAMAICA, PANAMA,
COLOMBIA, COSTA RICA,
GUATEMALA, HONDURAS,
NICARAGUA
CONNECTING FOR
PACIFIC COAST PORTS OF
COLOMBIA, ECUADOR,
PERU, CHILE,
MEXICO & CENTRAL AMERICA

From New York, Boston, Philadelphia, Baltimore, New Orleans.

SUBJECT TO CHANGE WITHOUT NOTICE.

This sailing list shows the times when steamers may be expected to sail from and arrive at the several ports, but their sailing or arrival at the time stated is not guaranteed, nor will the United Fruit Company hold itself responsible for any delay or consequences arising therefrom.

The time of connecting transportation lines is shown only for the convenience of the public. The Company will not be responsible for any errors or changes which may occur.

San Diego

California's Great Exposition Celebrating the Opening of the Panama Canal
California's Christmas Gift

IT is a big idea in gifts, and rather un-usual, but one in which all the peoples of the world may participate; one which comes to a full realization on the stroke of midnight at New Year's Eve and lasts until another New Year's Eve in 1916.

The greater part of the United States and Canada—and if you insist, the Northern hemisphere of the old world—is buried to-day under snow and ice, or soon will be. The song birds are gone, the flowers are gone and the balmy days are gone.

But on the Pacific Coast, near Old Mexico, lies a city where the birds are singing, where roses are in bloom and the oranges are ripe, where snow never comes in and where it is always June. This is San Diego, the Mecca of those who wish comfort and health and happiness—it is the land where one truly lives.

To this land came Spanish sailors and Spanish soldiers and Spanish settlers in the centuries which have passed, and from their life sprang the traditions which still rule their arts and architecture and romance.

And in that Spanish atmosphere of mission and cathedral, of quiet patio and gay fiesta, has been built San Diego's Exposition Beautiful.

THE PLAZA A

Panama California Exposition

Five hundred miles to the north lies San Francisco, where during the greater part of 1915 will be held another Exposition, also celebrating the opening of the Panama Canal, presenting to the world many features differing from the Exposition Beautiful—the two supplementing one another.

When California celebrates, the Golden State's enthusiasm requires two outlets.

This Is the West of Your Country

It is a West in which you find a civilization that pre-dates that of pre-historic Egypt; it is the Great West of the Grand Canyon, the Yosemite, the Yellowstone, the Painted Desert, the Great Trees; the Great West that is old, yet young. It is the West that you should see, and 1915 is the time for you to see it.

Throughout 1915 the San Diego Exposition Beautiful will be open, offering a gorgeous landscape of unchanging verdure, set with the flashing crimson and gold and purple of the Southwest coast, offering a dreamy renaissance of old Spain, with caballero and troubadour and señorita dwelling in the quaint balconies and plazas and patios of this magic city.

This is California's gift for 1915 for all the year. It cannot quite be delivered to your door on Christmas morning, but your nearest ticket agent will tell you all about it.

See that your ticket in 1915 reads San Diego

1915 All the Year

"Oh! España, como mi joven, corazon por ti latia en tiempos pasados."
—*Longfellow.*

"How much of my young heart, O Spain, Went out to thee in days of yore?"
—*Longfellow.*

1915 All the Year

PATIO ARTS AND CRAFTS BUILDING

IT APPEARS TODAY

"THERE ARE TWO KINDS OF TRAVEL:
FIRST CLASS AND WITH CHILDREN."
– ROBERT BENCHLEY

„ES GIBT ZWEI ARTEN
ZU REISEN: FIRST CLASS
UND MIT KINDERN."
– ROBERT BENCHLEY

1920·

« IL EXISTE DEUX
CLASSES POUR VOYAGER :
LA PREMIÈRE CLASSE,
ET CELLE AVEC DES
ENFANTS. »
– ROBERT BENCHLEY

1929

CHASING THE SUN

Following the devastation of World War I, the Lost Generation was ready for a good time.

IN HER BEST-SELLING NOVEL *GENTLEMEN PREFER BLONDES* (1925), ANITA LOOS SATIRIZED THE TRAVELS OF AMERICANS with a tale of two showgirls, Lorelei Lee, an enterprising gold-digger, and her friend, Dorothy, on a grand tour of Europe. As Lorelei describes the voyage: "I always love the ocean. I mean I always love a ship and I really love the *Majestic* because you would not know it was a ship because it is just like being at the Ritz."

Following the devastation of World War I, the Lost Generation was ready for a good time. Flappers and sheiks of the Jazz Age moved to a fast, syncopated beat. The literary smart set joked with a knowing patter — especially the Algonquin Round Table, the famed clique of successful young writers who lunched at New York's Algonquin Hotel.

Sumptuous ocean liners attracted passengers during this giddy era. Despite Prohibition, Americans would drink once a ship entered international waters. The French Line (Compagnie Générale Transatlantique) was the most exclusive and desirable. Its stunning *Ile de France* had the first entirely art deco interior. Throughout the decade, French Line passenger counts and revenues soared. It had 91,000 passengers in 1928, up from 20,000 in 1919.

American society was changing. There was a sense of freedom in the air, a kicking over of traces. Automobiles offered young people escape from the restrictions of their parents and communities. Women's emancipation only *started* with winning the vote in 1920. Jazz babies shortened their skirts, smoked in public, wore makeup, and frequented speakeasies. *Jazz*, after all, was often used as a slang term for sex. Sunbathing was all the rage. Travelers followed the sun from the tropics

Royal Hawaiian Hotel, ca. 1927

to the south of France, which was best reached by the exclusively first-class Train Bleu.

Hawaiian beaches called. The Matson Line opened the stunning "Pink Palace of the Pacific," the Royal Hawaiian Hotel, in 1927. This $4-million Spanish-Moorish confection was a dream of a tropical hotel, as imagined by the prominent New York architects Warren and Wetmore.

Meanwhile, railroads, seeking to maintain ridership, presented the Golden State as the new Eden. Absent during the war, advertising for trains came roaring back in the '20s, and long-distance travel statistics held firm throughout the decade. The Southern Pacific hired artist Maurice Logan for an ad campaign of iconic Western images. His first series had no trains—just a sun-kissed beauty sitting on a California beach, or riding a mule in Yosemite. In 1926, Hernando Villa designed the Santa Fe's distinctive logo, a proud Indian chief in a war bonnet, and it became the railroad's most indelible image.

In Florida, the developer Carl G. Fisher saw a mangrove swamp and envisioned the playground of Miami Beach. During a freezing New York winter, Fisher installed a sign in Times Square that flashed, "It's June in Miami." With the easy credit of the decade, the Florida land boom was on. But a devastating 1926 hurricane started deflating land values. Well before the 1929 crash, Florida's bubble had popped.

◄◄ *Scientific American*, 1925   ► Glacier National Park, 1921

1920

1923

1924

Spotlight hits Hawaii as world tour of Edward, Prince of Wales, stops at Matson Line's Moana Hotel

Alles blickt nach Hawaii, als Edward, Prince of Wales, auf seiner Weltreise im Moana Hotel der Matson Line absteigt

Hawaï est sous les projecteurs quand la tournée mondiale d'Edward, Prince de Galles, fait halte au Moana Hotel de la compagnie Matson Line

Longtime winter hot spot Hôtel du Cap in Antibes stays open for summer; Gertrude Stein and Alice B. Toklas visit Pablo Picasso

Der Winter-Hotspot Hôtel du Cap in Antibes bleibt im Sommer geöffnet; Gertrude Stein und Alice B. Toklas besuchen Pablo Picasso

L'Hôtel du Cap à Antibes, villégiature hivernale de choix, reste ouvert tout l'été ; Gertrude Stein et Alice B. Toklas rendent visite à Pablo Picasso

A Passage to India, E.M. Forster's novel about cultural differences separating British school-mistress and an Indian doctor

E.M. Forster veröffentlicht seinen Roman *Auf der Suche nach Indien* über eine britische Lehrerin und einen indischen Arzt

Un Passage vers L'Inde, roman d'E. M. Forster sur le fossé culturel entre une institutrice anglaise et un médecin indien

SONNENHUNGRIG

Nach den Verwüstungen des Ersten Weltkriegs
wollte es die Lost Generation besser haben.

IN IHREM ROMANBESTSELLER *GENTLEMEN PREFER BLONDES* VON 1925, EINER SATIRE AUF DIE REISEN DER AMERIKANER, ERZÄHLT ANITA LOOS VON ZWEI SHOWGIRLS – der unternehmungslustigen, aufs Geld versessenen Lorelei Lee und ihrer Freundin Dorothy – auf einer Bildungsreise durch Europa. Lorelei beschreibt die Reise so: „Das Meer mochte ich schon immer. Also, ich mag Schiffe, und die *Majestic* mag ich wirklich, denn man würde gar nicht merken, dass es ein Schiff ist, denn es ist dort wie im Ritz."

Nach den Verwüstungen des Ersten Weltkriegs wollte es die Lost Generation besser haben. Die literarischen Cliquen tauschten ihre Insiderwitze aus, speziell der Algonquin Round Table, ein legendärer literarischer Zirkel erfolgreicher junger Autoren, die im New Yorker Algonquin Hotel regelmäßig zu Mittag aßen.

Luxuriöse Linienschiffe verloren dennoch nicht ihren Reiz. Trotz Prohibition sprachen die Amerikaner dem Alkohol zu, sobald sich ein Schiff in internationalen Gewässern befand. Exklusivste und gefragteste Reederei war die French Line (Compagnie Générale Transatlantique). Ihre fantastische *Ile de France* besaß das erste vollständige Art-déco-Interieur. Buchungszahlen und Einnahmen schnellten nach oben, von 20 000 Passagieren 1919 auf 91 000 im Jahr 1928.

In den Vereinigten Staaten vollzog sich ein sozialer Wandel. Ein Gefühl der Freiheit lag in der Luft, eine radikale Abkehr vom Vergangenen. Autos ermöglichten den jungen Leuten eine Flucht vor den Einschränkungen ihrer Eltern. Das Erstreiten des Wahlrechts im Jahr 1920 war nur der *Startschuss* für die Emanzipation der Frau. Die „Jazz Babys" kürzten die Röcke, rauchten, trugen Make-up und hockten in Kneipen. *Jazz* benutzte man oft als Slangausdruck für Sex. Sonnenbäder waren der Hit. Man reiste der Sonne entgegen – von den Tropen bis nach Südfrankreich, das man am besten mit dem luxuriösen Le Train Bleu erreichte.

Auch die Strände von Hawaii lockten. Die Matson Line eröffnete 1927 den „Pink Palace of the Pacific", das Royal Hawaiian Hotel. Diese 4 Mio. $ teure spanisch-maurische Kreation war ein Traum von einem Tropenhotel, wie ihn sich die Architekten Warren und Wetmore ausgedacht hatten.

Um ihr Fahrgastaufkommen zu wahren, präsentierten die Eisenbahngesellschaften den Golden State als das neue Eden. Werbung für Bahnreisen, die es während des Kriegs nicht gegeben hatte, feierte in den 1920er-Jahren eine schwungvolle Wiedergeburt, sodass sich die Langstreckenstatistik gut behaupten konnte. Die Southern Pacific gewann den Maler Maurice Logan für eine Anzeigenkampagne mit ikonenhaften Bildern vom Westen. In der ersten Serie gab es gar keine Züge – nur eine von der Sonne geküsste Schönheit an einem kalifornischen Strand oder auf einem Esel in Yosemite. Hernando Villa entwarf 1926 das markante Logo der Santa Fe: einen stolzen Indianerhäuptling, der zum unauslöschlichen Sinnbild der Eisenbahn wurde.

In Florida erblickte der Baulöwe Carl G. Fisher einen Mangrovensumpf und träumte vom Tummelplatz Miami Beach. Mitten in einem bitterkalten New Yorker Winter warb Fisher mit einer Leuchtreklame auf dem Times Square: „In Miami ist es Juni". Angesichts leicht erhältlicher Kredite boomte das Grundstücksgeschäft in Florida. Nach einem verheerenden Hurrikan begannen die Grundstückspreise 1926 jedoch wieder zu fallen. Lange vor dem Börsenkrach von 1929 war die Blase namens Florida geplatzt.

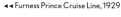
◀◀ Furness Prince Cruise Line, 1929   ▶ Hawaii Tourist Bureau, 1929

1925

1926

1926

First motel – or motorist's hotel – built in San Luis Obispo, California

Erstes Motel – oder „motorist's hotel" – im kalifornischen San Luis Obispo errichtet

Construction du premier motel – ou hôtel pour automobilistes – à San Luis Obispo, Californie

In wake of hurricane, Florida land boom goes bust

Ein Hurrikan bereitet den in Florida florierenden Grundstücksgeschäften ein Ende

À la suite d'un ouragan, la bulle immobilière de Floride explose

First run of the Chief—Santa Fe Lines' Chief deluxe limited train running from Chicago to Los Angeles

Erste Fahrt des Luxuszugs Chief der Santa Fe Lines von Chicago nach Los Angeles

Lancement du train Chief Deluxe de la compagnie Chief-Santa Fe Lines entre Chicago et Los Angeles

LA RUÉE VERS LE SOLEIL

Après les ravages de la Première Guerre mondiale, la « génération perdue » eut envie de s'offrir du bon temps.

DANS SON BEST-SELLER DE 1925 *LES HOMMES PRÉFÈRENT LES BLONDES,* **ANITA LOOS SE MOQUAIT DE LA FAÇON DE VOYAGER DES AMÉRICAINS À TRAVERS L'HISTOIRE DE DEUX DANSEUSES DE REVUE,** Lorelei Lee, une croqueuse de diamants pleine d'audace, et son amie Dorothy, parties pour une grande tournée d'Europe. Lorelei décrit le voyage en ces termes : « J'ai toujours adoré la mer. J'ai toujours aimé les bateaux, et si j'aime vraiment le *Majestic*, c'est parce qu'on n'a pas l'impression d'être sur un bateau, on se croirait au Ritz ».

Après les ravages de la Première Guerre mondiale, la « génération perdue » eut envie de s'offrir du bon temps. Les garçonnes et les rois de l'ère du jazz dansaient sur des rythmes endiablés tandis que l'intelligentsia littéraire plaisantait avec esprit et répartie, notamment dans le Cercle d'Algonquin, célèbre clique de jeunes écrivains à succès qui se retrouvaient pour déjeuner à l'hôtel Algonquin de New York.

Les paquebots somptueux attirèrent de nouveau les voyageurs. Fuyant la Prohibition, les Américains se mettaient à boire dès que leur bateau pénétrait dans les eaux internationales. La Compagnie Générale Transatlantique était la plus luxueuse et la plus demandée. Son impressionnant *Île de France* fut le premier paquebot aménagé dans le style Art Déco. Tout au long des années 1920, le nombre de passagers et les revenus de la compagnie explosèrent. En 1928, elle transporta 91 000 passagers, contre 20 000 en 1919.

La société américaine changeait aussi. Grâce à la voiture, les jeunes pouvaient échapper aux contraintes imposées par leurs parents et leurs communautés. L'émancipation des femmes ne *démarra* qu'avec leur droit de vote en 1920. Les jazzeuses raccourcirent leurs jupes, fumaient en public, se maquillaient et fréquentaient les bars clandestins. La dernière mode était au bronzage. Les voyageurs suivaient le soleil, des Tropiques au sud de la France, de préférence à bord du Train Bleu.

Les plages de Hawaï faisaient envie. En 1927, la Matson Line ouvrit l'impressionnant Royal Hawaiian Hotel, surnommé le « palais rose du Pacifique ». Cet édifice hispano-mauresque de 4 millions de dollars symbolisait l'hôtel tropical de rêve tel que l'avaient imaginé les grands architectes new-yorkais Warren et Wetmore.

Parallèlement, les compagnies de chemins de fer, toutes désireuses de conserver leur leadership, présentèrent la Californie comme le nouvel Eden. Absentes pendant la guerre, les publicités pour les trains firent un retour fracassant dans les années 1920, et les statistiques des trajets longue distance se maintinrent fermement tout au long de la décennie. La compagnie Southern Pacific recruta

◄◄ *World Traveler*, 1923   Hôtel du Cap, 1923

1926

Dude Ranchers Association founded in Cody, Wyoming, in response to popular interest in travel to American West

Dude Ranchers Association als Reaktion auf das große Interesse an Reisen in den Westen der USA gegründet

Fondation de la Dude Ranchers Association à Cody, Wyoming, en réponse à l'intérêt pour les voyages dans le Grand Ouest américain

1927

Elsa Maxwell retained by Prince of Monaco to create principality's social cachet as summer resort

Der Fürst von Monaco beauftragt die Journalistin Elsa Maxwell, das Fürstentum zu einem gefragten Sommerresort zu machen

Le Prince de Monaco demande à Elsa Maxwell de promouvoir sa principauté comme une destination estivale exclusive

1927

Maiden voyage of SS *Ile de France*, luxury ocean liner designed by Emile-Jacques Ruhlmann for French Line

Jungfernfahrt des von Emile-Jacques Ruhlmann für die French Line entworfenen Kreuzfahrtschiffs SS *Ile de France*

Croisière inaugurale de l'*Île de France*, luxueux paquebot conçu par Émile-Jacques Ruhlmann pour la Compagnie Générale Transatlantique l'artiste Maurice Logan pour concevoir une campagne publicitaire composée d'images symbolisant l'Ouest. Sur la première série, on ne voyait même pas de train, juste une beauté bronzée allongée sur une plage californienne ou chevauchant un mulet à Yosemite. En 1926, Hernando Villa imagina un logo original pour la ligne Santa Fe, un chef indien fièrement couronné d'une parure de plumes qui devint le symbole le plus indélébile de la compagnie.

Le promoteur immobilier Carl G. Fisher découvrit la mangrove de Floride et imagina Miami Beach. Pendant un hiver glacial à New York, il fit installer sur Times Square un panneau clignotant qui proclamait «C'est le mois de juin à Miami». Comme il était alors très facile d'obtenir un crédit, la Floride connut un boom immobilien, mais en 1926, un ouragan dévastateur commença à faire chuter la valeur des terres. La bulle de Floride éclata bien avant le crash de 1929.

Cunard, 1929

1928

1929

1929

Tango bursts from backstreets of Buenos Aires, Argentina; Paris swoons over singer Carlos Gardel

Der Tango macht sich aus den Hinterhöfen von Buenos Aires, Argentinien, hörbar; Paris wird vom Sänger Carlos Gardel verzaubert

Le tango déferle sur le monde depuis les rues de Buenos Aires, Argentine ; Paris se pâme devant le chanteur Carlos Gardel

Agua Caliente resort in Tijuana, Mexico, opens racetrack; Hollywood celebrities head south of border

Einweihung der Rennbahn des Agua Caliente Resort im mexikanischen Tijuana; zahlreiche Hollywoodstars hüpfen über die Grenze

L'Agua Caliente Resort de Tijuana, Mexique, ouvre un circuit automobile ; les célébrités d'Hollywood s'y pressent

Aviatrix Amelia Earhart promotes passenger airline service; with Charles Lindbergh founds Transcontinental Air Transport

Amelia Earhart, die schon früh Passagierflüge förderte, gründet gemeinsam mit Charles Lindbergh die Transcontinental Air Transport

L'aviatrice Amelia Earhart promeut les vols de passagers et fonde la Transcontinental Air Transport avec Lindbergh

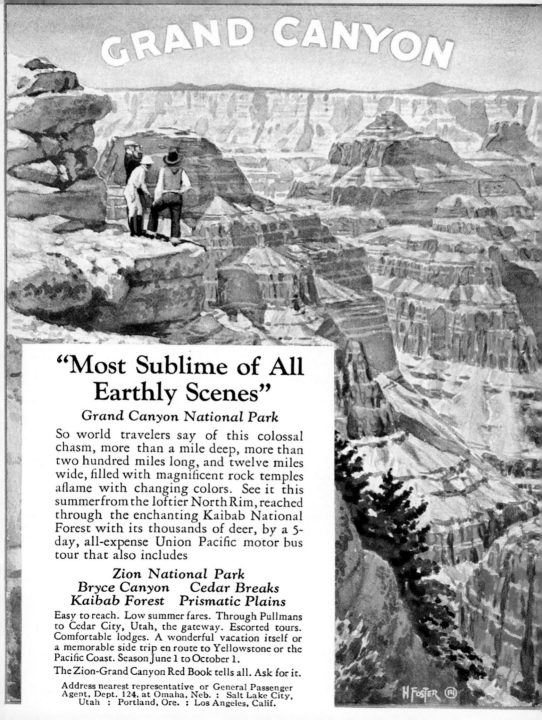

GRAND CANYON

"Most Sublime of All Earthly Scenes"

Grand Canyon National Park

So world travelers say of this colossal chasm, more than a mile deep, more than two hundred miles long, and twelve miles wide, filled with magnificent rock temples aflame with changing colors. See it this summer from the loftier North Rim, reached through the enchanting Kaibab National Forest with its thousands of deer, by a 5-day, all-expense Union Pacific motor bus tour that also includes

Zion National Park
Bryce Canyon   Cedar Breaks
Kaibab Forest   Prismatic Plains

Easy to reach. Low summer fares. Through Pullmans to Cedar City, Utah, the gateway. Escorted tours. Comfortable lodges. A wonderful vacation itself or a memorable side trip en route to Yellowstone or the Pacific Coast. Season June 1 to October 1.

The Zion-Grand Canyon Red Book tells all. Ask for it.

Address nearest representative or General Passenger Agent, Dept. 124, at Omaha, Neb. : Salt Lake City, Utah : Portland, Ore. : Los Angeles, Calif.

H FOSTER

Union Pacific Railroad, 1927

Travels to national park destination hotels and their breathtaking views increased in the '20s. The stunning Ahwahnee Hotel in Yosemite National Park opened in 1927, after two years of construction that required the most complicated trucking effort of its day.

In den 1920er-Jahren steuerte man immer häufiger die in Nationalparks gelegenen Landhotels mit ihren atemberaubenden Ausblicken an. Das prächtige Ahwahnee Hotel im Yosemite National Park wurde 1927 eröffnet – nach zweijähriger Bauzeit mit der kompliziertesten Transportlogistik jener Tage.

Dans les années 1920, les touristes affluaient dans les hôtels des parcs nationaux pour profiter de leurs panoramas époustouflants. L'impressionnant Ahwahnee Hotel du Parc National de Yosemite ouvrit en 1927, après deux années de construction qui nécessitèrent l'effort de camionnage le plus complexe de l'époque.

▶ Union Pacific Railroad, 1925

Sacred to the Indian
The Great White Throne, Zion National Park, held in awe as the abode of the Great Spirit.

The long hidden splendors of Zion National Park. Bryce Canyon and Cedar Breaks are yours

Here, in Southern Utah, are flaming canyons and jewelled amphitheatres painted in incredible colors by sun magic and the wizardry of wind and water. Here, too, is a lingering frontier of empurpled distances with quaint Mormon villages, Indians, wild horses, extinct volcanoes and mysterious cliff dwellings.

Season May 15 to October 15

Inaccessible a few years ago except to a few adventurous Americans, the Union Pacific has now made it possible to see it in comfort by providing sleeping car service, regular motor tours and the latest style of National Park lodges and dining rooms.

The trip is a memorable vacation adventure in itself, or may be made in connection with tours to Salt Lake City, Yellowstone National Park or the Pacific Coast.

Ask about low round trip summer fares.

Send For Free Booklet In Natural Colors
It is the only way we can tell you of the unbelievable coloring of this unique land; also contains complete practical information.

Address nearest Union Pacific Representative or General Passenger Agent at Omaha, Neb. :-: Salt Lake City, Utah :-: Portland, Ore. :-: Los Angeles, Cal.

Union Pacific

C A L I F O R N I A

WHEN your gorgeous autumn days are graying into winter...and that cold November twilight comes... well, winter's on the way...

Soon smart society is on the move, winging westward to the blue Pacific... to California, America's gay Riviera...playground of the world!

Come either to Los Angeles or San Francisco...and this whole enchanted land is at your feet—a land of sunshine and flowers, of highways that roll away like magic carpets through the mountains, along the sea...through fascinating, colorful cities . . . stately redwood forests. All California is your playground, infinitely varied...polo and golf, and five o'clock tea

in the patio...starry nights, with the slumberous roar of the surf. A land of sunny loveliness, June-like days—in California.

Los Angeles and its Hollywood, Pasadena and Beverly Hills, gay words . . . to the travel-wise . . . then San Diego, with Agua Caliente just over the border. And for good stylish loafing, which science calls heliotherapy, heed the call of the desert! Palm Springs...or Death Valley, with its enthralling beauty and vast brooding expanse of sand and silence... back to the ocean again at Santa Barbara, another favorite of the smart world.

San Francisco—flavor of Naples and Paris. Center of a brilliant social season... charming, cosmopolitan, sophisticated.

Nearby, you'll find paradise made fashionable at Monterey and Del Monte . . . Yosemite and Tahoe a night away, and just to the north the great Redwood Empire... duck and quail shooting, steelhead and salmon fishing...the kinds you read about in sport magazines.

Golf — all up and down the coast memorable green courses welcome you, from Eureka to Coronado and out on Catalina, 25 miles off shore.

California requests the pleasure of your company this fall and winter. Bring the youngsters—the schools are good.

Books picturing California will be sent on request. Write either of these organizations.

CALIFORNIANS, INC.
SEC. 1811. 703 MARKET STREET, SAN FRANCISCO

ALL-YEAR CLUB OF SOUTHERN CALIFORNIA
SEC. R-11. 1151 SO. BROADWAY, LOS ANGELES

◄ All-Year Club of Southern California, 1929

World Traveler, October 1923

Railroads saw the Golden State as the way to
maintain high ridership, since a bevy of travelers
followed the sun to California in the '20s. Al
Jolson, the biggest star of his day, recorded the
1924 hit "California, Here I Come." It sounded
like one long ad: "Where bowers of flowers
bloom in the spring!"

Die Bahngesellschaften setzten auf den Golden
State, um ihr hohes Fahrgastaufkommen zu
wahren, denn in den 1920er-Jahren folgte
ein ganzer Schwarm von Reisenden der
Sonne nach Kalifornien. Al Jolson, der größte
Gesangsstar seiner Zeit, nahm 1924 den Hit
„California, Here I Come" auf. Er klang wie
eine lange Werbeanzeige: „Where bowers of
flowers bloom in the spring!"

Les compagnies de chemins de fer voyaient
dans le « Golden State » un moyen de conserver
un nombre maximum de passagers, car dans
les années 1920, beaucoup de voyageurs
suivaient le soleil jusqu'en Californie. Al Jolson,
la plus grande star de son époque, enregistra
le tube « California, Here I Come » en 1924.
On aurait dit une longue réclame publicitaire :
« Where bowers of flowers bloom in the spring! »
(« Là où des berceaux de fleurs éclosent au
printemps ! »)

HOLLYWOOD

BY-THE-SEA

The gay Broad Walk along the ocean's edge passes directly in front of the Hollywood Hotel.

Enjoy Your

HOLLYWOOD BY-THE-SEA lends itself to gaiety outdoor recreation in variety such as you sel find in a summer vacation land. From morning u evening Hollywood's guests make merry on Beach Broad Walk—in surf and Casino pool—on fish grounds and golf course—in yachts and motor craft .

At night, when myriad lights transform the ocean fr into a great white way, Caesar La Monaca's Hollyw Band adds to the enjoyment of the merry crowds— the music of Arnold Johnson's famous orchestra quick dancing feet, as cool sea breezes freshen bodies tired fr the sports of the day . . . . .

In dining rooms and lobbies of brilliant hotels, at

HOLLYWOOD RESORT AND INDUSTRIAL BOARD

On the Ocean • • On the Florida East Coast Railro

in FLORIDA

Swim here in the great pool of the Bathing Casino—or in the surf and sea, as you prefer.

...cation Here

...lendid Country Club, on the roof garden of the Holly-
...od Hotel on the Beach, or outdoors under the stars,
...e accumulated cares of workday life magically fall away
...d hearts are light again . . . . .

...cation days are always fair at Hollywood By-the-Sea,
...d nights are always cool. Here vacation dreams really
...me true. The gaiety that every normal life craves and
...e glow of health that only the great outdoors can give,
...ait you here—whether your stay be brief or permanent.
...xurious, hospitable hotels will add to the pleasure and comfort
...your visit. Special low cost Hollywood summer excursions
...ake possible a trip to this seaside wonderland on a very mod-
...ate vacation budget. Just sign and mail the coupon for com-
...te information.

...W. YOUNG, *President* • Hollywood, *in* Florida

On the Dixie Highway

Hollywood summer excursions by boat and rail offer wonderful vacation opportunities. Mail this coupon for full information.

YOUR SUMMER VACATION

MAIL THIS COUPON TODAY

HOLLYWOOD RESORT AND INDUSTRIAL BOARD
Hollywood, *in* Florida

Please mail me full information about low cost
summer excursions to Florida, with free illustrated
folders.

Name _____

Street _____

City _____ State _____

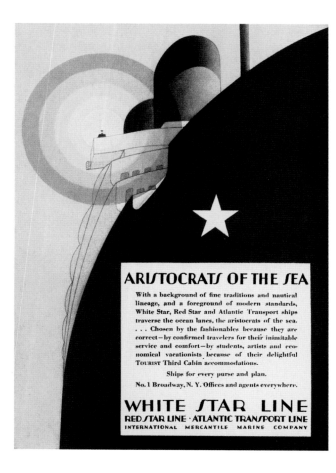

ARISTOCRATS OF THE SEA

With a background of fine traditions and nautical
lineage, and a foreground of modern standards,
White Star, Red Star and Atlantic Transport ships
traverse the ocean lanes, the aristocrats of the sea.
. . . Chosen by the fashionables because they are
correct—by confirmed travelers for their inimitable
service and comfort—by students, artists and economical vacationists because of their delightful
TOURIST Third Cabin accommodations.

Ships for every purse and plan.

No. 1 Broadway, N. Y. Offices and agents everywhere.

WHITE STAR LINE
RED STAR LINE · ATLANTIC TRANSPORT LINE
INTERNATIONAL MERCANTILE MARINE COMPANY

◄◄ Hollywood By-the-Sea, Florida, 1925

Developer Joseph Young planned his Hollywood By-the-Sea down to its boardwalk and
business district. Young's version of his "Dream
City" was on the ocean—not inland like its West
Coast namesake. Started in 1920, it flourished
during the Florida boom, with 36 apartment
buildings, almost 2,500 houses, and 252 commercial buildings by 1926.

Joseph Young plante sein Hollywood-By-
the-Sea von der Uferpromenade bis zum
Einkaufsviertel. Youngs „Traumstadt" lag
allerdings am Meer und nicht im Binnenland
wie ihr Namensvetter von der Westküste. Die
1920 gegründete Siedlung profitierte vom Flo-
ridaboom; 1926 besaß sie 36 Wohnblocks, fast
2500 Häuser und 252 Geschäftsgebäude.

Le promoteur immobilier Joseph Young
imagina tous les détails de son Hollywood
By-the-Sea, jusqu'à sa promenade en front de
mer et son quartier d'affaires. La « ville de rêve »
de Young se trouvait au bord de la mer, et non
dans les terres comme son homonyme de la
Côte Ouest. Lancé en 1920, le projet prospéra
pendant le boom immobilier de Floride et
comptait 36 immeubles résidentiels, près de
2500 maisons et 252 immeubles commer-
ciaux dès 1926.

◄ International Mercantile Marine Company,
1928

► Life, 1927

Life

Tourists' Number

August 18 1927
Price 15 cents

TraVel

SEPTEMBER

1924

35 cents a co

$4.00 a y

Travel, 1924

In the race between cars and trains, automobile travel miles surpassed train travel by 1920. Railroads fought back with express "flyers" that offered exclusive first-class service. But, by 1930, there were 26.7 million cars, one for every 4.5 people, in the United States, an amazing increase from 4,000 in 1900.

Im Wettrennen zwischen Auto und Zug hatte das Auto hinsichtlich der zurückgelegten Kilometer 1920 erstmals die Nase vorn. Die Bahngesellschaften konterten mit schnellen „Flyers", die einen exklusiven Erste-Klasse-Service boten. Doch in den Vereinigten Staaten gab es 1930 bereits 26,7 Millionen Autos, rund 22 pro 100 Einwohner, ein immenser Zuwachs gegenüber nur 4000 im Jahr 1900.

Dans la course entre trains et voitures, la route l'emporta sur le rail en kilomètres parcourus en 1920. Les compagnies ferroviaires réagirent en lançant des trains express exclusivement première classe. En 1930, on comptait 26,7 millions de voitures aux États-Unis, soit une pour 4,5 personnes, contre seulement 4000 en 1900.

▶ New York Central, 1926

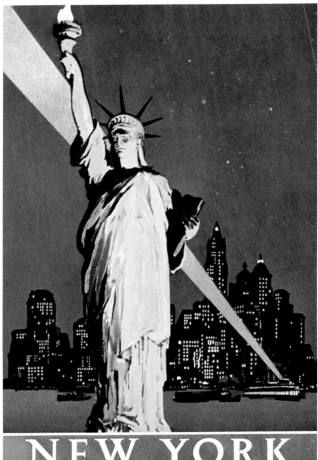

NEW YORK
The WONDER CITY *of the* WORLD
NEW YORK CENTRAL LINES

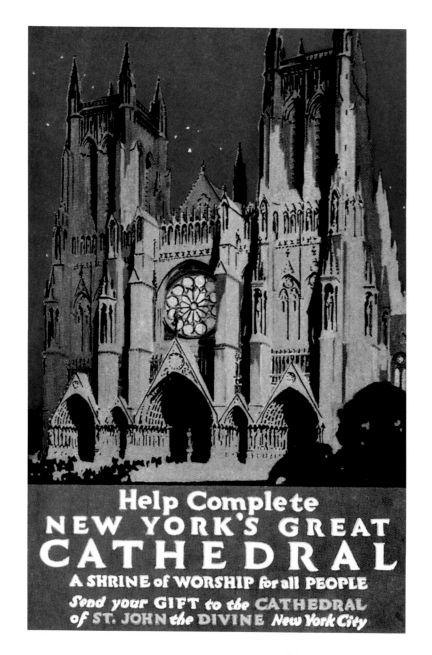

Cathedral of St. John the Divine, 1925

Evanston Lighthouse
By the Elevated Lines

Chicago Illinois Rail, 1925

HOMEWARD BOUND
by SOUTH SHORE LINE

TRAINS FROM CHICAGO OPERATED OVER THE ILLINOIS CENTRAL RAILROAD
from RANDOLPH, VAN BUREN, 12ᵗʰ 43ʳᵈ 53ʳᵈ AND 63ʳᵈ STREET STATIONS AND KENSINGTON

South Shore Line Trains, 1926   ▶ North Shore Line, 1925

Land of Romance

～ and a Great Exposition

ANCIENT MOORISH TEMPLES... Magnificent "Castles in Spain" ... land of Romance—Play ... Wonder places all, where time has lent its graceful charm to enchant you!

Travelling in Spain is like a wonderful dream... the wonders of history parading before your eyes!

And you may live amidst this historical grandeur, this romance—in modern comfort—at moderate cost!

Visit the great "International Exposition of Barcelona" and see the greatest collection of art, science and industry of all times. Housed in buildings that took eight years to build and at a cost of $22,000,000. Spain has perfectly blended her own architecture, centuries old, with all that is beautiful in the "Moderne."

Spain—Barcelona—should be on your itinerary for your tour in 1929.

[Barcelona—Paris, 23 hours ... London, 30 hours ... Berlin, 39 hours. Motor Tours on 40,000 miles of hard surface roads! Rail transportation reduced.]

INTERNATIONAL
EXPOSITION
BARCELONA

May to December

1929

For further information address any Tourist Bureau, or M. Ventura, American Delegate, Steinway Hall, 113 West 57th Street, New York City

◀ International Exposition Barcelona, 1929

South African Government Railways, 1929

During the 1920s, the French Riviera became the place to go during the summer. Here, South African Government Railways wants some of these flocks of tourists to head to a Riviera farther south—in Durban, South Africa.

In den 1920er-Jahren wurde die französische Riviera zum bevorzugten Sommerziel. In dieser Anzeige versucht die staatliche südafrikanische Eisenbahngesellschaft einen Teil dieser Touristenscharen an eine weiter südlich gelegene Riviera zu locken – nach Durban in Südafrika.

Pendant les années 1920, la Côte d'Azur devint le dernier endroit à la mode pour passer l'été. Ici, la compagnie South African Government Railways tente de faire descendre ces foules de touristes bien plus au sud, à Durban, en Afrique du Sud.

DELIGHTFUL DURBAN

CHARMINGLY different, this gem-like Riviera in the Garden Province of South Africa . . . Gay, colorful, joyful Durban . . . Here health and pleasure prosper in a setting of sparkling sunshine, zestful climate, the amazing blue of the Southern sky, the dancing waters of the Indian ocean.

Luxurious hotels overlook spacious stretches of beach and a beautiful harbor alive with white-bellied sails of pleasure craft, with warships, whalers, windjammers . . . Delightful golf and yachting clubs . . . Sailing, sea bathing, surfing, angling, polo, cricket, horse-racing, motoring, high-class concerts, theatres . . . all catering happily to the lovers of sport, recreation, leisure.

Durban's attractions provide an exquisite interval in a tour of South Africa's many wonders . . . Matchless Victoria Falls . . . Zimbabwe's mysterious ruins . . . Kimberley's famous diamond mines . . . Marvelous Cango Caves . . . The gold mines of the Rand . . . Drakensberg Mountains . . . The Valley of a Thousand Hills . . . The great Kruger Big Game Preserve . . . and Historic Good Hope, the "Cape Beautiful."

Send for fully illustrated booklet to

SOUTH AFRICAN GOVERNMENT RAILWAYS
11 Broadway, New York City

◄◄ Burlington Route, 1923

National Motorist, 1929

The membership magazine of the Automobile Club of America reflects the decade's passion for sunbathing. Before the 1920s, fair skin was one hallmark of a "lady," since workers labored under the hot sun. But in the Industrial Age, workers went into factories. Fashion reversed— a sun-kissed complexion was desirable.

Die Mitgliederzeitschrift des Automobile Club of America bezeugt die aufkommende Begeisterung fürs Sonnenbaden. Bis etwa 1920 war helle Haut gleichsam das Gütesiegel einer „Lady", in Abgrenzung von den im Freien tätigen Arbeitern. Im Industriezeitalter indes ging man zum Arbeiten in die Fabrik, und die Mode kehrte sich um, sodass man nun einen von der Sonne verwöhnten Teint anstrebte.

Le magazine des membres de l'Automobile Club of America reflète la passion des bains de soleil qui naquit dans les années 1920. Auparavant, une lady digne de ce nom se devait de garder le teint pâle pour se différencier de la classe ouvrière qui travaillait sous un soleil de plomb, mais les ouvriers ayant rejoint les usines depuis la Révolution Industrielle, la mode s'inversa. La tendance était désormais au bronzage.

◄ Northern Pacific Railway, 1929

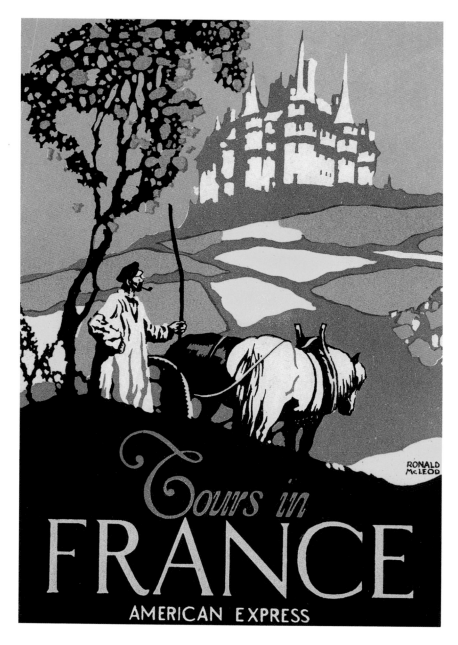

Tours in **FRANCE**

AMERICAN EXPRESS

American Express, 1926

American Express, 1927

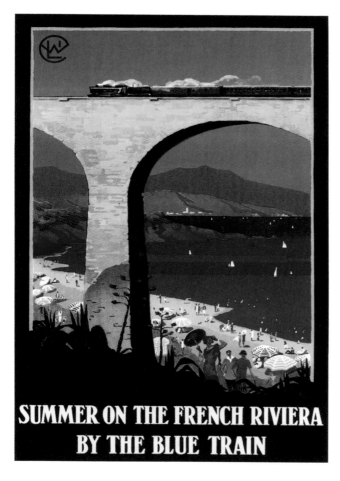

SUMMER ON THE FRENCH RIVIERA BY THE BLUE TRAIN

South of France, 1928

Starting in 1922, the Train Bleu made the journey to the south of France as hot as the destination. This "train of paradise" seemed like one big party, for all 80 passengers had connecting luxury compartments. It inspired a Diaghilev ballet, with story by Jean Cocteau and costumes by Coco Chanel.

Ab 1922 verkehrend, machte Le Train Bleu die Reise nach Südfrankreich so aufregend wie das Ziel selbst. Die Fahrt mit dem „Paradieszug" glich einer großen Party, denn für sämtliche 80 Fahrgäste gab es miteinander verbundene Luxusabteile. Der Zug inspirierte Diaghilew zu einem Ballett mit Libretto von Jean Cocteau und Kostümen von Coco Chanel.

Lancé en 1922, le Train Bleu ralliait le sud de la France, qui était alors la destination à la mode. Ce « train paradisiaque » ressemblait à un grand salon mondain sur roues, les compartiments de luxe des 80 passagers étant communicants. Cela inspira un ballet à Diaghilev, avec livret de Jean Cocteau et costumes de Coco Chanel.

▶ Cannes, ca. 1925

OSHKOSH "*Chief*" TRUNKS

Hotchkotch? . . . Oochkooch? "Better to be guilty of mispronunciation than travel with anything less than the best trunk in the world." That's what hundreds of experienced French travelers say who have a perfectly terrible time pronouncing the name "OSHKOSH."

THE TRUNK *in the picture is an Oshkosh "Chief" Wardrobe. The name "Chief" means the best trunk that Oshkosh knows how to make. The people of Mars may have discovered how to produce a better trunk than this, but they haven't told anyone on earth about it yet. A handsome descriptive booklet, "The Chief of Trunks," is free. For a copy, address the Oshkosh Trunk Company, 445 High Street, Oshkosh, Wisconsin.*

Oshkosh Trunks, 1926

Travel in the early '20s usually meant extended stays and formal dinners. Travelers needed trunks—often several. Oshkosh was noted for well-made pieces—this ad might be a sly reference that it was the "Louis Vuitton of America." Top of its line was the Chief, made of waterproof duck cloth. In 1927, as travel patterns shifted, Oshkosh began making smaller hand luggage.

Reisen bedeutete Anfang der 1920er-Jahre meist einen längeren Aufenthalt und förmliche Diners. Hierzu benötigte man einen Schrankkoffer – oft gleich mehrere. Womöglich birgt diese Anzeige der für ihre gute Qualität bekannten Firma Oshkosh einen unterschwelligen Hinweis auf ihren Status eines „Louis Vuitton von Amerika". Beim Topmodell „Chief" bot imprägniertes Segeltuch zusätzlichen Schutz. Als sich das Reiseverhalten änderte, begann Oshkosh 1927 mit der Fertigung von Handgepäck.

Au début des années 1920, le voyage était en général synonyme de longs séjours et de dîners chics. Les voyageurs avaient souvent besoin de plusieurs malles. Oshkosh se distingua par ses produits de bonne facture : cette publicité sous-entend peut-être que la marque était le « Louis Vuitton d'Amérique ». Le Chief, son produit le plus haut de gamme, était en toile imperméable. En 1927, quand la façon de voyager évolua, Oshkosh se mit à fabriquer des bagages à main plus petits.

▶ Coral Gables, Florida, 1926

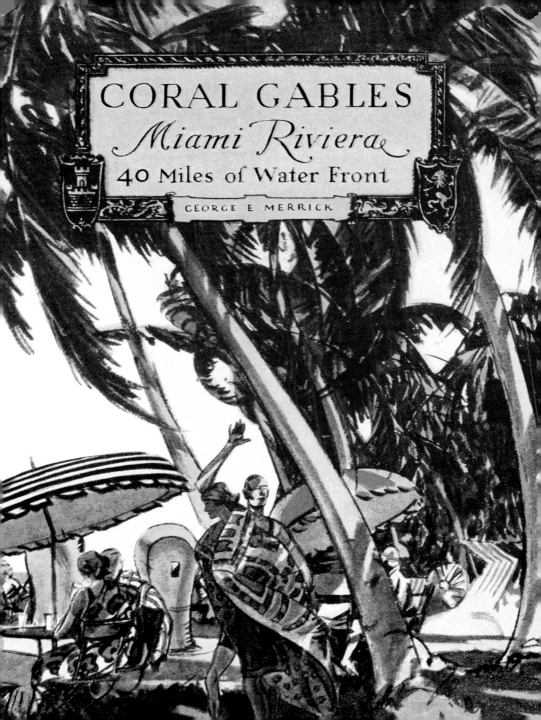

CORAL GABLES
Miami Riviera
40 Miles of Water Front

GEORGE E MERRICK

CORAL GABLES
Miami Riviera
40 Miles of Water Front
GEORGE E. MERRICK

Coral Gables, Florida, 1926

Coral Gables, influenced by the City Beautiful movement, was envisioned by the developer George Merrick in the languid Mediterranean revival style. Propelled by the Florida boom, $7 million in land was sold, 65 miles of roads constructed, and more than 600 homes built between the town's inception in 1921 and incorporation in 1925.

Beeinflusst durch die „City Beautiful"-Bewegung, ist Coral Gables eine Kreation des Städteplaners George Merrick im lässigen Stil des Mediterranean Revival. Angetrieben durch den Boom in Florida, wurden zwischen den ersten Anfängen 1921 und der Stadtgründung 1925 Land für 7 Mio. $ verkauft sowie 100 Straßenkilometer und mehr als 600 Häuser gebaut.

Influencé par le mouvement urbaniste City Beautiful, le projet Coral Gables au style néo-méditerranéen langoureux est né de l'imagination du promoteur immobilier George Merrick. Sous l'impulsion du boom immobilier de Floride, la vente de terrains s'eleva à 7 millions de dollars, 105 kilomètres de routes furent construits et plus de 600 maisons bâties entre la création de la ville en 1921 et son incorporation en 1925.

▶ Coral Gables, Florida, 1925

CORAL GABLES
Miami Riviera
40 Miles of Water Front
GEORGE E. MERRICK.

Society's Winter Paradise.... Hawaii

The Hawaii Tourist Bureau

San Francisco, Calif.	Los Angeles, Calif.
1119 Monadnock Building	655T Chamber of Commerce Building
MATSON Line *from* San Francisco	**LASSCO** Line *from* Los Angeles
Portland and Seattle	in Southern California

535 FIFTH AVE.	NEW YORK	730 SO. BROADWAY	LOS ANGELES
140 SO. DEARBORN	CHICAGO	521 FIFTH AVE.	NEW YORK
215 MARKET ST.	SAN FRANCISCO	119 W. OCEAN AVE.	LONG BEACH
723 W. SEVENTH ST.	LOS ANGELES	140 SO. DEARBORN	CHICAGO
1805 ELM ST.	DALLAS, TEXAS	685 MARKET ST.	SAN FRANCISCO
1319 FOURTH AVE.	SEATTLE	213 E. BROADWAY	SAN DIEGO, CALIF.
82½ FOURTH ST.	PORTLAND, ORE.	609 THOMAS BLDG.	DALLAS, TEXAS

Any travel agent will gladly give you full particulars and arrange your bookings

CORAL SANDS gleam today with gay Cosmopolites lured from the far reaches of the earth. The throbbing colors of Deauville, Cannes, famed watering places of the world, merge with the lavish tints of the South Seas ↝↝↝ their glistening greens and tropic golds and the million shifting shades between. The sparkle of Continental smartness is on great hotels that jewel the shore at Waikiki ↝↝↝ Everywhere is the zest of anticipation ↝↝↝ the vibrant thrill that marks the pre-holiday season in the Paradise Isles.

¶ Sophisticates enticed by the bizarre have opened the season each year a little earlier. They have come to know the rapture of Christmas under a velvet sky ↝↝↝ windows ablaze in the palaces of departed Hawaiian Kings ↝↝↝ clear-throated carols ascending to pendant stars that glow like orbs of fire through the fronds of swaying palms ↝↝↝ They come in the mellow beauty of autumn to linger until languorous spring bursts into the crashing colors of Hawaiian summer ↝↝↝ For them winter is only a fiction ↝↝↝ They know tonight the miracle of a moon of molten silver pouring its translucent sheen over majestic mountains and dancing waters ↝↝↝ the haunting harmony of sobbing steel-guitars and plaintive voices that rise and fall on vagrant breezes that drift in from the sea.

¶ They have learned that Hawaii is just a *few days* away ↝↝↝ a land of enchantment at the end of a blissful interlude of sun and sea and sky on luxurious liners as proud as any that float. They know it as the magic place where shimmering rainbows drape verdant golf courses ↝↝↝ where friendly beach-boys weave native hats or conquer racing waves, erect on charging surf-boards ↝↝↝ where sporty denizens of the deep lurk in constant challenge to the mettle of the ardent fisherman, or idle days may be dreamed away in tropic bowers still primitive and unspoiled.

¶ *You can go from any of the four great gateways of the Pacific in four to six days, according to the liner selected. And you do not have to bother with passports or other formalities. Hawaii is an integral part of the United States—as much so as your own State.*

REST IN BERMUDA

The rest and quiet for which your soul longs, await you here. Bermuda is a haven of peace, for it is almost alone in allowing no automobiles, railroads and street cars, and it is blessed with the world's most equable climate.

The winter temperature averages between 60° and 70°.

Unique as a rest resort, Bermuda also offers rare recreation the year 'round—unexcelled golf, tennis, bathing, sailing, fishing, riding, driving, cycling, sightseeing among natural marvels. The sea gardens, magical caves, natural arches, cathedral rocks, and marine grottos, vie in interest with the lavish displays of exotic flowers, the rare trees and plants, the white coral roads, the pink beaches, and the 17th-century homes and gardens.

Two days from New York—no passports. Excellent hotels and boarding places, and furnished cottages. Booklet from the Furness Bermuda Line, 34 Whitehall Street, New York, The Royal Mail Steam Packet Company, 26 Broadway, New York, or any travel bureau, or

THE BERMUDA TRADE DEVELOPMENT BOARD
250 Park Avenue, New York
(A Department of the Bermuda Government, which
has authorised the publication of this advertisement.)

*Those who have crossed more than once
invariably choose their ship with care*

S.S.		S.S
RELIANCE	AND OTHER SPLENDID STEAMERS	RESOLUTE
ALBERT BALLIN		DEUTSCHLAND

UNITED AMERICAN LINES
(HARRIMAN LINE)
joint service with

HAMBURG AMERICAN LINE

Write for fascinating travel booklet P. Q.

39 BROADWAY, NEW YORK

171 W. RANDOLPH ST., CHICAGO   230 CALIFORNIA ST., SAN FRANCISCO

United American Cruise Line, 1924

HAVANA

Here's a trip abroad~
not far away~not too expensive

WHEN winter comes, the travel-wise start south to Cuba. Here is the one winter resort that offers *all* the modern pastimes of the complete vacation—*all* the benefits of travel in the bracing sunshine of the tropics—with the *added* pleasure of an environment that is entirely foreign—different—a thorough change of scene which means a complete getting away from the things you're tired of and carries you into the sparkle, the freedom, the fascinating atmosphere of the old world. They're coming now, by train, by highway, by water, by air, to the pleasures, interests and new experiences that characterize life in the "Pearl of the Antilles" . . . Havana has earned the reputation, "Smartest City in America." Out of this setting of early Spanish colonialism has risen an ultra-modern metropolis of a half-million persons, with every facility for accommodating and entertaining its throngs of winter vacationists . . . deluxe hotels, grand boulevards, the gorgeous Prado, imposing theatres, the opera, broad highways radiating for hundreds of miles through scenic countryside . . . brilliant social life and every summer sport that's known to the out-of-doors—golf, tennis, polo, hunting — deep sea fishing, swimming, yachting — horse racing at famous Oriental Park—the thrilling jai-a-lai, fastest of games—every sport doubly delightful in entrancing tropical surroundings. Here are new health and new pleasures for all the family. (There are good American day and boarding schools for the children). Here is mental rejuvenation for the American business man; a radical change from the routine . . . an opportunity to *forget* business, with the comfortable knowledge that if need be, a phone call can bring him quickly back to his desk. Plan *now* to visit Cuba, the *ultimate* in winter travel!   :   :   :

For information, etc., any travel bureau, any railroad, steamship or airplane ticket office or the National Tourist Commission, Havana.

Cuban National Tourist Commission, 1929

Havana was known as the "Paris of the Caribbean." During Prohibition it rivaled Miami as a tourist center, for Cuba's legal alcohol was only a short hop from many big East Coast cities. Cuba also offered something more: Its colonial past signaled a promise of sultry and voluptuous experiences.

Während der Prohibition machte Havanna, das „Paris der Karibik", Miami als Touristenmagnet Konkurrenz, denn Kubas legaler Alkohol war von vielen Großstädten an der Ostküste nur einen Katzensprung entfernt. Doch Kuba bot noch mehr: Seine koloniale Vergangenheit verhieß sinnenfrohe Ausschweifungen.

La Havane passait pour être le « Paris des Caraïbes ». Pendant la Prohibition, elle concurrençait Miami en tant que centre touristique car Cuba, où la consommation d'alcool était autorisée, ne se trouvait qu'à un saut de puce de nombreuses grandes villes de la Côte Est. L'île avait aussi autre chose à offrir : son passé colonial était une promesse d'expériences sensuelles et voluptueuses.

▶ Cunard, 1929

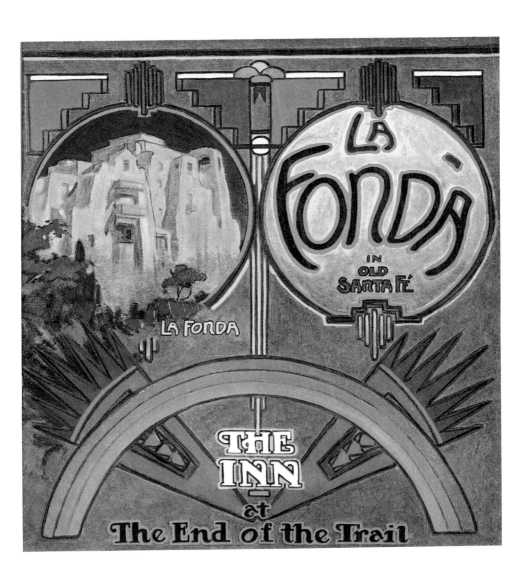

The St. Charles Hotel, 1923   La Fonda Inn, 1927

Your stop in China takes you back 1000 years

By HARRY A. FRANCK*

"CHINA, a world in itself. An ancient civilization that has come down to us almost intact. It is as if the social life of the pre-Christian era had been shifted into neutral and placed in a museum, not as a dead world's junk but still teeming with life, that we might see how our remote ancestors lived. For with all its recent furor to overtake the procession of what we perhaps mistakenly call modern progress, the great land of half a billion people is still essentially in the hand-making and barter stage . . .

"You cannot, of course, even if you try, miss Shanghai, where to cross the street separating the foreign concessions from the native city will instantly carry you back a thousand years. Thence great foreign steamers will take you up the Yang Tze Kiang, the "River Son of the Sea," if you like; modern trains to Peking. inimitable among world's cities. There is only one Peking. Charm of ancient ways, a culture and social deportment quite as advanced as ours, yet so different that it has won for the West the term "barbarian." Street-straddling arches like the materialization in permanent form of some extravaganza, hundreds of thousands of men and boys trotting between the shafts of vehicles bearing hundreds of thousands of others on many a strange errand . . . pages would not suffice merely to catalogue the incredibly quaint, the thrilling, the wonder producing sights—and sounds—to be found within those triple gigantic walls that surround what was long the Forbidden City . . ."

Harry A. Franck

DOLLAR AND AMERICAN STEAMSHIP LINE MAIL LINE

Typical Moroccan Outdoor Market Scene

Exterior of Transatlantique Hotel at Biskra

Along the White Roads
above the Mediterranean

ON'T you wish sometimes that life weren't so conventional? Wouldn't you like to slip back a thousand years and find a strange, white city, basking in topaz sunshine above a sapphire sea — a city with all the color in the world adrift in its narrow streets?

Wouldn't you like to sit in a cool blue and white courtyard in Algiers while a sand diviner tells your fortune? Wouldn't you like to wander past the twisted red and black pillars of the Street of the Perfumers in Tunis? Wouldn't you like to mount a mule and go slowly, slowly, down a reed-roofed street in Fez, with the sunshine filtering through in wide gold squares?

Wouldn't you like to watch the Ouled Naïls, the only women who can wander with unveiled faces, go out from their red-striped tents to dance on the hearts of men?

Wouldn't you like to buy rose-pink embroideries in Salé, rich old rugs, squares of glazed turquoise tiling like mermaids' jewels, high-backed crimson saddles with winking brass mountings—and even a bit of candy from the bronze pirate who cries with such musical pathos, "Oh Allah, Allah, send me many people with sweet teeth" . . . . ?

All this only twenty-six hours from Europe, and Europe six days from America! You step on board a French Liner in New York and are under French Line management until you see the Statue of Liberty again. Steamships, hotels, motor cars to run you right out into the Sahara. All guaranteed by those red funnels with black tops that stamp the service sterling. . . . . In the meantime, drop a line for information. The booklets are a trip in themselves.

French Line

Compagnie Générale Transatlantique, 19 State Street, New York

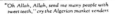

"Oh Allah, Allah, send me many people with sweet teeth," cry the Algerian market venders

Offices and agencies in principal cities of Europe and the United States

"SPEED IS THE CRY OF OUR ERA,
AND GREATER SPEED, ONE OF
THE GOALS OF TOMORROW."
– NORMAN BEL GEDDES

1930·

STREAMLINING
THE JOURNEY

Henry Dreyfuss reconceived every element —
from locomotive to dinner china, down to the sugar-
cube wrappers.

OUT OF THE FINANCIAL MAELSTROM OF THE GREAT DEPRESSION CAME A BELIEF IN THE POWER OF PURE DESIGN. "Brute force," said the industrial design luminary Raymond Loewy, "can have a very sophisticated appearance, almost of great finesse, and at the same time be a monster of power."

As leading industrial designers honed the shape of trains—transforming them down to the cocktail shakers—they also sped trains up. The first lightweight, streamlined train, the Union Pacific Railroad's City of Salinas (or M-10,000) left the station in February 1934. Months later, the elegant Burlington Zephyr had its first run, zooming to Chicago for the Century of Progress Exposition. Henry Dreyfuss redesigned every aspect of the New York Central Line's Mercury in 1936. But this was only a dress rehearsal for his overhaul of the 20th Century Limited. He reconceived every element—from locomotive to dinner china, down to the sugar-cube wrappers—on the deluxe, streamlined train that sped from New York to Chicago in 16 hours. Meanwhile, the Pennsylvania Railroad commissioned Raymond Loewy to redesign the GG1 electric locomotive in 1936. His torpedo-shaped S-1 for the Broadway Limited dazzled visitors to the 1939 New York World's Fair.

The Union Pacific Railroad's owner, Averell Harriman, on the other hand, wanted more than just a train designed—he wanted to create the destination. In 1936 he opened the Sun Valley Lodge, the first U.S. ski resort. A mix of Hollywood royalty and actual royalty hit the slopes in Ketchum, Idaho.

Airplane travel also took off in the '30s. In 1930, Boeing introduced air stewardesses, to make travel more congenial. The next year, Igor Sikorsky designed and built the first Clipper for Pan

Greyhound, 1938

American World Airways. These flying boats, which could land on water, offered an opulent ride at an opulent price. For example, the price from San Francisco to Manila was $1,710 round trip in 1937 — more than many people then earned in a year. Meanwhile, the popular new Douglas DC-3 captured the nation's fancy with its shimmering, stream-lined aluminum body, soundproofed cabins, ventilation ducts, upholstered seats, and high cruising altitude. As many as 28 passengers could soar coast-to-coast in 15 hours — the first airplane to turn a profit carrying only passengers.

Flying, however, only accounted for 7.6% of the long-distance travel market in 1936 — early airplane passengers were roughing it in pursuit of speed. At the other end of the luxury spectrum was the SS *Normandie*, the biggest, swiftest, most sophisticated vessel afloat, which first set sail in 1935. This French Line ship had an innovative hull design by Vladimir Yourkevitch, for a smoother voyage. But it was the art deco and streamline moderne interiors by leading French artists like Jean Dunand, Raymond Subes, and Jean Dupas that held the public's attention.

These luxuries — available, it is true, only to first-class passengers — and the many technological advances made travel better despite the severe economic turbulence. That sense of hope carried into the 1939 New York World's Fair. Its theme, "The World of Tomorrow," was sunny and optimistic about the transportation wonders to come.

◄◄ Bermuda, 1934   ► Italian Line, 1934

1931

1931

1934

Waldorf Astoria opens in New York; last major hotel planned in U.S. before stock market crash

Eröffnung des Waldorf Astoria in New York als letztes großes Hotel, das in den USA vor dem Börsenkrach geplant wurde

Ouverture du Waldorf Astoria à New York, le dernier grand hôtel américain dont la construction avait été planifiée avant le krach boursier

Greyhound Corporation formed; by 1936 will be first bus company with routes across U.S.

Gründung der Greyhound Corporation, die 1936 als erste Busgesellschaft ein flächendeckendes Streckennetz offerierte

Création de Greyhound Corporation : dès 1936, elle s'impose comme la première compagnie d'autocars proposant des itinéraires à travers tous les États-Unis

Cunard and White Star merge

Fusion der Reedereien Cunard und White Star

Fusion des compagnies Cunard et White Star

LOB DER STROMLINIE

Henry Dreyfuss erfand quasi alles neu – von der Lok über das Tafelgeschirr bis zum Würfelzuckerpapier.

DAS FINANZDESASTER DER WELTWIRTSCHAFTSKRISE HATTE ZUR FOLGE, DASS MAN AN DIE WIRKUNG REINER FORMEN ZU GLAUBEN BEGANN. „Rohe Gewalt", so Raymond Loewy, die Lichtgestalt des Industriedesigns, „kann sehr raffiniert wirken, fast von großer Finesse und doch zugleich vor Kraft strotzend."

Während führende Industriedesigner die Konturen der Züge glätteten (und sie bis hinab zu den Cocktailshakern verwandelten), wurden die Züge automatisch schneller. Der erste dieser leichten, stromlinienförmigen Züge war der ab Februar 1934 verkehrende City of Salinas (oder M-10 000) von Union Pacific Railroad. Wenige Monate später trat der elegante Burlington Zephyr seine erste Fahrt an, indem er nach Chicago zur Weltausstellung „A Century of Progress" raste. Henry Dreyfuss überarbeitete 1936 den Mercury der New York Central Line in sämtlichen Details. Doch dies war nur die Generalprobe für seine Generalüberholung des 20th Century Limited. Für diesen stromlinienförmigen Luxuszug, der in 16 Stunden von New York nach Chicago flitzte, erfand Dreyfuss quasi alles neu – von der Lok über das Tafelgeschirr bis zum Würfelzuckerpapier. Ebenfalls im Jahr 1936 wurde Raymond Loewy von Pennsylvania Railroad beauftragt, der Elektrolok GG1 ein neues Design zu verpassen. Und 1939 verblüffte seine torpedoförmige S-1 für Broadway Limited die Besucher der Weltausstellung in New York.

Averell Harriman, Eigentümer der Union Pacific Railroad, wollte mehr als einen neu designten Zug, er wollte ein Reiseziel kreieren. 1936 eröffnete er mit der Sun Valley Lodge das erste Skiresort der USA. Prominente jeglicher Provenienzen frequentierten die Hänge in Ketchum, Idaho.

◄◄ Lockheed, 1939   Palm Beach, Florida, 1937

Auch Flugreisen nahmen in den 1930er-Jahren einen Aufschwung. Boeing präsentierte 1930 die ersten Stewardessen, um das Reisen angenehmer zu gestalten. Igor Sikorsky baute ein Jahr später den ersten Klipper für Pan American World Airways. Diese Flugboote (sie können auf dem Wasser landen) boten einen opulenten Trip zu einem opulenten Preis. So zahlte man 1937 für ein Rückflugticket von San Francisco nach Manila 1710 $ – mehr als viele damals in einem Jahr verdienten. Derweil begeisterte die neue Douglas DC-3 die Nation mit ihrem glitzernden stromlinienförmigen Alurumpf, schallgedämmten Kabinen, Lüftungsdüsen, gepolsterten Sitzen und großer Reiseflughöhe. In nur 15 Stunden gelangten 28 Passagiere von Küste zu Küste – im ersten Flugzeug, das mit der ausschließlichen Personenbeförderung Profit machte. Flugreisen machten 1936 jedoch nur 7,6 % des Langstreckenmarktes aus. Am

1932

1934

1935

Marlene Dietrich in *Shanghai Express*: "It took more than one man to change my name to Shanghai Lily"

Marlene Dietrich in *Shanghai Express*: „Es brauchte mehr als nur *einen* Mann, um mich in Shanghai Lily zu verwandeln"

« Il a fallu plus d'un homme pour me rebaptiser Shanghai Lily », dit Marlene Dietrich dans *Shanghai Express*

Union Pacific Railroad's M-10,000 is first lightweight, streamlined train; together with Zephyr, reenergizes train travel

Als erster leichter Zug verleiht der M-10 000 von Union Pacific Railroad mit dem Zephyr den Bahnreisen neuen Schwung

Le M-10 000 de l'Union Pacific Railroad est le premier train léger et aérodynamique ; avec le Zéphyr, il relance le voyage en train

New SS *Normandie* is biggest, fastest, most sophisticated vessel afloat, with innovative hull by Vladimir Yourkevitch

Mit ihrem innovativen Rumpf von Wladimir Yourkewitsch ist die neue SS *Normandie* das größte und schnellste Schiff der Zeit

Avec sa coque innovante conçue par Wladimir Yourkevitch, le nouveau Normandie est le navire le plus grand et le plus rapide alors à flot anderen Ende des Luxussegments begegnen wir mit der 1935 in Dienst gestellten SS *Normandie* dem größten, schnellsten und fortschrittlichsten Schiff der Zeit. Wladimir Yourkewitsch hatte diesem Passagierdampfer der French Line einen innovativen Rumpf verpasst, der eine ruhigere Fahrt ermöglichte. Nachhaltigen Eindruck hinterließen indes die Art-déco- und Streamline-Moderne-Interieurs von führenden französischen Künstlern wie Jean Dunand, Raymond Subes und Jean Dupas.

Dieser allerdings nur den Passagieren der ersten Klasse gebotene Luxus sowie die zahlreichen technologischen Fortschritte machten das Reisen trotz der schweren ökonomischen Turbulenzen angenehmer. Auch die Weltausstellung 1939 in New York zeugte von Hoffnung, denn sie gab unter dem Thema „Die Welt von morgen" einen optimistischen Ausblick auf die künftigen fantastischen Verkehrsmittel.

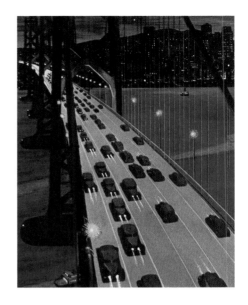

Californians Inc., 1937 ▶▶ Matson Line, 1934

1935

1937

1937

Glen Martin designs flying boats – the M-130, or China Clipper; Norman Bel Geddes redesigns interiors for Pan Am

Glen Martin entwirft Flugboote wie M-130 oder China Clipper; Norman Bel Geddes überarbeitet für Pan Am die Interieurs

Glen Martin invente des bateaux volants – le M-130, ou le China Clipper ; Norman Bel Geddes reconçoit les intérieurs de la Pan Am

Italian Line acquires SS *Rex* and SS *Conte di Savoia*; this ad is essence of haute deco, but their interiors are grandly classical

Die Italian Line erwirbt die SS *Rex* und SS *Conte di Savoia*; trotz Anzeige im Haute-Déco-Stil im Innern aber klassisch

La Società di Navigazione italienne achète le *Rex* et le *Conte di Savoia* ; contre toute attente, les intérieurs des navires restent très classiques

San Francisco's iconic Golden Gate Bridge opens to the public

Einweihung der Golden Gate Bridge, des neuen Wahrzeichens von San Francisco

Ouverture au public du Golden Gate Bridge, l'emblème de San Francisco

NEW ADVENTURE

A view of Sydney harbor . . . evoking admiration for Australia and the youthful vitality of its young civilization . . . playing . . . building . . . achieving a new order on the world's oldest continent. Strange contrasts—almost within sound of today's busy traffic—unique survivals of human and animal life found in no other part of the world. A voyage to this South Seas continent offers a *new adventure*.

Join a Matson *"South Pacific Cruise" personally escorted all-inclusive-cost—to Australia! via Hawaii! Samoa! Fiji! New Zealand!* Never before in travel! A 46-day cruise from California, *every month of the year.* No more than 5 days between ports. Smart elegance of magnificent liners…"Mariposa" or "Monterey"…emphasizing your enjoyment of the voyage. Similar attractive fares if you travel independently. ☆ *Your travel agent is an authority, see him for information, or any of our offices.*

The OCEANIC STEAMSHIP COMPANY
MATSON LINE

VOYAGE ET PROGRÈS TECHNOLOGIQUE

Henry Dreyfuss en reconçut chaque élément, de la locomotive à la vaisselle en porcelaine, en passant par les sachets de sucre.

LE MAELSTRØM FINANCIER DE LA GRANDE DÉPRESSION ENGENDRA UNE GRANDE CONFIANCE DANS LE POUVOIR DU DESIGN ÉPURÉ. « La force brute », déclara le visionnaire du design industriel Raymond Loewy, « peut avoir un aspect très sophistiqué, voire extrêmement raffiné, tout en étant un monstre de puissance ».

Quand les grands designers industriels aiguisaient la forme des trains – les transformant dans leurs moindres détails jusqu'aux shakers à cocktail – ils en accéléraient aussi la vitesse. Le City of Salinas (ou M-10 000) d'Union Pacific Railroad, premier train léger et aérodynamique, fut lancé en février 1934. Quelques mois plus tard, l'élégant Burlington Zephyr vivait son baptême du rail en filant vers Chicago pour l'exposition « Un Siècle de Progrès ». Henry Dreyfuss reconçut chaque aspect du Mercury de la New York Central Line en 1936, un exploit surpassé par la transformation qu'il imposa au 20th Century Limited. Il réinventa le moindre élément de ce train aérodynamique de luxe qui reliait New York à Chicago en 16 heures, de la locomotive à la vaisselle en porcelaine, en passant par les sachets de sucre. En 1936, la compagnie Pennsylvania Railroad demanda à Raymond Loewy de reconcevoir la locomotive électrique GG1. En 1939, la S-1 en forme de torpille qu'il inventa pour le Broadway Limited éblouit les visiteurs de l'Exposition Universelle de New York.

Quant à Averell Harriman, propriétaire de l'Union Pacific Railroad, il ne se contenta pas d'inventer un train : il créa une destination. En 1936, il inaugura Sun Valley Lodge, la toute première station de sports d'hiver du pays. Un mélange d'élite hollywoodienne et de têtes couronnées déferla alors sur les pistes enneigées de Ketchum, Idaho.

Les années 1930 virent aussi le décollage du voyage aérien. En 1930, Boeing recruta des hôtesses de l'air pour rendre les voyages plus agréables. L'année suivante, Igor Sikorsky conçut et construisit le premier Clipper pour la compagnie Pan American World Airways. Ces « bateaux volants » capables de se poser sur l'eau proposaient des voyages de luxe à prix exorbitants. Par exemple, l'aller-retour San Francisco/Manille coûtait 1710 dollars en 1937, un montant supérieur au salaire annuel de l'Américain moyen. Pendant ce temps, le nouveau Douglas DC-3 enflamma l'imagination du pays grâce à son fuselage en aluminium scintillant, ses cabines insonorisées, ses conduits d'aération, ses sièges rembourrés et sa haute altitude de croisière. Capable de transporter 28 passagers d'une côte à l'autre en 15 heures, ce fut le premier avion à devenir rentable en transportant seulement des passagers.

En 1936, les vols en avion ne représentaient toutefois que 7,6 % du marché des voyages longue distance. Sur le marché du luxe, le *Normandie*, navire le plus grand, le plus rapide et le plus sophistiqué alors à flot, effectua sa première traversée en 1935. Le paquebot français possédait une coque innovante conçue par Vladimir Yourkevitch pour voyager plus confortablement. Ce furent toutefois ses intérieurs Art Déco modernes et épurés signés par de grands artistes français comme Jean Dunand, Raymond Subes et Jean Dupas qui retinrent l'attention du public.

Tous ces luxes – certes uniquement accessibles aux passagers de première classe – et les nombreux progrès technologiques améliorèrent les conditions de voyage en dépit de sévères turbulences économiques. Ce sentiment d'espoir se refléta lors de l'Exposition Universelle de New York en 1939. Son thème, « Le Monde de Demain », rayonnait d'optimisme quant aux futures merveilles de l'industrie du transport.

▶ Italian Line, 1939   ▶▶ Thompson Products, 1935

1937

1937

1939

Hindenburg disaster, killing 36 people, essentially ends passenger travel by dirigible

Die Hindenburg-Katastrophe mit 36 Toten bedeutet letztlich das Ende für Reisen per Luftschiff

La catastrophe du Hindenburg, 36 morts, met quasiment un terme au transport de passagers par dirigeable

The Danish aristocrat Isak Dinesen, aka Karen Blixen, writes *Out of Africa* about her life in Kenya, to worldwide acclaim

Die dänische Aristokratin Isak Dinesen (Karen Blixen) erlangt Weltruhm mit *Afrika, dunkel lockende Welt* über ihr Leben in Kenia

L'aristocrate danoise Isak Dinesen écrit *La Ferme Africaine.* Ce livre racontant sa vie au Kenya est plébiscité dans le monde entier

World War II begins

Ausbruch des Zweiten Weltkriegs

Début de la Seconde Guerre mondiale

◄ Southern California, 1934

Southern California, 1935

The biggest movie stars of the '30s were exquisitely aerodynamic. Actresses like Marlene Dietrich, Claudette Colbert, and Carole Lombard had such hollowed cheekbones and sharply sculpted jaws that they could have posed for the hood ornaments on fancy, super-chic 1930s cars of the time. The kind few people were buying, except in movies.

Auch die größten Filmstars der 1930er-Jahre waren überaus aerodynamisch. Schauspielerinnen wie Marlene Dietrich, Claudette Colbert und Carole Lombard besaßen derart hohle Wangen und markante Kinnpartien, dass sie als Kühlerfiguren der tollsten Schlitten jener Zeit hätten posieren können. Von der Art, wie sie sich kaum jemand zulegte, außer in den Kinofilmen.

Les plus grandes stars de cinéma des années 1930 étaient d'une beauté aérodynamique. Des actrices comme Marlene Dietrich, Claudette Colbert et Carole Lombard avaient les joues tellement creuses et les mâchoires si sculptées qu'elles auraient pu inspirer les décors de capots des voitures de luxe super chic de la décennie. Du genre que peu de gens achetaient, sauf dans les films.

HOLLYWOOD *alone is worth the trip*

A BRILLIANT premiere in Hollywood. At intermission, the smart world fills the forecourt. Celebrities from the four corners of the earth. A scene you'll remember the rest of your life...

But the studios and the stars are just one part of this many-sided Southern California vacation. Tomorrow you're aquaplaning on a mile-high lake, deep in the pine forest. Next day, basking on a sandy beach or sailing to Catalina's palm-fringed shore.

Each day, new adventures. Golf, racing, tennis, polo—all in fascinatingly unfamiliar surroundings. Interesting cities: Los Angeles, Pasadena, Long Beach, Glendale, Beverly Hills, Pomona, Santa Monica. Flowers, orange groves, vineyards. Secluded resorts. Missions the Spanish Padres built...the peace and mystery of "Mother Mexico."

Give yourself this stimulating *change* this summer. You can do it easily even in a 2-weeks vacation, and costs are ridiculously low. Remember too, summer days in Southern California are rainless, and you'll sleep under blankets at night.

Free automatic trip planner

Your Southern California trip plans itself through this unique new book which gives you the whole story from the time you leave home till you're back again: What to see and do, over 100 pictures, maps, itemized cost schedules, etc...impartial information not available elsewhere.

ALL-YEAR CLUB OF SOUTHERN CALIFORNIA

Come to California for a glorious vacation. Advise anyone not to come seeking employment, lest he be disappointed; but for tourists, the attractions are unlimited.

SOUTHERN CALIFORNIA

All-Year Club of Southern California, Div. C-4, 1111 So. Broadway, Los Angeles, Calif.
Send me *free* book with complete details (including costs) of a Southern California vacation. Also send free routing by □ auto, □ rail, □ plane, □ bus, □ steamship. Also send free booklets about counties checked: □ Los Angeles, □ Santa Barbara, □ Orange, □ Inyo, □ Riverside, □ San Diego, □ Ventura, □ Imperial, □ Mission Trails, □ San Bernardino.
Name _____ Street _____
City _____ State _____

Isles of Repose

FOR VETERANS OF THE FAIR

When you've "done" the World's Fair, and you feel pretty well "done" yourself, come to this nearby tranquil retreat, Bermuda.

Nothing occurs with rush or clatter in this coral Arcady next door. Life is thrilling enough at bicycle pace. Motor traffic is banned by a humane Parliament, along with smoke-belching chimneys, fumes, and like disturbers of the peace.

Here, in this land of fun and flowers, is the balm for all your sorrows (including hay-fever). Even the climate beguiles you. Forever pleasant, it offers year-round indulgence in your favourite sports . . . golf . . . sailing . . . game fishing . . . tennis . . . bathing on rose-tinted beaches.

As a fillip to the Fair, nothing could be more fitting than a sojourn in this spot so beautifully strange.

BERMUDA IS NEAR THE NEW YORK WORLD'S FAIR . . . BY SEA OR BY AIR — Luxury liners travel from New York to Bermuda in 40 hours . . . a round-trip total of nearly 4 days of shipboard life. Sailings from Boston, too. • Splendid new transatlantic planes now take off from New York and Baltimore, Maryland, and descend at Bermuda 5 hours later . . . an enchanting experience in the sky. • A wide choice of accommodations is provided by Bermuda's many hotels and charming cottages. • No passport or visa is required.

Bermuda
PLEASURE ISLAND

FOR BOOKLET: *Your Travel Agent, or The Bermuda Trade Development Board, 30 Rockefeller Plaza, N.Y.C., or Victory Bldg., Toronto.*

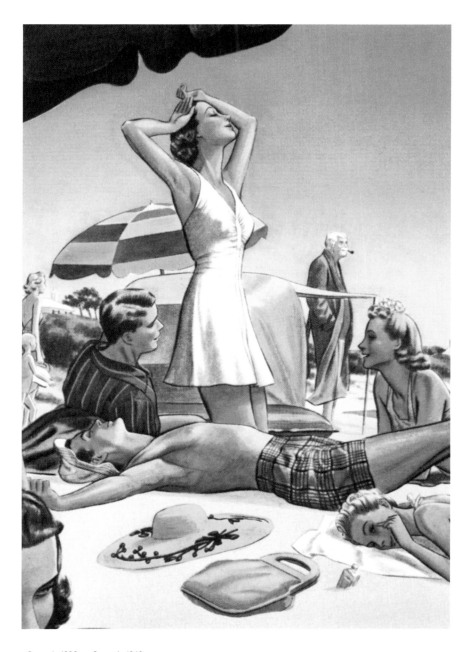

◄ Bermuda, 1939   Bermuda, 1940

Lady in Waiting

She might have served at the court of Versailles, this femme de chambre from Brittany. Pleasant and deft and courteous, she invents a hundred little unobtrusive attentions to make life a luxurious affair. For she is bred, through long apprenticeship, in the French Line tradition of service. ● Every voyager on France-Afloat is accorded such devotion as Royalty itself enjoys. Merely to wish is to be obeyed. There is a whole regiment of attentive stewards and stewardesses . . . who not only speak English, but seem actually to interpret one's unspoken whims. And every attendant, from the four-foot page-boys to the maître d'hôtel, is concerned, personally and intimately, with life's amenities. ● How could a French Line crossing be anything but Sybaritic? The food, for example, is considered by connoisseurs to be the flower of French cuisine . . . and it is served with an engaging and appropriate grandeur. (Enter caviar . . . cupped by the claws of a life-size eagle sculptured in gleaming ice!) Everything about France-Afloat . . . the atmosphere, the appointments, the company . . . contributes to a thoroughly successful crossing. ● May we point out that in spite of its many luxuries, a French Line passage costs no more? Any travel agent will be glad to arrange your booking . . . and there is no charge to you for his services. . . . French Line, 19 State Street, New York City.

MONTAGE CREATED FOR THE FRENCH LINE BY HALICKA, PARIS

French Line 🇫🇷

PARIS. June 9 and 30, July 21, August 11 and 30, September 18, October 6   ●   ILE DE FRANCE. June 16, July 7 and 28, August 18, September 9 and 29, October 20   ●   LAFAYETTE. June 13, July 3, August 25, September 15   ●   CHAMPLAIN June 2 and 23, July 15, August 4, September 22

French Line, 1934

This French Line ad describes the voyage as being "sybaritic," for the company's sumptuous first-class luxuries were heralded. Even in 1934, when the Great Depression was crushing the world economy, wealthy travelers sought out this line—and a subsidy from the French government helped keep it afloat.

Diese Anzeige der French Line spricht von einer „schwelgerischen" Reise, um die in der ersten Klasse gebotenen Annehmlichkeiten zu verkünden. Ungeachtet der Weltwirtschaftskrise entschieden sich betuchte Reisende noch 1934 für diese Reederei, die durch Finanzspritzen des französischen Staates über Wasser gehalten wurde.

Cette publicité pour la « French Line » présente le voyage comme « voluptueux » pour vendre le luxe première classe de la compagnie. Même en 1934, alors que l'économie mondiale souffrait de la Grande Dépression, les voyageurs fortunés plébiscitaient cette compagnie. Le gouvernement français lui octroya une subvention pour la garder à flot.

▶ French Line, 1931

Good-Bye to all that!

RACKETS and riveters ... cross-town traffic and subways ... brownstone fronts with basement entrances ... conferences and conventions and sales charts ... six o'clock friends and parlor games ... aren't you in your soul of souls fed up with them?

The sulphur and molasses season is at hand. Now is the time when executives come back from lunch wondering why nothing tastes good any more. Now is the time, also, when smart people give themselves a taste of good salt air and a few weeks abroad.

"Seymour," they say (if their budget includes a Seymour), "get out the trunks. We're off on the Vasty Deep." Or if, like most of us, they have no Seymour, they just pack a few bags, hail a taxi, and say: "Pier 57, North River."

And presto! the moment they set foot on deck, they're in France! ... Bronzed and mustachioed tars, whose Breton forefathers saw America before Columbus ... well-trained English-speaking servants within call ... all is well-ordered for these fortunate travelers. They speed eastward ... eating marvelous food ... basking ... walking ... dancing ... and in general doing whatever they darn well please. And they step ashore feeling already a different person altogether!

Ask your travel agent about voyaging on France Afloat ... and as the skyline vanishes from view, wave your hand, sniff the salt breeze, and say: "Good-bye to all that!" The French Line, offices in the larger cities of the United States and Canada, or at 19 State Street, New York City.

French Line

ILE DE FRANCE, April 8, April 30 • • LAFAYETTE, April 16, May 21 • • DE GRASSE, April 5, May 10
ROCHAMBEAU, April 30 • • PARIS, May 14 • • • FRANCE (West Indies Cruise, April 8), April 22, May 27

Lido after dark

THE CONTE DI SAVOIA . . . MIDNIGHT!

THE miraculous Southern Route sun has gone down . . . and the scene changes utterly. Instead of beach slacks . . . it's "white tie and tails". Instead of deck tennis, fencing, traps . . . it's music and champagne . . . or Asti Spumante, if you prefer to "do as the Romans do", as you probably will. For of course this is an Italian ship, offering all the warmth and subtlety of Italy's wines and table delicacies as well as those of other countries. Daytime Lido brought first fame to the Italian Line, with its sweeping play-decks and pools. Lido after dark brings the crowning mark of elegance to your Wintertime outdoor crossing.

Choose the great Rex, the gyro-stabilized Conte di Savoia, or the charming Roma, for an express voyage. Or enjoy the more leisurely route of the Vulcania or Saturnia, with their eight or nine extra ports to entertain you on the way. All are true Lido leaders . . . by day or night!

The leading **TRAVEL AGENTS** in your city are our representatives. Consult them freely—their services are gratis. Or apply to our nearest office: New York, Philadelphia, Boston, Cleveland, Chicago, Los Angeles, San Francisco, New Orleans, Montreal, Toronto.

ITALIAN LINE

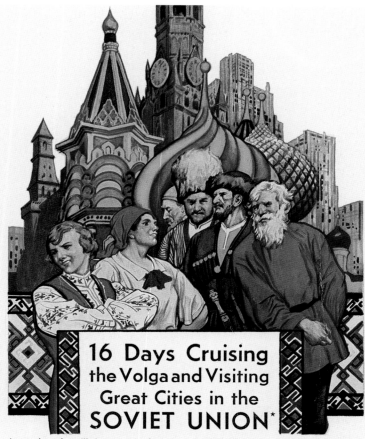

16 Days Cruising
the Volga and Visiting
Great Cities in the
SOVIET UNION*

An experience that will give you a trip of remarkable contrasts ranging from Tartar villages to the new social and industrial planning of vital Soviet cities. *Leningrad* with its palaces and museums . . . *Moscow* with its tremendous activities . . . *Nizhni-Novgorod* with its ancient romance and huge modern projects . . . 4 days on the mighty Volga following the course of many nationalities, traditions, and cultures . . . *Stalingrad* with its gigantic metal and tractor works . . . and then by return train to *Moscow*.

INTOURIST provides everything—hotels, meals, all transportation, sightseeing, theatre tickets, Soviet visa, and the services of English-speaking guides.

Other tours of unusual interest: *Moscow and Leningrad*, 5 days, $70; 7 days, $85. *Caucasus and Crimea*, 24 days, $240 up; *Volga, Caucasus and Crimea*, 30 days, $300 up. *Caucasus and Georgia*, 20 days, $200 up. Three tours to *Turkestan*. Industrial Tours.

★ $192 for two together, Second Class; $240 for one alone. Greatly reduced rates for groups of three and four together.

Write for General Booklet X4.   INTOURIST, Inc., 261 Fifth Avenue, New York ● 304 N. Michigan Boulevard, Chicago ● 756 S. Broadway, Los Angeles. ● *Or see your own travel agent.*

TRAVEL IN THE SOVIET UNION

Intourist, Inc., 1935   ▶ *Travel*, ca. 1930

Hawaii WILL LIVE IN YOUR HEART
forever

Matson Line to *Hawaii*

NEW ZEALAND • AUSTRALIA • via SAMOA • FIJI

Complete details of exhilarating Matson South Pacific voyages may be
secured from all Travel Agents or Matson Line—Oceanic Line; New York,
Chicago, San Francisco, Los Angeles, San Diego, Seattle, Portland.

*Hawaiian hotel reservations at the beautiful Royal Hawaiian and Moana at Waikiki may
now be made when you book steamer passage. An added convenience for Matson travelers.*

S. S. LURLINE • S. S. MARIPOSA • S. S. MONTEREY • S. S. MALOLO

Hawaii's floral beauty photographed in natural co

THE ISLANDS OF *Hawaii*

★ Oahu, Honolulu's island, is one of the four main counties of the Hawaiian group. The others—Kauai, Maui and Hawaii—share Oahu's advantages, but offer their own individual beauty and diversion.

HUBERT MACK   COPYRIGHT HAWAII TOURIST BUREAU 1938

★ *At play in Honolulu. Natural color photograph taken in Hawaii*

Waikiki—*the world's famous beach is only part of Hawaii's great diversity!* All of her islands are rimmed by superb beaches . . . white sands, black sands, "barking" sands . . . shaded by slanting coco-palms, washed by lazy surf. You may swim in perfect comfort at any time by clock or calendar . . . midnight or noon . . . January or June!

Behind her shorelines, high-speed motor-roads wind through verdured canyons . . . past plantation-lands . . . and climb to the inspiring summits of great volcanoes.

Behind her gaiety and varied pleasures is *Hawaii, the community,* modern and American. A community of fine schools . . . lovely homes . . . *shops that are fashion centers.* A land of boundless energy . . . imparting to all an unique joy of living.

When you turn westward to these isles like no other place in the world . . . let us know your sailing-date, that we may welcome you . . . with scented necklaces fresh woven from our native flowers . . . the Aloha *lei* greeting, proud tradition of Hawaii! Nowhere else does a community say "how-do-you-do" with such sincerity and grace. *Write us by all means.*

From routine to rapture in an instant-change! Swift, luxurious steam-ships sailing from Los Angeles, San Francisco or Vancouver, B. C. speed over this glorious sea-way in less than five days. Our booklet, "Nearby Hawaii" and "Tourfax" bulletin contain complete information, invaluable in planning your visit. Free, from your railway, steam-ship, or travel agent, or Hawaii Tourist Bureau, 40 Main Street, San Francisco, Calif.; 722 West Olympic Boulevard, Los Angeles, Calif.

This Bureau, with headquarters at 765 Bishop Street, in Honolulu, is a non-profit organization, maintained by

THE PEOPLE OF HAWAII

to enable you to obtain accurate information on any subject concerning the entire Territory of Hawaii, U. S. A.

◄ Matson Line, 1938   Hawaii Tourist Bureau, 1936

Here I am -- the fellow who said he would never fly !

"If I'd thought it was anything like this, I'd have been flying long ago! Here I am, enjoying undreamed-of travel comforts, seeing beauty I never knew existed, saving *days* of time! It's not costing me a penny more, but I'm sure *getting more!*"

Most everyone who flies has at one time said: "*I'll never fly!*" But wisdom whispered: "Don't be too sure. It's a *big* thing! Better try it and see." And so they flew . . . and alighted from their first flights, elated, discoverers of a new world! You, too, have only to *fly* to know that travel by air is a reality for *thousands* every day and night the whole year around, and that the sooner you adopt flying, the sooner you catch up with other modern-day folks! American Airlines, Inc., Dept. E-20, 20 North Wacker Drive, Chicago.

Serving America's Major Cities From Coast to Coast

American Airlines, 1939

By the end of the '30s, airplanes had begun to change the nation's travel plans. Air passengers no longer had to rough it, since planes now offered a far smoother ride, as well as temperature control, soundproofing, and stewardesses. This wealthy businessman might well have been a likely passenger.

Im ganzen Land sah sich das Reiseverhalten ab Ende der 1930er-Jahre durch das Flugzeug zunehmend beeinflusst. Flugreisende mussten nun nicht mehr einiges einstecken, denn die neuen Maschinen boten einen weitaus ruhigeren Flug sowie Temperaturregulierung, Schalldämmung und Stewardessen. Dieser betuchte Geschäftsmann könnte durchaus als Passagier infrage gekommen sein.

À la fin des années 1930, l'avion avait commencé à modifier les projets de voyage des Américains. Les passagers aériens n'avaient plus à voyager à la dure, car les avions étaient désormais plus confortables, insonorisés, équipés du chauffage, de la climatisation et même d'hôtesses de l'air. Ce riche homme d'affaires aurait fait un passager tout à fait crédible.

► American Airlines, 1939

►► Pennsylvania Railroad, 1938

☆ The amazing speed and superb comfort of Flagship travel and the dependability of American's nation-wide day-and-night service provide a striking example of the American public *getting what it wants*. There are many who are not yet aware of the extent, the economy or the convenience of air travel. To these people, regular Flagship patrons say: "Fly once, and you'll fly always!" Call your Travel Agent today for Flagship schedules and fares. Or phone the nearest office of American Airlines, Inc.

AMERICAN AIRLINES *Inc*
ROUTE OF THE FLAGSHIPS

AMERICAN AIRLINES INC.
SYSTEM MAP

■ AMERICAN AIRLINES ══ CONNECTING LINES

PENNSYLVANIA RAILROAD PRESENTS

A FLEET OF MODE

ERE'S THE FLEET OF MODERNISM!
(Standard Time)
BROADWAY LIMITED

, New York	5:00 P.M.
, Philadelphia	6:20 P.M.
, Chicago	8:00 A.M.
, Chicago	3:30 P.M.
, Philadelphia	7:09 A.M.
, New York	8:30 A.M.

THE GENERAL

, New York	3:40 P.M.
, Philadelphia	5:09 P.M.
, Chicago	7:50 A.M.
, Chicago	3:15 P.M.
, Philadelphia	8:01 A.M.
, New York	9:30 A.M.

LIBERTY LIMITED

, Washington	5:10 P.M.
, Baltimore	5:55 P.M.
, Chicago	8:35 A.M.
, Chicago	3:10 P.M.
, Baltimore	8:02 A.M.
, Washington	8:50 A.M.

"SPIRIT OF ST. LOUIS"

, New York	5:15 P.M.
, Philadelphia	6:38 P.M.
, Washington	5:30 P.M.
, St. Louis	12:42 P.M.
, St. Louis	12:15 P.M.
, Washington	9:55 A.M.
, Philadelphia	8:24 A.M.
, New York	9:50 A.M.

l trains air-conditioned. P.R.R.
ury Coaches and Improved Section
pers on all trains except the all-room
llman train — Broadway Limited.

Bar Lounge: Designed in collaboration with the Pullman Company by Raymond Loewy, creator of smart modern interiors. Interestingly placed divans .. conversation corners in richly cushioned fabrics .. low broad upholstered settees .. venetian blinds .. a magnificent mural, facing long triple-panelled mirrors .. a fan-wise bar within easy hail. Soft shades predominate in the color scheme and lighting which are soothing, not flamboyant.

Master Suites (on Broadway and Liberty Limiteds) Something entirely new in private accommodations. Two rooms, not one. The first, a handsome lounge in soft colors, with radio and other modern furnishings (at night, twin beds); the second, a private bathroom with shower.

VISM

Observation Cars: Here the designer's art is conspicuously evident. Cresc shaped divans . . low tabourets . . deep carpeting . . lounge chairs inform arranged, the lighting soft but radiant. The whole effect distinctively casua in a smart club. A richly appointed buffet adjoins the main lounge. Anyt missing? Yes, the open observation platform. Now it is glass-enclosed lux

INTO SERVICE WEDNESDAY, JUNE 15, 1938, LED BY A NEW AND FINER

BROADWAY LIMITED

First All-Room Train in History . . Daily Between New York and Chicago . . 16 Hours!

CK TRAINS are reborn—a whole fleet of them. t innovations in comfort and style. Even car s and dimensions change. All this, achieved by oration of Pennsylvania Railroad and Pullman any engineers and Raymond Loewy, noted designer.

's all yours to enjoy in air-conditioned travel on lvania Railroad routes uniting New York, Phila- a, Baltimore, Washington and other leading cities Chicago and St. Louis.

w types of private accommodations, a wider than ever before available on any train. In ad- to new versions of drawing rooms, compart- double bedrooms, you now have . . the Master

Suite, the Roomette, the Duplex. Each has a definite individuality, and all have nice soft beds — 6 feet, 5 inches long — and private toilet facilities.

Nor is that all. New personality is given the fleet leader . . *Broadway Limited*. Staffed with valet, barber, mani- curist, maid and train secretary, this leader becomes an all-room Pullman train. Privacy for every passen- ger. New-style diners, too—excitingly different. Faster schedule also — New York to Chicago in 16 hours!

Coupled with the new electrified mileage east of Harrisburg, this *Fleet of Modernism* now makes travel on the Pennsylvania Railroad even more attractive than ever before. Enjoy it!

Roomettes give you private little world of you own. Comfortably compac this accommodation pro vides . . personal toilet an washing facilities, illumi nated mirror, enclosed ward robe and, at night, a full length bed which dips dow at your finger's touch

BY DAY *a cheery sitting roo*
BY NIGHT *a cozy bedroor*

ennsylvania Railroac

SHORTEST ROUTE BETWEEN EAST AND WEST — HEAVIEST RAIL, FINEST ROADBED IN AMERICA. YOU CAN SLEEP

Why 20,000 people missed their boats

You don't want to keep sailing dates in Hawaii. Waikiki's clock is easily forgotten. It doesn't seem important. You try to recall those troublesome affairs you should be going home to worry about. Oh well—there'll be another ship . . . how do the old timers say "later"? . . . *mahope!*

Another swim, another saunter along the hibiscus trail. Let's take a boat to Kona tomorrow and troll for sword-fish at Napoopoo. Let's fly over to Maui or have an afternoon at Hanalei beach on Kauai. One more go at the surf-board and hula. One more night under the coco palms, the moon making rainbows against the mountains —the sea whispering of nights drifting by and other nights to come.

Let Hawaii's tropic sunshine, its balmy fragrant breezes wash old gritty trouble out of your mind. From the moment your ship swings into Hono-

lulu harbor and hospitable Hawaii greets you with her fragrant flower leis of friendship you become a new person.

Your winter playground will be a land glowing with the color of a million flowers—a warm sea that substitutes the white crests of lazy waves

for winter snows. There'll be tropical fruit—papaia, bananas, lychee, mangoes, passion fruit. Fern jungles; plantations of sugar, coffee and pineapple. Volcanoes, scarred with freak lava flows, rise to craters large enough to hold a city.

$275 or less, can well cover the expense of an 18-day round trip from the Pacific Coast ports of Los Angeles, San Francisco and Vancouver. This low cost will allow: first-class accommodations on board ship, a good hotel or cottage, your meals and a bit of sightseeing. Will you write us for proof?

HAWAII

HAWAII TOURIST BUREAU

(HONOLULU, HAWAII, U. S. A.)

1514 A RUSS BUILDING, SAN FRANCISCO

The Hawaii Tourist Bureau will, on request, mail you FREE, authoritative information about the Islands, costs, what to see and do, etc. For a special booklet on Hawaii, illustrated in full color, with picture maps, send 10c to defray cost of handling.

Hawaii Tourist Bureau, 1932

This ad promises that you can leave your troubles behind, for Hawaii was indeed far away. But after Amelia Earhart's first solo flight between Hawaii and California in 1935, air travel developed. Franklin D. Roosevelt was the first president to visit Hawaii, staying at Matson's luscious Royal Hawaiian Hotel in 1934.

Diese Anzeige verspricht, dass man seine Sorgen zurücklassen kann, denn Hawaii war in der Tat weit entfernt. Doch Amelia Earharts erster Alleinflug 1935 von Hawaii nach Kalifornien bildete gleichsam den Startschuss für die Flugreisen. Franklin D. Roosevelt besuchte 1934 als erster US-Präsident Hawaii und übernachtete in Matsons reizendem Royal Hawaiian Hotel.

Cette publicité promettait que vous pouviez laisser vos soucis loin derrière vous, puisque Hawaï se trouvait littéralement très loin. En 1935, après le premier vol en solitaire d'Amelia Earhart entre Hawaï et la Californie, les liaisons aériennes se développèrent. Franklin D. Roosevelt fut le premier Président à visiter Hawaï. Il séjourna au splendide Royal Hawaiian Hotel de la compagnie Matson en 1934.

▶ Dollar Steamship Lines, 1935

Christmas Present

*A happy, carefree cruise Round the World...
designed to your order... starting whenever
you choose... taking 85 days to two years.*

Luxurious Living
ALONG THE SUNSHINE ROUTE

World-famed President Liners have broad play-decks and an outdoor swimming pool... every stateroom outside (with real twin beds)... menus made up from the best the whole wide world affords.

Visits to 21 Fascinating Ports
PHILIPPINE DUGOUT AND VINTAS

Exciting days and nights in the great cosmopolitan ports of Cuba and Panama, California, Hawaii, Japan, China, the Philippines, Malaya, India, Egypt, Italy, and France... 14 fascinating far-flung countries.

Stopovers and Sidetrips Anywhere
PEKING SIDETRIP

Weekly sailings from New York, Los Angeles and San Francisco allow stopovers and sidetrips anywhere en route... continuation on the next or another of these world's only regular-world-cruising ships.

Low Shore Costs
INDIA HAS BRAND NEW THRILLS

Ask your own Travel Agent for all details. Or write Dollar Steamship Lines, 604 Fifth Avenue, New York; 110 South Dearborn Street, Chicago; 311 California Street, San Francisco. Offices in other principal cities.

Round the World
CRUISES TO ORDER

COST JUST $**854** FIRST CLASS

·

DOLLAR
Steamship Lines

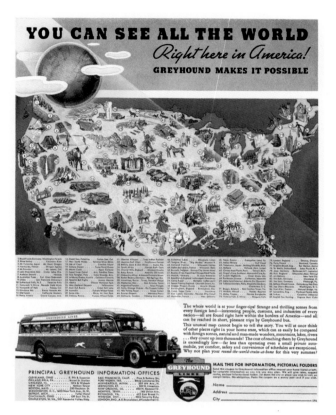

Greyhound, 1932

Buses were considered a good alternative to trains. One of the Depression's biggest movies acknowledged this. Claudette Colbert stars as a runaway heiress in *It Happened One Night* (1934). She meets a reporter (Clark Gable) on the bus from Florida to New York. Love and many Oscars ensue.

Der Bus galt als eine gute Alternative zum Zug – so auch in einem der größten Kinoerfolge jener Zeit: *It Happened One Night* (*Es geschah in einer Nacht*, 1934) mit Claudette Colbert als Erbin auf der Flucht, die im Bus von Florida nach New York einem Reporter (Clark Gable) begegnet. Liebe und zahlreiche Oscars folgten.

Le bus était considéré comme une bonne alternative au train, comme le prouve l'un des plus grands films de la Dépression. Dans *New York-Miami* (1934), Claudette Colbert incarne une héritière en fuite qui rencontre un reporter (Clark Gable) dans un bus reliant la Floride à New York. S'ensuivirent une célèbre histoire d'amour et de nombreux Oscars.

Over the King's Highway

—we roll . . seeing the Golden State

by Greyhound . . . old Missions, blue Pacific, guardian mountains, giant trees

A STRANGE cavalcade halts in the shade of lordly oaks . . stalwart Spaniards in glittering armor and polished helmets. At their right, sun-flooded hills . . . at their left, the flashing blue Pacific. Their black-bearded captain glances back along the path . . . "A brave trail we are breaking, Cavaliers!" he shouts. "We will call it El Camino Real—the Royal Road—in honor of our King!"

That was 163 years ago. Today, the thousands who travel California's Mission Trail, by Greyhound Bus, find that it has truly earned its proud title. This broad paved road extends northward from San Diego through Los Angeles * and Santa Barbara to San Francisco's Golden Gate . . . revealing old Spanish Missions,

shining Monterey Bay, giant redwood trees whose sheer height takes the breath. Greyhound Lines offer not merely the best way to reach Pacific Coast points from anywhere in the Nation. It is the only public transportation with a half-dozen optional routes from ocean to ocean . . . and from Canadian cities to Mexico.

This is the restful, time-saving way for short trips, too. Greyhound buses are healthfully warmed by Tropic-Aire heaters. Exceptionally comfortable chairs recline to any desired position for relaxation or sleep. Frequent rest and lunch stops are scheduled on every trip . . . terminals are right downtown.

45,000 miles of Greyhound routes cover the United States. They will serve you best on business trips, week-end visits or winter excursions to California, colorful Southwest, Gulf Coast, Florida. And remember—every ticket means a substantial saving!

Above—Tinted photograph of Santa Barbara Mission—one of the most beautiful and well-preserved of them all. *At right*—A glimpse of the Pacific through graceful palms. Greyhound offers a delightful 3-Day Tour of the Mission Trail between Los Angeles and San Francisco.

* By all means, come to the Olympic Games at Los Angeles, July 30th to August 14th, this year. And see the Rodeo at Salinas, July 20th to 24th . . . . a rip-roaring flashback to cowboy days!

GREYHOUND
Lines

MAIL THIS TODAY

These Greyhound Lines Serve the Whole Nation . . . .

CENTRAL·GREYHOUND
E.11 St. & Walnut Ave., Cleveland, Ohio

PACIFIC·GREYHOUND
9 Main St., San Francisco, Calif.

NORTHLAND-GREYHOUND
509 6th Ave., N., Minneapolis, Minn.

PENNSYLVANIA-GREYHOUND
Broad St. Station, Philadelphia, Pa.

PICKWICK-GREYHOUND
917 McGee St., Kansas City, Mo.

SOUTHLAND-GREYHOUND
Pecan & Navarro Sts., San Antonio, Tex.

ATLANTIC·GREYHOUND
601 Virginia St., Charleston, W. Va.

CAPITOL-GREYHOUND
405 American Bldg., Cincinnati, O.

SOUTHEASTERN-GREYHOUND
Lexington, Kentucky

EASTERN·GREYHOUND
Nelson Tower, New York City

RICHMOND-GREYHOUND
42 E. Broad St., Richmond, Va.

CANADIAN GREYHOUND
1004 Security Bldg., Windsor, Ont.

Send this coupon to the nearest Greyhound office, listed at left, for attractive pictorial booklets on California □, or 52 page booklet, "America's Scenic Highways" □. Any other information desired:

Name

Address

SP-2

TRAVEL AT REDUCED RATES TO YOUR FAVORITE
SUMMER RESORT
IN *Pullman* SAFETY & COMFORT

◄ Pullman-Standard, 1937   Pullman-Standard, 1937

AMERICA ON PARADE

SKY CHIEF   SKY QUEEN   SKY MASTER   SUN RACER

SKY KING   SKY EMPRESS

Every day and every night scores of passengers on TWA are gaining new apprecia-
tion of America's beauty. They thrill to the spectacle of California —are speechless
at the splendor of Grand Canyon from the sky. The whole colorful West —Sky City
of Acoma, Inscription Rock, Boulder Dam, Enchanted Mesa, Painted Desert —delight
beyond all expectation. Even the fertile farmlands of the Mississippi Basin are surprisingly interesting. And the approach to New York, the world's greatest city, presents a view that cannot be surpassed.

On business or pleasure, by day or by night, your flight across America via TWA
will seem all too short. Douglas Skyliners on all schedules, each equipped with Gyro-
Pilots and Automatic Stabilizers, assure smooth, steady, comfortable flight. Call any
TWA office, Pennsylvania R. R., or leading hotels and travel bureaus.

fly **TWA**

◄ TWA, 1935

SS *Normandie*, French Line (Albert Sébille), 1935

This shimmering jewel of the French Line was the fastest and biggest ship at sea. Her lavish art deco and streamline moderne interiors, by leading French artists like Raymond Subes and Jean Dupas, captured the sophisticated travelers' fancy. The vast first-class dining room featured 12 lighting pillars by Lalique.

Dieses funkelnde Juwel der French Line war das schnellste und größte Schiff der Zeit. Verschwenderische Art-déco- und Streamline-Moderne-Interieurs von führenden französischen Künstlern wie Raymond Subes und Jean Dupas fanden Anklang bei den kultivierten Passagieren. Der gewaltige Speisesaal erster Klasse glänzte mit zwölf Lichtsäulen von Lalique.

Ce joyau éblouissant de la Compagnie Générale Transatlantique était le bateau le plus grand et le plus rapide du monde. Signés par des artistes français tels Raymond Subes et Jean Dupas, ses intérieurs Art Déco somptueux, modernes et épurés enflammèrent l'imagination des voyageurs les plus raffinés. L'immense salle à manger de première classe comptait 12 piliers d'éclairage en cristal de Lalique.

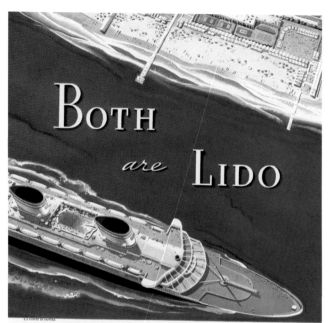

BOTH *are* LIDO

S.S. CONTE DI SAVOIA

The Lido of Venice . . . and the Lido of Italian liners . . . are sisters under the sun! The famed strip of golden, warm sands, splashed by the turquoise of the Adriatic and set off by the glories of Venice across the Lagoon . . . sees its splendor, its color, its charm, its Lido life mirrored on the sweeping decks of the super-liners Rex and Conte di Savoia . . . leaders of the equally famed Italian Line fleet!

Smart Europe flocks to Venice's Lido "in season". Smart America more and more is flocking to the Italian Line's Lido in all seasons—because of the outdoor delights, the mildness, the serene comforts of the Southern Route crossing, at any time of the year.

Soon you will be going abroad again. This time, give your trip the added glamour of a Lido crossing . . . and the added 1000 miles or more of Mediterranean cruising at no added cost. There are two ways to go—a direct, express crossing to Naples, Genoa or Nice on the Rex or Conte di Savoia . . . or a leisurely itinerary embracing as many as ten fascinating ports on the popular Roma, Saturnia or Vulcania. And at the end of your Lido voyage, fast trains will speed you to European capitals!

*   *   *

The leading **TRAVEL AGENTS** in your city are our representatives. Consult them freely—their services are gratis. Or apply to our nearest office: New York, Philadelphia, Boston, Cleveland, Chicago, San Francisco, New Orleans, Montreal, Toronto.

Italian Line, 1937

The Italian Line was called "the Riviera afloat," and, for emphasis, swimming pools were sur-rounded by sand and decks were dotted with large beach umbrellas. Grandly classic inte-riors, as well as the sand, may have reminded passengers of the Lido, the Venice beach.

Die Italian Line wurde auch „schwimmende Riviera" genannt. Wie um dies zu betonen, ver-teilte man Sand rund um die Schwimmbecken und übersäte die Decks mit großen Strand-schirmen. Stattliche klassische Interieurs und auch der Sand mögen den Gast an Venedigs Strand, den Lido, erinnert haben.

La Società di Navigazione était surnommée « la plage en pleine mer ». D'ailleurs, ses piscines étaient entourées de sable et ses ponts équipés de grands parasols. Les grandioses intérieurs classiques et le sable rappelaient peut-être le Lido – la plage de Venise – aux passagers.

▶ Alaska, 1935

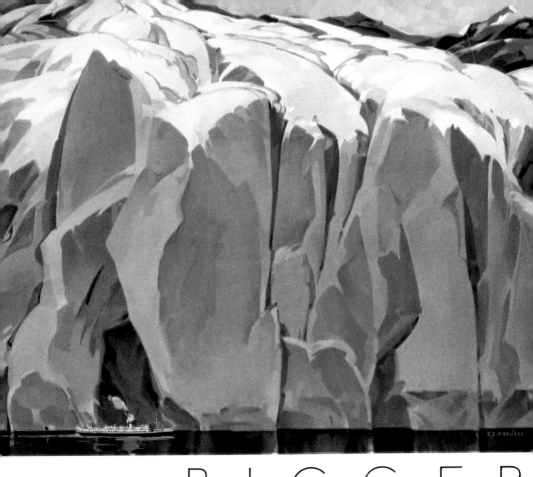

THE GLACIERS ARE B I G G E R

The largest glaciers in the world are along the coast of Alaska. You can snowball upon them in summer—yet in June and July, wild flowers in profusion fringe their edges!

A most unusual country is Alaska. Imagine, if you will, a land where a baseball game can be played at midnight without artificial light! Where totem poles stand next to telephone poles in modern towns. Where vines grow three inches over night, in gardens near glacial fields of ice.

Travel by train across America. We have *air-conditioned* trains which are cool, clean, quiet and safe. Relax as you ride. Arrive at Seattle, refreshed and ready to sail. How much vacation time have you? Two weeks, three, or four? We can give you an Alaskan trip to exactly fit your time and pocketbook. And nowhere in the world can you find a vacation paradise to equal this enchanted land. May we figure costs from your home town?

in ALASKA

For free Alaska literature, write any of The All-American Services to Alaska:

Pan Am Clipper, 1938

Well-suited for the Clipper. These passengers, clearly too wealthy to be brought down by the Great Depression, are boarding a Clipper, the boat-plane that soared across the Pacific and Atlantic. Juan Trippe, the Pan Am chairman who developed the Clipper, was continually looking to keep his airline out ahead.

Genau richtig: Diese Passagiere, eindeutig zu reich, um von der Weltwirtschaftskrise in die Armut getrieben zu werden, steigen gerade in eine flinke Clipper ein – jenes Flugboot, das auf dem Pazifik wie Atlantik verkehrte. Juan Trippe, Chef von Pan Am und Entwickler der Clipper, war stets darauf bedacht, dass seine Fluglinie die Nase vorn hatte.

Bien habillés pour le Clipper : ces passagers, apparemment trop riches pour souffrir de la Grande Dépression, embarquent à bord d'un Clipper, le « bateau volant » qui traversait le Pacifique et l'Atlantique. Juan Trippe, le Président de la Pan Am qui développa le Clipper, cherchait constamment à préserver la longueur d'avance de sa compagnie aérienne.

▶ United Air Lines, 1930

▶▶ Western Railroads, 1935

NEW WORLD'S RECORDS BY UNITED AIR LINES

☆ With a new fleet of 3-mile-a-minute, Wasp-powered Boeings, United Air Lines is giving the fastest service ever maintained with multi-motored planes. New York-Chicago is a morning, after-noon or evening flight. Chicago-Pacific Coast an overnight journey. And New York-California a trip of less than one day. These are world's records.
☆ The public's response to this service is to use it. During 1933 United Air Lines carried approximately 125,000 passengers. Another world's record.
☆ United's new Boeing planes make every provision for the passengers' comfort. Heated spacious cabins.

60,000,000 MILES FLYING EXPERIENCE

CALIFORNIA TO NEW YORK . . . 20 HRS.
3 flights daily each way
CHICAGO TO NEW YORK . . . 4¼ HRS.
10 flights daily each way
CALIFORNIA TO CHICAGO . . . 14½ HRS.
3 flights daily each way
FT. WORTH-DALLAS TO CLEVELAND . . . 9 HRS.
2 flights daily each way
LOS ANGELES TO SEATTLE . . . 8 HRS.
2 flights daily each way

(West bound schedules slightly longer due to prevailing winds.)

Consult new United Air Lines' time table for schedule to intermediate and off-line points

UNITED AIR LINES
Subsidiary of United Aircraft & Transport Corporation

☆ Adjustable reclining chairs for relaxation or for sleeping during night flights.
☆ United Air Lines' year-round service utilizes every known aid to avigation. Multi-motored planes manned by two transport pilots. Two-way radio. Direc-tive radio beam. Lighted airways. Fre-quent weather reports.
☆ Fly with United Air Lines — the fastest and most interesting way to travel. ☆ For schedules, tickets or res-ervations to 137 cities . . . call United Air Lines' ticket offices, Hotel Porters, Travel Bureaus, Postal or Western Union. ☆ Air Express — Phone Air Ex-press Division, Railway Express Agen-cy. Use Air Mail — it speeds business.

Stewardess service. Lunches served oil-it included in economical fares.

Two veteran pilots (averaging 4,000 hours of flying) on every multi-motored plane.

Now

REAL TRAVEL ECONOMY

Basic fares on Western Railroads are as low as 2c per mile round trip for sleeping car travel; correspondingly low for coaches and chair cars. Sleeping car accommodations one-third lower; no surcharge. Special bargains in Summer Excursion tickets on sale daily. All-Expense Tours available at railroad ticket offices and tour agencies. Ship your auto at reduced rates and travel in comfort by train. Your dollar goes farther on Western Railroads. See any railroad ticket agent.

TRAVEL BY TRAIN

to PACIFIC NORTHWEST • ALASKA • CALIFORNIA • SAN DIEGO EXPOSITION • AMERICAN ROCKIES • DUDE RANCHES • OZARKS • TEXAS GULF COAST • NORTH WOODS AND LAKES • SOUTHWEST • OLD MEXICO • NATIONAL PARKS • RESORTS OF EVERY CHARACTER

WESTERN TRAINS
are *Air-Conditioned*
... FARES IN THE WEST ARE LOW ...

● The Golden West is calling all Americans this year with a lavish list of wonderful attractions easily reached on air-conditioned trains. • Air-conditioning on wheels! The greatest contribution to travel comfort in 25 years! . . . Providing air so cool and clean that you look and feel "fresh as the breath of spring—*while* you travel and *when* you arrive." . . . Luxurious cars so quiet you relax at once into a delighted sense of well-being. . . . Air-conditioning makes the *finest* travel service in the world. And Western Railroads have made it the *most economical.* • All principal trains west of Chicago, St. Louis, Memphis and New Orleans have been air-conditioned. Western Railroads have spent millions of dollars in this improvement. But it costs you *not one penny extra.* These trains also offer incomparable dining car service at prices surprisingly modest. • So travel in the West this summer and really see America. Travel by train and enjoy ideal weather from the moment you leave regardless of climatic conditions en route. Save money. Save time. Travel at ease, in comfort and peace of mind. Train schedules are dependable. Train travel is safer. • Don't be satisfied with less modern transportation. For train travel in the West costs so little, offers so much.

On your Western Tour by train see at least one National Park

Consult any railroad representative for rates, routes, schedules or literature on places to visit

Visit Quaint Old Mexico

Keep Cool in the Rockies

Play on Pacific Beaches

See the National Parks

Walk Among the Big Trees

Plan Now

FOR A GLORIOUS TRIP
TO
GERMANY

• Turn romantic pages of history in Germany. The time-mellowed ruins of ancient castles, the tomb of Charlemagne, the elaborate Guild Halls of medieval cities, the Romanesque and Gothic cathedrals of Cologne, Freiburg, Worms and Speyer, and Frederick the Great's palace of Sanssouci . . . these and many others . . . What glories of the past they echo! . . . What message of romance they bring you—as you tour through Germany . . . while operas and festivals, stage-craft and symphonies evidence in word and music the undying genius of Goethe, Wagner, Beethoven and Bach.

But the world marches on in Germany, also . . . Here you will find 20th Century progress. Or all modern sports and many that are uniquely German — piloting gliders on the Wasserkuppe or breasting the Rhine in a Faltboat. Then, too, there are great cities like Berlin, with their gay night life, splendid theatres, hotels and restaurants . . . And centers of culture, art and merrymaking like Munich, as famed for its museums as for its brew . . . Dresden, Nürnberg, Frankfurt, Stuttgart, Bayreuth, Weimar — all with a connotation of their own.

As for scenery: the Bavarian Alps, the Black Forest, Harz and Thuringia . . . the castles and vineyards of the Rhine and its gentle-flowing tributaries, the fruit trees and gardens of the Bergstrasse, the lovely sweep of sea and sky along the Baltic and North Sea. And the charm of Germany's famous health resorts.

All this you can enjoy, and more . . . in perfect comfort whether in hotel, train or steamer . . . good living at moderate prices, *still further reduced by the use of registered Travel Marks.* And the German Railroads grant you *60% reduction of rail fares.* Now is the time to see Germany. Begin planning your trip today.

Travel on swift streamliners of the German Railroads. The famous "Flying Hamburger" covers 186 miles in 137 minutes. All Rail fares reduced 60%.

CONSULT YOUR TRAVEL AGENT AND WRITE FOR BOOKLET 48

GERMAN RAILROADS INFORMATION OFFICE
665 Fifth Avenue at 53rd Street, New York, N. Y.

65

German Railroads Information Office, 1938   ▶ Hamburg-American Line, 1934

Fastest Way to France, England, Germany

Bremen · Europa

Special sailing **Columbus** June 29th

Ireland · England · France · Germany

The "Famous Four" Expresses

A sailing every Wednesday Midnight

New York   Deutschland
Hamburg   Albert Ballin

Cabin Liners

to Ireland France Germany

Berlin ... St. Louis ... Stuttgart

he
ience

avigation
th
he
t
he
ving

ur
al
avel
ent, or

 Hamburg-American Line   •   **North German Lloyd**

Workers' Club, Moscow

16 Days in 4 Great Cities
of the SOVIET UNION $192*

TRAVEL IN THE
SOVIET UNION

Intourist, Inc., 1931

XIth
OLYMPIC
GAMES
AUGUST 1·16th
BERLIN

GERMANY

● Olympic Year is the World's Festive Year in Germany. The XIth Olympic Games are centered in a grand programme of exciting attractions: The Bayreuth Wagner Festival Plays, the Munich Opera Festivals, International Olympic Art Exhibitions, brilliant theatricals, interesting expositions and conventions. German genius for organization has timed these events so that you can enjoy them during a glorious vacation in Germany. In addition: Scenic grandeur and natural beauty . . . famous health resorts . . . romantic castles . . . picturesque folk festivals . . . medieval towns . . . cosmopolitan cities . . . the Rhine. Modern travel comfort and the traditional hospitality of the land of Wanderlust and Gemütlichkeit. Railroad fares reduced 60% and Registered Travel Marks at low rates. Write for booklet 83.

GERMAN RAILROADS INFORMATION OFFICE
665 Fifth Avenue at 53rd Street, New York

German Railroads Information Office, 1936

HARPER'S BAZAAR

June · 1933

SUMMER FASHIONS

SPECIAL REDUCED FARES
Low Summer Rates

....TO THE ORIENT

• Never before have such attractive rates to the Orient been offered to the American public. Round trip summer rates to Yokohama are now equivalent to approximately one-and-one-half minimum rates first, cabin, second, and tourist classes.
• De luxe first, second, and cabin classes from San Francisco and Los Angeles via Honolulu. Every comfort of the twentieth century on great new express motor liners. Magnificent dancing salons ...tiled swimming pools...gymnasiums...public rooms, the work of European stylists...and menus that would make any languid appetite laugh in eager anticipation. • Also

splendid new cabin and tourist cabin motor liners almost as luxurious ... from Seattle and Vancouver direct to Japan.

JAPAN, CHINA and the PHILIPPINES
From Pacific Coast to Japan and Return

FIRST CLASS	CABIN CLASS	TOURIST CABIN
• $465 •	$375 •	$195UP •

Now is the time to see the wonderful lands of the East. Full details as to rates and the exceptional service given on N.Y.K. ships are described in beautifully illustrated literature. Call or write to Department 19.

N·Y·K·LINE
(Japan Mail)

New York, 25 Broadway, 545 Fifth Avenue San Francisco, 551 Market Street · Seattle, 1404 Fourth Avenue · Chicago, 40 North Dearborn Street · Los Angeles, 605 South Grand Avenue · or any Cunard Line office. Consult your local tourist agent. He knows.

"TO TRAVEL IS TO DISCOVER THAT EVERYONE IS WRONG ABOUT OTHER COUNTRIES." —ALDOUS HUXLEY

„REISEN IST DAS ENTDECKEN, DASS ALLE UNRECHT HABEN MIT DEM, WAS SIE ÜBER ANDERE LÄNDER DENKEN." —ALDOUS HUXLEY

1940

SIEGERMACHT USA

Als die Waffen wieder ruhten, griff man gern auf die schon vor dem Krieg erfundene Klimaanlage zurück. Plötzlich ließ es sich in warmen Gefilden besser aushalten, und Orte wie Palm Springs boomten.

IM ANSCHLUSS AN DEN ANGRIFF DER JAPANER AM 7. DEZEMBER 1941 AUF PEARL HARBOR ERKLÄRTE PRÄSIDENT FRANKLIN D. ROOSEVELT DEUTSCHLAND UND JAPAN DEN KRIEG. Die Vereinigten Staaten begannen unverzüglich mit den Vorbereitungen. Die Rationierung von Benzin und Kautschuk ließ die Urlaubsreisen binnen weniger Wochen fast auf Null zurückgehen, während die US-Industrie auf Rüstungsgüter umgestellt wurde. Zwischen dem Beginn der Weltwirtschaftskrise und dem Ende des Zweiten Weltkriegs entstand lediglich ein modernes Stadthotel, nämlich das Washington Statler (das heutige Capital Hilton) von 1943. Der US-Geheimdienst wurde bereits in der Planungsphase hinzugezogen, damit Roosevelt und seine New-Deal-Administration dort sicher waren. Der Haupteingang lag nach hinten, es gab eine versteckte Zufahrt und einen speziellen Lastenaufzug, der die Karosse des Präsidenten direkt auf die Etage mit dem Tanzsaal beförderte.

Als der Krieg 1945 zu Ende war, beeilte sich Amerika, die verlorene Zeit aufzuholen. So konnten etwa die Greyhound Bus Lines nach Raymond Loewys Entwürfen für den Silversides-Bus mit der Produktion beginnen. Das verschlankte Hunde-Logo verdankt sich ebenfalls Loewy.

Auch griff man gern auf die schon vor dem Krieg erfundene Klimaanlage zurück. Nun ließ es sich in warmen Gegenden besser aushalten. Orte wie Palm Springs boomten. Das Image der Wüstenstadt als Spielwiese der Elite zeigt sich am Beispiel Frank Sinatras. Als der Sänger 1946 seine erste Million gemacht hatte, ließ er sich ein voll klimatisiertes Haus in der Wüste bauen. Der Entwurf von E. Stewart Williams – geduckt, mit Flachdach und viel Glas – war der Inbegriff des aufkeimenden Modernismus von Palm Springs.

UN MONDE EN GUERRE

L'après-guerre vit l'adoption d'une invention d'avant-guerre : l'air conditionné. Les climats chauds devinrent soudain plus attirants, et Palm Springs, entre autres, connut une ère de prospérité.

APRÈS LA TRISTEMENT CÉLÈBRE ATTAQUE DE PEARL HARBOR LE 7 DÉCEMBRE 1941, LE PRÉSIDENT FRANKLIN D. ROOSEVELT DÉCLARA LA GUERRE À L'ALLEMAGNE ET AU JAPON. Les États-Unis se mobilisèrent immédiatement pour entrer dans la Seconde Guerre mondiale. En quelques semaines, le rationnement d'essence et de caoutchouc paralysa quasiment tout le marché des voyages de loisir alors que l'industrie américaine se concentrait sur l'effort de guerre.

Entre le début de la Grande Dépression et la fin de la Seconde Guerre mondiale, on ne construisit qu'un seul hôtel moderne : le Washington Statler (aujourd'hui le Capital Hilton), en 1943. Sa conception nécessita les conseils des services secrets afin que l'hôtel puisse accueillir Roosevelt et son administration du New Deal. L'entrée principale se trouvait derrière l'hôtel, avec une allée couverte pour les voitures et un ascenseur spécial qui emmenait directement la voiture présidentielle à l'étage de la salle de conférence.

Après la signature de l'Armistice en 1945, l'Amérique était impatiente de rattraper le temps perdu. Par exemple, la compagnie Greyhound put lancer la production des cars Silversides conçus par Raymond Loewy. Ce dernier donna aussi un look plus moderne au logo de chien.

L'après-guerre vit l'adoption d'une invention d'avant-guerre : l'air conditionné. Les climats chauds devinrent soudain plus attirants, et Palm Springs, entre autres, connut une ère de prospérité. Son image de ville désertique transformée en terrain de jeu pour l'élite fut immortalisée par Frank Sinatra, qui s'y fit construire une maison climatisée en 1946 dans le désert après avoir gagné son premier million. Le design d'E. Stewart Williams – maison basse à toit plat avec portes en verre ouvrant l'espace sur l'extérieur – représentait la quintessence du mouvement moderniste de Palm Springs. La même année, Billy Wilkerson ouvrit le Flamingo de Las Vegas, premier hôtel climatisé du pays qui abritait sous le même toit un casino, une boîte de nuit et des suites. Pour que les joueurs perdent la notion du temps, il n'y avait aucune horloge dans le casino. Entre 1941 et 1944, les revenus issus du jeu augmentèrent de 56 %. Le gangster Bugsy Siegel, également financier du Flamingo, prit alors conscience de tout l'argent que pouvait rapporter le tourisme, en particulier le jeu (Lucky Luciano fit de même pour Cuba quand il accueillit une réunion de grands parrains à l'Hotel Nacional de La Havane en 1946). Lors de l'ouverture de l'aéroport McCarran Field de Las Vegas en 1948, la capitale mondiale du jeu était déjà une destination touristique internationale.

Pendant cette période, les hôtels bien établis bénéficièrent d'un rafraîchissement d'après-guerre. Le Beverly Hills Hotel fit appel à l'architecte Paul R. Williams pour des rénovations et des extensions en 1947. La décoratrice de la haute société Dorothy Draper supervisa au Greenbrier Hotel, établissement du XIXe siècle situé en Virginie Occidentale, un réaménagement de deux ans couronné en 1948 par un gala de réouverture de trois jours qui vit chanter Bing Crosby avec le Duc de Windsor à la batterie.

Crosby contribua très largement au succès de la saga des films *En Route*. *En Route vers Singapour* (1940) marqua le début du duo Crosby et Bob Hope. Les aventures de ces deux naufragés se poursuivirent dans *En Route pour le Maroc* (1942) et *En Route pour Rio* (1947). Si ces deux-là arrivaient à s'en sortir dans les pays exotiques, alors tout le monde le pouvait. La démocratisation du voyage s'accélérait.

◄◄ TWA, 1946   ► Matson Line, 1949

1947

1948

1948

Paul R. Williams revamps Beverly Hills Hotel; banana leaf wallpaper and pink-green-and-white color scheme soon iconic

Paul R. Williams verleiht dem Beverly Hills Hotel ein neues Gesicht; Bananenblatt-Tapeten setzen neue Maßstäbe

Paul R. Williams relooke le Beverly Hills Hotel; feuilles de bananier et tons de rose/vert/blanc deviennent ses emblèmes

Air India granted international flying privileges when India gains independence

Air India erhält internationale Flugrechte, als Indien die Unabhängigkeit erlangt

Air India se voit octroyer des droits de vol international quand l'Inde gagne son indépendance

Greenbrier Hotel's gala reopening party after two-year redecoration; Bing Crosby sings, Duke of Windsor plays drums

Wiedereröffnungsgala des Greenbrier Hotels nach zweijährigem Umbau: Bing Crosby als Sänger, der Herzog von Windsor am Schlagzeug

Gala de réouverture du Greenbrier Hotel avec Bing Crosby au micro et le Duc de Windsor à la batterie

Golden hours under the sparkling Pacific sun bring a new sense of peace on the Lurline

Discover a new life...vibrant, gay, relaxed...
CRUISE TO HAWAII ON THE NEW LURLINE

atchless days on the loveliest ship afloat. The Lurline gives you ery shipboard comfort and enjoyment. Beautiful surroundings... w friends... deck games, swimming, sun-bathing, dancing... star-ed nights. Food and service are superb.

Then the Islands ... like green jewels in the Pacific. Yours to explore, yours to know ... their gentle life, their flower-fragrant air, their warm beaches. Here's a vacation cruise you will never forget. Let your travel agent plan it now.

Matson Lines Offices: *New York • Chicago • San Francisco*
Los Angeles • Seattle • Portland • San Diego • Honolulu

Matson

San Francisco and Los Angeles TO HAWAII

For the SWORDS of today...

and the PLOWSHARES of tomorrow...

The swords of 1941 are fast and deadly fighting airplanes. Their blades are the whirling, powerful propellers that rocket them through the air at unprecedented speeds in defense of nations.

In building these airplanes Lockheed is doing a patriotic duty. But hopefully, Lockheed looks to the day when these blades will cleave new paths to commerce, peace and expanded industry.

LOOK TO *Lockheed* FOR LEADERSHIP <u>IN</u> BOTH

LOCKHEED AIRCRAFT CORPORATION   BURBANK, CALIF.

◄◄ The Milwaukee Road, 1947

Lockheed, 1941

Even as Lockheed was gearing up for the war economy, producing the squadrons of planes needed to fight the Germans and Japanese, the aircraft manufacturer was already betting that there would be pent-up travel demand when World War II ended. Americans enjoyed travel for pleasure all too much.

Bereits während sich Lockheed auf den Krieg einstellte, um die Unmengen von Flugzeugen zu produzieren, die man im Kampf gegen Deutschland und Japan brauchte, setzte der Flugzeughersteller auf den zivilen Nachholbedarf nach Kriegsende. Dafür fanden die Amerikaner einfach zu viel Gefallen an Vergnügungsreisen.

Même quand Lockheed travaillait à l'effort de guerre en produisant les escadrons d'avions requis pour combattre les Allemands et les Japonais, le constructeur se doutait déjà que la demande en voyages aériens augmenterait considérablement après la fin de la Seconde Guerre mondiale. Les Américains aimaient trop voyager pour le plaisir.

► Martin Aircraft, 1945

Hi, mommy... flying's fun!

Just look at that smile! Whether you're 6 or 60, on pleasure or business, it'll be fun to travel by Martin airliner! No crowds, no noise, no dirt . . . the big Martin transport will be air-conditioned, sound-proofed, clean as a whistle! And such a quick trip! No long, tiring hours wasted en route. With a young hostess to watch over her . . . a big, soft seat to curl up in . . . an individual reading light and full-view window . . . she'll be as snug and comfortable as in an armchair at home!

SO DEPENDABLE, TOO!

On new Martin airliners, radar "will see" through rain, snow, fog or darkness. Special heating units will melt ice before it can form on wings, tail or propeller. Two Pratt & Whitney engines deliver nearly the horsepower of all 4 engines of many former wartime bombers; on only one of these big power-

plants, high-flying Martin airliners could soar a third of a mile above the nation's highest mountain. For speed, luxury and dependability, no plane of its type can surpass a Martin airliner!

THE GLENN L. MARTIN COMPANY, BALTIMORE 3, MARYLAND

FLY VIA MARTIN TRANSPORT ON THESE GREAT AIRLINES!

Capital (PCA)	•	Eastern	•	Chicago & Southern
Braniff	•	United	•	Northwest	•	Delta
Dodero (Argentina)	•	Panagra	•	Commander
		Cruzeiro do Sul (Brazil)		

Builders of Dependable ★ *Aircraft Since 1909*

Wings for Your Wishes

"Wish I were in New York . . . wish I were in California . . . wish I were at home . . . wish I could have a longer vacation."

SIR . . . or Madam, there's a genie who grants such wishes! He's the helpful individual who reserves space for you on TWA. To summon him, simply use the magic dial of your telephone. In about the time it takes to say TWA, you'll find yourself set to travel on wings.

And it's luxury travel that you'll like every mile and every minute.

Flying TWA, you find a new note of hospitality in the air. You enjoy a personal radio . . . tempting food. And from take-off to landing you are pleasantly aware of the precision and thoughtfulness that mark *the airline run by flyers.*

Long known as the shortest, fastest coast-to-coast airline, we now offer *four* timely transcontinental flights each way every day . . . three "through Skysleepers" and the famous scenic daylight flight over majestic Grand Canyon. And city-to-city "commuter schedules" have been increased to get you there and back the

same day. For example . . . *eighteen* flights daily, New York-Pittsburgh! Use TWA to gain time in your business. Use it for pleasure. *And watch this airline for great new things to come.*

FAST FLIGHT FACTS

LOS ANGELES TO NEW YORK
Shortest time: 15 Hrs. 41 Min. Fare . . $149.95

LOS ANGELES TO CHICAGO
Shortest time: 11 Hrs. 29 Min. Fare . . $105.00

CHICAGO TO PITTSBURGH
Shortest time: 2 Hrs. 27 Min. Fare . . $23.95

NEW YORK TO PITTSBURGH
Shortest time: 2 Hrs. 23 Min. Fare . . $21.00

The **TRANSCONTINENTAL** *Line*
and Western Air, Inc.
10 RICHARDS ROAD, KANSAS CITY, MISSOURI

TWA, 1940

A New World in Travel

IT'S almost like traveling on the wings of a wish...this skimming through the air in the big, fast ships of TWA. You simply step aboard and before you can begin to believe it, *you're there.*

You travel so smoothly, surrounded by such luxury, that you thoroughly enjoy every minute aloft. That's because TWA has been doing things for you!

On Skyclub or Skysleeper, you'll find hospitality that is truly distinctive of TWA. Appetizing meals, restful appointments, a personal radio, alert attention to your every wish...nothing is omitted that could add to your pleasure. And you'll be glad to know, too, that TWA is *the airline run by flyers.* You'll sense this fact throughout the ship...and in every member of the crew.

For long distance travelers, TWA now offers *four* transcontinental flights daily. But you don't have to take a *long* trip to know the pleasure of flying TWA. For the shortest, fastest coast-to-coast airline has also stepped up "commuter" schedules from city-to-city. Make use of this service... for business, for pleasure. And watch this airline run by flyers *for great new things to come.*

FAST FLIGHT FACTS

NEW YORK TO PITTSBURGH
Shortest time: 2 Hrs. 23 Min. Fare ... $21.00
PITTSBURGH TO CHICAGO
Shortest time: 2 Hrs. 56 Min. Fare . . $23.95
CHICAGO TO LOS ANGELES
Shortest time: 12 Hrs. 24 Min. Fare . . $105.00
DAYTON TO CHICAGO
Shortest time: 2 Hrs. 3 Min. Fare . . . $14.70
NEW YORK TO MINNEAPOLIS
Shortest time: 7 Hrs. 40 Min. Fare ... $61.45

The **TRANSCONTINENTAL** *Line*
and Western Air, Inc.

TWA, 1941

Revolutionary Rockets!

Authorities predict that aircraft designs of tomorrow will be of the advanced rocket type. The new rocket models will permit much higher speeds at much higher altitudes. Thus new developments which require light alloys keep opening up avenues for improved products. The Bohn organization is one of the world's largest and leading specialists in the engineering and fabrication of aluminum, magnesium and brass products. When peace comes, Bohn metallurgists and engineers should be helpful to you in designing your products for tomorrow.

BOHN ALUMINUM AND BRASS CORPORATION
GENERAL OFFICES — LAFAYETTE BUILDING • DETROIT 26, MICHIGAN
Designers and Fabricators
ALUMINUM • MAGNESIUM • BRASS • AIRCRAFT-TYPE BEARINGS

BOHN

Bohn, 1945   ▶ TWA, 1940

Broader Wings

TO SPAN THE NATION... And the graceful sweep of their arrival

marks an epochal advance in air travel. TWA's new Boeing Stratoliners are here! And with them come spaciousness, smoothness, luxury and speeds never before known along any commercial airway in the nation. By presenting Stratoliners today, TWA again, as in the past, is first to put the proved into practice, once more demonstrating that Progress goes hand in hand with Precision on the airline run by flyers.

TRANSCONTINENTAL & WESTERN AIR, Inc.

The TRANSCONTINENTAL *Line*

TWA *Stratoliner*

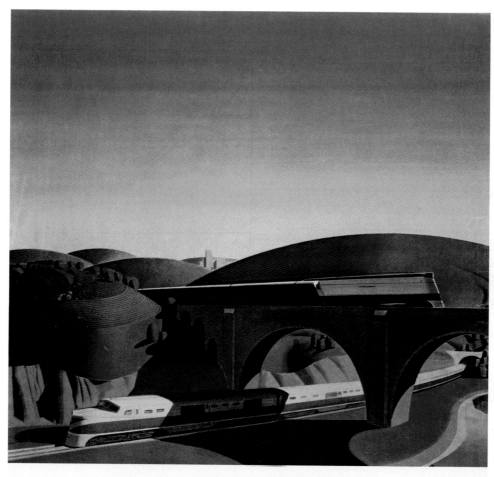

Two Trains of Thought

Sometimes we think Diesel-Liners are better for a certain purpose. Sometimes we think Steam-Liners are better. We play no favorites. We have no preferences. We make no snap judgments. We study each problem separately, and come up with our answer. Sometimes it's a Diesel-Liner. Sometimes it's a Steam-Liner. Whichever it is, we build it. It will do the job it was intended to do. And it will be one of the world's finest, most modern locomotives.

AMERICAN LOCOMOTIVE

DIESEL · STEAM · ELECTRIC

American Locomotive Company, 1941 ▸ California Zephyr, 1949

…us comfort at money-saving new VISTA-DOME chair coaches.

Feminine as a boudoir is the women's lounge. Men's lounges equally complete.

Enjoy Delicious Meals and personalized service in the California Zephyr's beautiful dining car.

…ENIC WAY TO CALIFORNIA

…AKE THE VISTA-DOME *California Zephyr*

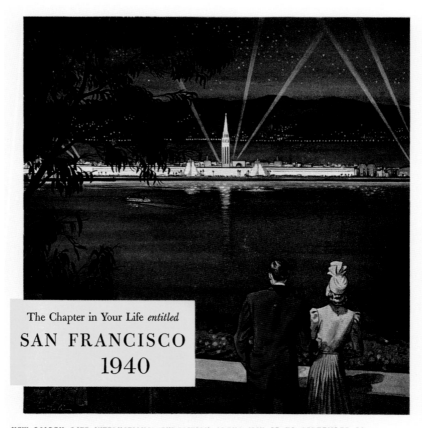

The Chapter in Your Life *entitled*

SAN FRANCISCO
1940

NEW GOLDEN GATE INTERNATIONAL EXPOSITION OPENS MAY 25 TO SEPTEMBER 29

One night this summer we'd like to take you up on Telegraph Hill to show you San Francisco's million lights, and Treasure Island framed by the world's two largest bridges.

Here, all that you ever dreamed about this City suddenly comes true. About you is the high-piled, storied metropolis that sprang from a Spanish pueblo overnight. There, the Golden Gate through which the 'Forty-Niners came from all the countries of the earth, bringing their customs and their tastes to linger on in the Latin Quarter, Chinatown and in a dozen other foreign colonies. These are the hills, so steep that cable cars were invented to climb them. And there, in the middle of the Bay...the world's most beautiful World's Fair.

This magic night you will remember always, as you will remember all your other nights and days in San Francisco...and on Treasure Island, with its lovely courts and gardens, exciting Gayway, fine new art exhibit, the Aquacade and the deeply moving pageant, *America! The Cavalcade of a Nation.*

In San Francisco you will dine around the world, dance where modern music was born, explore Golden Gate Park...Fishermen's Wharf...the long Embarcadero...

We've just prepared a new illustrated book that tells the whole exciting story of this City, its Exposition and the wonderland so close to San Francisco: the groves of giant Redwoods, Yosemite National Park, Lake Tahoe and the Land of Gold; hospitable Del Monte and sunny Santa Cruz, on Monterey Bay.

Send the coupon today for your free copy of this book. Find out how low all costs are here. See how easily and quickly you can come over smooth highways, or by train or plane or boat.

New Golden Gate International Exposition, 1940

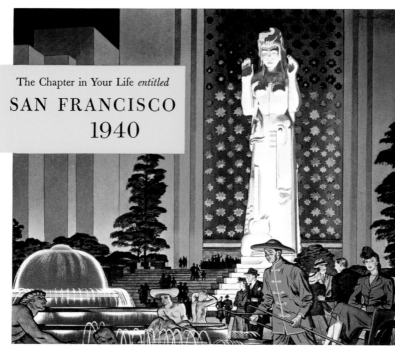

The Chapter in Your Life *entitled*

SAN FRANCISCO
1940

Court of Pacifica on Treasure Island

NEW GOLDEN GATE INTERNATIONAL EXPOSITION OPENS MAY 25

The people of San Francisco ... of all California, cordially invite you to the new Golden Gate International Exposition on Treasure Island, May 25 to Sept. 29, 1940.

We promise you that this new World's Fair will be more beautiful, even, than the one that thrilled so many million visitors last year. We promise you more entertainment, and more rare treasures from far Pacific lands. We promise you days and nights you'll cherish all your life. Days in the lovely courts of

You'll ride merry cable cars

Treasure Island, gay with flowers and fountains. Days exploring San Francisco's hilly streets; shopping in Chinatown; strolling the romantic Embarcadero. The never-to-be-forgotten day you walk, or ride, across the Golden Gate on the longest span in the world.

Nights of fun in famous restaurants and cocktail lounges high above the City's million lights. Enchanted nights in the glowing fairyland of Treasure Island. The breathless night you stand on Telegraph Hill to watch the battle fleet weave their searchlights against the stars.

Send this coupon for our new illustrated guide book, "The Chapter in Your Life entitled San Francisco." It includes chapters about the thrilling vacationlands near San Francisco: Del Monte on the Monterey Peninsula and Santa Cruz, Yosemite National Park, the Redwood Empire, Lake Tahoe and the Land of Gold, the Shasta-Cascade Wonderland and all the rest. Find out how quickly you can come by highway, train or plane; how little this grand vacation really costs.

You'll play by Monterey Bay

★ CALIFORNIANS INC.

Dept. 104, 703 Market St., San Francisco, Calif.
Please send your new, free 1940 vacation book.

Name_____

Street_____

City_____

State_____

New Golden Gate International Exposition, 1940

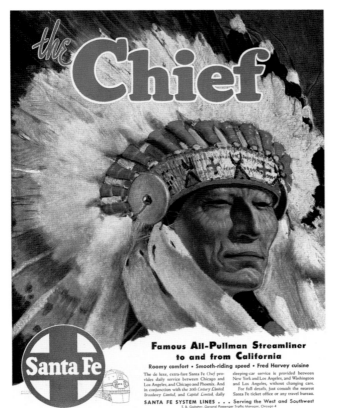

the **Chief**

**Famous All-Pullman Streamliner
to and from California**

Roomy comfort • Smooth-riding speed • Fred Harvey cuisine

The de luxe, extra-fare Santa Fe *Chief* provides daily service between Chicago and Los Angeles, and Chicago and Phoenix. And in conjunction with the *20th Century Limited Broadway Limited*, and *Capital Limited*, daily

sleeping-car service is provided between New York and Los Angeles, and Washington and Los Angeles, without changing cars.
For full details, just consult the nearest Santa Fe ticket office or any travel bureau.

SANTA FE SYSTEM LINES . . . Serving the West and Southwest

T. B. Gallaher, General Passenger Traffic Manager, Chicago 4

Santa Fe

Santa Fe Railway, 1947

U.S. railroads raked in big profits during the war, and expected this passenger surge to continue when fighting stopped. The Sante Fe Chief express service to California roared again. But with competition from cars and planes, Americans had many forms of travel to choose from. Train ridership never fully recovered.

Die Bahngesellschaften strichen während des Kriegs satte Profite ein und erwarteten auch nach Ende der Kampfhandlungen einen Fortbestand der Passagierflut. So verkehrte die Expresslinie Santa Fe Chief wieder nach Kalifornien. Angesichts der Konkurrenz durch Auto und Flugzeug hatten die Amerikaner die Qual der Wahl, sodass sich die Zahl der zivilen Bahnpassagiere nie wieder ganz erholte.

Les compagnies ferroviaires américaines amassèrent de gros bénéfices pendant la guerre, et s'attendaient à ce que cette hausse du trafic se poursuive après la fin du conflit. La ligne express Chief de la compagnie Sante Fe reprit du service vers la Californie. Avec la concurrence de la voiture et de l'avion, le train ne retrouva jamais vraiment ses anciens niveaux de fréquentation.

► Santa Fe Railway, 1949

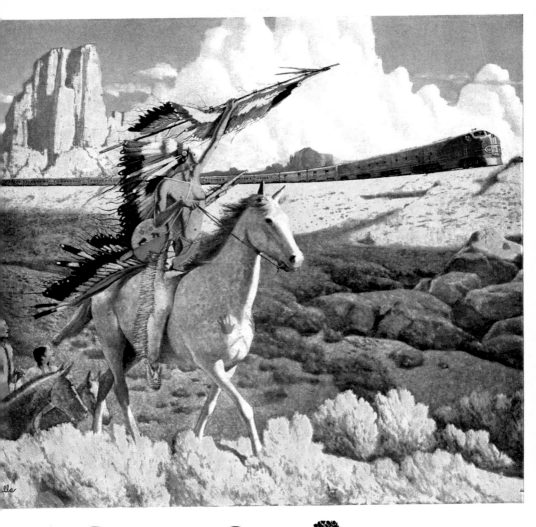

The Chiefs

BETWEEN CHICAGO AND THE WEST AND SOUTHWEST

Santa Fe

Headed by the *Super Chief* and *The Chief,* the Santa Fe great fleet of trains between Chicago and California offers a choice of fine accommodations to satisfy every taste and fit every pocketbook. And between Chicago and Texas, it's the *Texas Chief.*

For smooth-riding comfort...friendly hospitality... delicious Fred Harvey meals...fascinating scenery...travel Santa Fe—*the Chief Way!*

R. T. Anderson, General Passenger Traffic Manager, Santa Fe System Lines, Chicago 4, Illinois

Step into the New World

Air travelers have said that in stepping into the modern airliner—for almost any kind of trip—they step into a new world.

It is a compact world, easy to get about in. You are picked up in one city—or on one continent—and set down in another with the smooth, effortless magic we used to associate only with fairy tales.

It is a world of quiet efficiency, where a man can get his work done in a hurry . . . without breathless haste . . . a kind of executive efficiency that will be much needed in days to come. And the Airlines will be superbly equipped to provide it, with still larger and faster planes, newer standards of service and at *radically reduced fares.*

For many months, war has been the Airlines' business because most of their passengers and cargoes have been *in that business.* But air transportation will speed them back to the cherished ways of peace just as readily as it has helped speed the nation to victory.

When you travel by Air *make reservations early; please cancel early if plans change.* When you use Air Express *speed delivery by dispatching shipments as soon as they're ready* by calling Air Express Division of Railway Express Agency. AIR TRANSPORT ASSOCIATION, 1515 Massachusetts Avenue, N. W., Washington 5, D. C.

➤ ➤ ➤

This advertisement is sponsored by the nation's airlines and leading manufacturers in the aviation industry

THE AIRLINES OF THE UNITED STATES
LEADING THE WORLD IN AIR TRANSPORT

◄ The Airlines of the United States, 1945

American Airlines, 1946

With the end of World War II, civilian air travel
was on the rise. Flights were now far more
comfortable. American Airlines was an early
adopter when it came to stewardesses—they
had been on American flights since 1933.

Mit Ende des Zweiten Weltkriegs bekamen
zivile Flugreisen Aufwind. Und die Flüge waren
nun auch viel komfortabler. American Airlines
entschied sich schon früh für Stewardessen,
die es auf amerikanischen Flügen bereits seit
1933 gab.

Après la fin de la Seconde Guerre mondiale,
le transport de passagers civils augmenta.
Les vols en avion étaient désormais beaucoup
plus confortables. American Airlines fut l'une
des premières compagnies à embaucher des
hôtesses de l'air – elles égayaient les vols américains depuis 1933.

Fifty Millions for New Wings!

United's famous Main Line Airway is handling the greatest volume of traffic in history. To meet this demand and to bring air travel to still more people, United operates a growing and versatile fleet of modern transports—twin-engined Mainliner 180's for intercity frequency and convenience—four-engined Mainliner 230's for medium and long range flights. To these will be added the great new 300-mile-an-hour, four-engined Mainliner 300's and 340's, and the fast twin-engined Mainliner 303's. United Air Lines is spending $50,000,000 for the latest and finest flying equipment—planes that will set new standards of speed, comfort and luxury in coast-to-coast air travel.

 United Air Lines holds the Award of Honor, presented by the National Safety Council, for having flown more than a billion and a half passenger miles without a fatal accident.

THE MAIN LINE AIRWAY
Passengers · Mail · Express · Freight

UNITED AIR LINES

AIR MAIL NOW 5c

◄ United Air Lines, 1946

The Airlines of the United States, 1945

The war was not quite over when this ad ran. But U.S. airlines were already positioning themselves as key to winning the peace—just they were vital to winning the war.

Der Krieg war noch nicht ganz vorüber, als diese Anzeige erschien. Und schon positionierten sich die US-Fluglinien als Schlüssel zum Gewinn des Friedens – so wie sie entscheidend zum Gewinn des Kriegs beigetragen hatten.

La guerre n'était pas encore tout à fait terminée quand cette publicité fut diffusée, mais les compagnies aériennes américaines se positionnaient déjà comme indispensables pour gagner la paix, tout comme elles l'étaient pour gagner la guerre.

"SEND THESE, THE HOMELESS, TEMPEST-TOST TO ME.
I LIFT MY LAMP BESIDE THE GOLDEN DOOR!"
—*Inscription on the Statue of Liberty*

Welcome Home !

And now her lifted beacon hand bids welcome to her own. She gazes out to sea upon a mighty fleet of transports of the air, filled with her valiant sons returning from a work well done.

She bestows her benediction alike upon those who are home to stay and those who still must fight—but whose task will be done more quickly because their paths to Tokyo are the highways of the sky.

With compassionate eyes she looks upon the dawn of brighter days when all men everywhere will once more turn to paths of peace and these same transports of the air will span the far-flung continents in friendly trade between the nations of the world.

On foreign battlefields our boys have found their wings and henceforth they will fly. They will want this means of travel in their daily lives—in fields of commerce—in leisure hours with days to spend in distant places hitherto beyond the reach of modest means.

Yes, air transportation which has so ably met the needs of war will play no little part in building a finer and a better land in which these men will find that peace and freedom for which they fought. Welcome home!

When you travel by Air make reservations early; please cancel early if plans change. When you use Air Express speed delivery by dispatching shipments as soon as they're ready. Air Transport Association, 1515 Massachusetts Avenue, N. W., Washington 5, D. C.

This advertisement is sponsored by the nation's airlines and leading manufacturers in the aviation industry

THE AIRLINES OF THE UNITED STATES
LEADING THE WORLD IN AIR TRANSPORT

HIGH ROAD TO ROME

*As in a winged chariot, you sweep across the Coliseum, where
gladiators fought it out more than 1800 years ago. In a single glance,
your view encompasses St. Peter's glistening dome and the majestic Vatican.
All this awaits you at the end of today's high road to Rome,
a swift new road that TWA has shortened to less than a day and a half.
And though you marvel at such speedy travel, you find it far
from breathless. You find, instead, that 40,000,000 miles of
international flying, with 9,000 overocean flights included, have taught
TWA crews how to make it mighty easy going. See your
local travel agent or TWA ticket office for information.*

TRANS WORLD AIRLINE

Direct one-carrier service to Newfoundland · Ireland · France · Switzerland · Italy · Greece · Egypt · Palestine
Trans-Jordan · Iraq · Saudi Arabia · Yemen · Oman · India · Ceylon · Portugal · Spain · Algeria · Tunisia · Libya

◄ TWA, 1946   TWA, 1946

OLD FAMILIAR FRIENDS

Rommel was knocking at the gates of Alexandria when TWA crews
first landed their war-cargoed planes on Egyptian airfields. Now,
in the air wake of such historic armadas, great Sky Chiefs wing there
from America's shores in the stretch of a day and a half.
The peace of mind you feel as you travel springs from a huge backlog
of such world-spanning experience. Twenty years of flying—more than
9,000 overocean flights—40,000,000 miles of international travel—
all recommend TWA as today's most satisfying way to see the world.
From California to Cairo, for first-class travel call on the nearest
TWA ticket office—or your travel agent.

TWA
TRANS WORLD AIRLINE

Direct one-carrier service to Newfoundland • Ireland • France • Switzerland • Italy • Greece • Egypt • Palestine
Trans-Jordan • Iraq • Saudi Arabia • Yemen • Oman • India • Ceylon • Portugal • Spain • Algeria • Tunisia • Libya

TWA, 1946   ▶ Pan Am, 1941

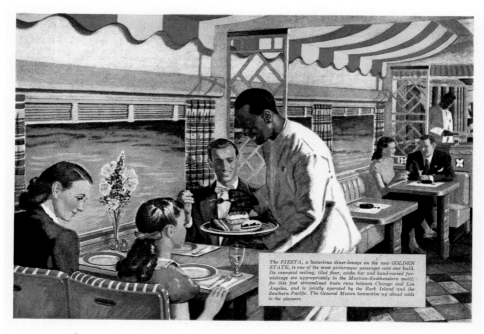

The FIESTA, a luxurious diner-lounge on the new GOLDEN STATE, is one of the most picturesque passenger cars ever built. Its canopied ceiling, tiled floor, adobe bar and hand-carved furnishings are appropriately in the Mexican-Southwestern motif for this fast streamlined train runs between Chicago and Los Angeles, and is jointly operated by the Rock Island and the Southern Pacific. The General Motors locomotive up ahead adds to the pleasure.

Quiet Sunday dinner—100 miles an hour

WHEN a train powered by a General Motors Diesel locomotive glides into — or out of — a station, there's not even a ripple in the glass of water at your elbow.

You travel with a new smoothness — and a new speed, too. Often, on the straightaways, your train may make 100 miles an hour.

General Motors locomotives have also brought a new cleanliness to travel — no soot and cinders to mar your appearance; no clouds of smoke and steam to mar your view.

They have held, for several years, the records for on-time arrivals.

That's why it is easy to see why 200 of America's finest, fastest name

trains are headed by General Motors power.

Easy to understand why better trains follow General Motors locomotives.

See the Electro-Motive Exhibit at the Chicago Railroad Fair.

ELECTRO-MOTIVE DIVISION

GENERAL MOTORS · LA GRANGE, ILL.

Home of the Diesel Locomotive

GM
GENERAL MOTORS
LOCOMOTIVES

HOLIDAY/SEPTEMBER

General Motors Locomotives, 1948

The Texas Special, crack train operated jointly by the Frisco and the Katy lines, runs between St. Louis, Dallas and San Antonio. The mecca of liberty-loving Americans who visit San Antonio is the Alamo, cradle of Texan independence where, in 1836, originated the inspiring battle-cry, "Remember the Alamo!"

See America First Class

THERE'S one sure way to see America first class — pick out trains with a General Motors Diesel locomotive up ahead.

For these General Motors locomotives give a smoother ride. Trains start and stop without annoying jerks or jolts.

You'll make your time count for more, too, because of faster, "on-time" schedules. And you'll see more because no smoke or steam will mar your view.

That's why General Motors locomotives are heading 197 of the nation's fastest, finest trains — and that's a majority of the Diesel-powered crack trains in the United States.

You'll find, as so many other smart travelers find, that *"Better trains follow General Motors locomotives."*

ELECTRO-MOTIVE DIVISION

GENERAL MOTORS • LA GRANGE, ILL.

Home of the Diesel Locomotive

GM
GENERAL MOTORS
LOCOMOTIVES

HOLIDAY/FEBRUARY

A luxurious compartment on the
TWENTIETH CENTURY LIMITED

For more than two years, five famous trains on the New York
Central has been powered by a General Motor locomotive on
its daily run, 910 miles each way, between Harmon, N.Y. and
Chicago. Also powered by GM Diesels are the Central's Knickerbocker and Southwestern, between Harmon and St. Louis.

"There's something really good about this morning!"

She feels as rested and relaxed this morning as she would had she slept in her own bed at home.

There are two reasons:

Modern trains follow modern locomotives. Since General Motors Diesel locomotives were introduced thirteen years ago, modernization of passenger equipment has made dramatic strides. But the locomotive itself deserves part of the credit. The flow of power in a GM Diesel locomotive is so smooth that you ride through the night without jerks at starting and stopping. You glide to a stop—start so smoothly that you would need to watch the landscape to know when your train starts to roll.

That is one of the many reasons why experienced travelers choose the trains with GM power up ahead.

And you can ride through the night—on a transcontinental journey—without a single change of locomotives.

And the savings in operating costs have enabled the railroads to provide extra comforts for passengers.

Fact is, the entire economy of the nation benefits as the railroads approach closer and closer to complete dieselization—the traveling public, shippers, investors and the railroads themselves.

"Better trains follow better locomotives"

ELECTRO-MOTIVE DIVISION
LA GRANGE, ILL.
GENERAL MOTORS

GM GENERAL MOTORS
DIESEL POWER

◄ General Motors Locomotives, 1947

Pennsylvania Railroad, 1944

Advertising for vacation train travel virtually stopped during World War II, as in World War I. But here the Pennsylvania Railroad uses the immense U.S. mobilization effort to talk about the quality of its service. During World War II, U.S. railways moved 43 million armed service members in 114,000 special troop trains.

Die Werbung für Ferienreisen mit dem Zug kam nach dem Ersten nun auch im Zweiten Weltkrieg praktisch zum Erliegen. Hier indes bedient sich Pennsylvania Railroad der intensiven landesweiten Kriegsvorbereitungen, um die Qualität ihres Service herauszustellen. Im Zweiten Weltkrieg wurden insgesamt 43 Millionen Soldaten in 114 000 speziellen Truppenzügen befördert.

Pendant la Seconde Guerre mondiale comme au cours du précédent conflit international, les publicités pour les voyages en train disparurent pratiquement de la circulation. Ici, la compagnie Pennsylvania Railroad tire néanmoins parti de l'immense effort de mobilisation américain pour communiquer sur la qualité de ses services. Durant la Seconde Guerre mondiale, les trains américains accueillirent 43 millions de soldats dans 114 000 convois affectés au transport de troupes.

◄ Alcoa Steamship Company, 1949

Matson Line, 1941

Before the war, American popular culture had presented the pleasures awaiting tourists in Hawaii. Bing Crosby introduced the hit "Blue Hawaii" in his movie *Waikiki Wedding* (1937) and MGM's tap sensation Eleanor Powell danced across the Lido deck of an ocean liner in *Honolulu* (1939). So the Japanese attack on Pearl Harbor on December 7, 1941, had been viewed as an even more devastating blow. Here, Matson wants travelers to focus on comfortable future trips to the tropical paradise.

Vor dem Krieg hatte die amerikanische Populärkultur den Touristen die Annehmlichkeiten Hawaiis schmackhaft gemacht. Bing Crosby landete einen Hit mit „Blue Hawaii" in seinem Film *Waikiki Wedding* (1937), und MGMs Steppsensation Eleanor Powell tanzte über das Lido-Deck eines Ozeandampfers in *Honolulu* (1939). So wurde der japanische Angriff auf Pearl Harbor am 7. Dezember 1941 zu einem umso vernichtenderen Schlag. Hier möchte Matson die Aufmerksamkeit der Urlauber auf das tropische Paradies lenken.

Avant la guerre, la culture populaire américaine reflétait les plaisirs attendant les touristes à Hawaï. Bing Crosby chanta le tube « Blue Hawaii » dans le film *L'Amour à Waikiki* (1937) et Eleanor Powell, la reine des claquettes de la MGM, dansa sur le pont d'un paquebot transatlantique dans *Honolulu* (1939). L'attaque de Pearl Harbor par les Japonais le 7 décembre 1941 n'en fut donc que d'autant plus dévastatrice. Ici, la Matson cherche à focaliser l'attention des voyageurs sur le confort de leurs futurs voyages vers ce paradis tropical.

TOWARD A RICHER TOMORROW

Matson's business is transportation — its specialty, joining Mainland America
and the lovely Islands of Hawaii through ever-improving standards of
travel. And looking toward a future, bright with the promise of fresh
peacetime progress, its plans encompass still finer things — the finest
travel facilities that can be provided by air or by sea.

Matson KNOWS THE PACIFIC

MATSON LINES TO HAWAII AND THE SOUTH PACIFIC
SAMOA · FIJI · NEW ZEALAND · AUSTRALIA

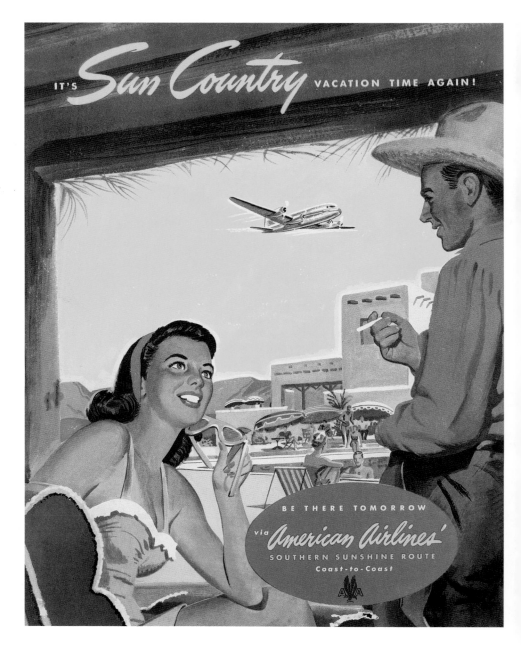

American Airlines, 1946 ▸ American Airlines, 1947 ▸▸ American Locomotive Company, 1946

LOOK WHAT'S COMING IN AMERICA

THE THEATRE THAT TRAVELS 90 MILES AN HOUR

Among the new wonders promised the rail traveler in the very near future is a club car that converts into a rolling movie theatre.

By day, you'll relax in a luxurious lounge. In the evening, you'll sit back and watch a latest Hollywood release as you speed on your journey.

This is no dream, but one of the many new features of trains which are in production right now. Conveniences and comforts like special playrooms for children. Telephone service for passengers en route. Roomier, more comfortable sleeping quarters than you ever dreamed of.

Such developments are part of a mode tion program estimated at $1,600,000,000 greatest ever undertaken by America's rail And you'll enjoy them not on some dist morrow, but as soon as the modern p trains hit the rails.

American Locomotiv

EW TRAINS!

MOTIVES AS REVOLUTIONARY AS THE TRAINS THEY PULL

To power your great new postwar trains, American Locomotive is building a line of Diesel-Electrics as revolutionary in design as the trains themselves.

These locomotives are the result of important wartime research. They will be *years* ahead in speed, power, smoothness, and economy of operation—super locomotives to handle every hauling job a railroad has.

For over the years, American Locomotive has been responsible for a large share of the basic new improvements in locomotives. Alco built America's *first* Diesel-Electric back in 1925. Alco built the record-breaking locomotives that are pulling so many crack trains today.

And soon, when you board the new postwar trains powered by American Locomotive, you'll be behind the finest locomotives ever built!

ompany *Sets the Pace for America's New Trains*

.. and for the people

FINER BUS TRAVEL OVER AMERICA'S BROAD HIGHWA

In this nation, more than anywhere else in the world, highways are the heritage of all the people—a most vital part of their livelihood and their happiness.

And intercity buses—which have carried nearly three billion wartime passengers since Pearl Harbor—seek constantly to bring to the people of America the full benefits of their priceless highway heritage. Through the years, intercity buses have extended the convenience and economy of highway travel to the people of every State. They take millions to and from their daily employment. They bring trade and prosperity to small towns and giant cities alike. They lead the way to all the scenic grandeur of America.

All who depend upon bus transportation may count on the bus lines to keep pace with the continuing development of America's highways, which are growing steadily longer, and smoother and broader. Bus operators already have completed plans for spacious new terminals, and inviting new wayside inns.

And in the buses themselves, the greatest advances in travel comfort yet known can be achieved through important changes in bus size and design. Plans call for wider, roomier seats for greater riding ease . . . increased leg room . . . wider aisles . . . thicker wall insulation for better control of inside temperatures. Engineering progress would, at the same time, enhance the traditional safety of bus travel with larger brakes, wider tires and increased road stability.

These and a host of other improvements are just around the "bend in the road" for the millions of people whose social and economic welfare is daily enriched by bus transportation.

To assure that better day of travel, highway authorities all over America are now considering progressive steps to modernize regulations enacted in the days of narrow highways. Their revision of outmoded limitations on bus size and design will permit the finest and safest public travel ever known on the highways.

Write for the new and interesting booklet, "Modern Highways and How They Can Serve You Better."

MOTOR BUS LINES

THIS TIME.... HOME !

Another Great Job for the Bus Lines . . . the One We Like the Best!

With an honorable discharge tucked in his pocket, he's making the most thrilling trip of his life. Even his wounds are almost forgotten, for this is that long-dreamed-of bus trip home! He is one of a growing number of veterans now returning to civilian life ... a vanguard of the millions who will be back later on.

Intercity buses carried the majority of these men to their induction centers ... served them on leave and furlough trips. Now it is our privilege to carry them home again. Among all the wartime jobs we have, this is the one we like the best.

Because it gives flexible, convenient service to every city and town along 390,000 miles of highways, bus transportation is the returning veteran's natural choice. Usually, he can step right aboard a bus at

his Army Separation Center and, shortly after, step out near his home.

And just as intercity buses serve our men in uniform from induction to homecoming so, too, do they serve millions of war workers and essential travelers of every type. This movement of manpower by intercity bus is all-important in relieving other public transportation of an overwhelming wartime load ... in helping to keep the home front strong. More than two billion passengers have been carried since the war began!

In order to accomplish this, some travel conveniences have had to be sacrificed for a while. But when war jobs are finished, the public can look forward to the finest bus transportation that has ever been known along the highways. A better day is coming tomorrow!

MOTOR BUS LINES OF AMERICA

NATIONAL ASSOCIATION OF MOTOR BUS OPERATORS, WASHINGTON, D. C.

◄ Motor Bus Lines of America, 1946   Motor Bus Lines of America, 1945

Roy Hewitt

Winter under the warm Cuban sun

Hotel Nacional de Cuba HAVANA

The Nacional, supreme luxury hotel of the tropics,
is the winter center of cosmopolitans from all over
the world. By day, the gay Cabana Sun Club, two
swimming pools, tennis, shuffleboard and other
recreation in the Nacional's 13 flowering acres. By night,
dance and be entertained in the Nacional's
new L'Arboleda night club and restaurant. There's no end to
the things to do in the glamorous life of Havana,
fun-capital of Latin America.

All the colour and romance of a

foreign land, yet only mi...

by air from the mainland!

A Kirkeby Hotel

Hotel Nacional de Cuba, 1948

This stunning Spanish-Moorish hotel with a nightclub and casino was considered one of the best in the Caribbean—and cited as a center of mob control in Cuba. In 1946, the gangster Lucky Luciano called a meeting of powerful mobsters there to decide how to divvy up gambling money on this voluptuous island.

Dieses famose spanisch-maurische Hotel mit Nachtclub und Kasino galt als eines der besten in der gesamten Karibik – und als kubanischer Treffpunkt der Gangsterbosse. Lucky Luciano traf sich hier 1946 mit einigen Größen, um das auf der verlockenden Insel mit illegalem Glücksspiel eingesackte Geld aufzuteilen.

Ce surprenant hôtel hispano-mauresque avec night-club et casino était considéré comme l'un des meilleurs des Caraïbes, ainsi que comme une plaque tournante de la mafia à Cuba. En 1946, le gangster Lucky Luciano y organisa une réunion de grands parrains pour débattre des moyens de détourner l'argent du jeu sur cette île de volupté.

▶ Statler Hotel, 1943

SALUTE

TO A NEW MEMBER
OF AN OLD FAMILY

HOTEL Statler
WASHINGTON, D. C.

ONLY BY HIGHWAY
you'll meet these 'Amazing Americans' at home!

ALONG U. S. HIGHWAY 66, one of several Greyhound routes through the heart of the Southwest, Indians still weave their beautiful rugs and blankets, hammer out unique silver jewelry, and offer bright-colored pottery made with their own hands.

Put yourself in this picture, *this Fall!*
The setting is in the vast and colorful Southwest ... an Indian rug weaver plies her skilled fingers as her ancestors have done for uncounted centuries ... the girl from the waiting bus tries on one of the rainbow-tinted blankets, and gives her own big-city version of an Apache war whoop!

Such friendly scenes are typical of travel by highway, in the sun-drenched land of the first Americans. It's an interesting fact that many Indian tribes, with their fascinating customs and costumes, can still be seen along the highways, not only in the Southwest, but in the evergreen

Northwest, among the Great Lakes, in the Midwest, in Florida, and even in New England! Greyhound trips and "Amazing America" Tours introduce you pleasantly to just such interesting people and places in all the 48 states, and in Canada. Whatever your reason for traveling — pleasure, business, or personal — we invite you to go the way that will help you to meet the real America ... *and real Americans!*

TIMELY TIP: Early Fall, after the mid-summer rush, is the best time for travel of any kind. Transportation is less crowded, weather is milder, there is more room in hotels and resorts.

and remember... By Highway means By Greyhound!

GREYHOUND

◄ Greyhound, 1945

Greyhound, 1946

After the war, Greyhound was able to institute the design changes that Raymond Loewy had devised before World War II. Production finally started on the sleek new Silversides motorcoach design. The company also began using Loewy's streamlined image of its running dog logo.

Nach dem Krieg konnte Greyhound das von Raymond Loewy noch in Friedenszeiten erdachte neue Design umsetzen. Endlich konnte man mit der Fertigung des neuen, schnittigen Silversides-Busses beginnen. Und man begann, Loewys verschlanktes Windhund-Logo zu verwenden.

Après la guerre, Greyhound réussit à intégrer les modifications conçues par le designer Raymond Loewy avant 1939. La compagnie lança enfin la production de son nouveau modèle de car Silversides aux lignes épurées. Elle commença aussi à utiliser le logo de chien qui court remanié par Loewy.

WHEN THEY
Re-discover
AMERICA...

They'll find fun, friendship, beauty — by Highway

Just as American men and women have worked side-by-side in the shock of battle — as they have toiled together in the din of war plants — so they will one day re-discover the magnificent land for which they have fought ... *still side-by-side!*

They will make their re-discovery trips by highway — because *only the highways* intimately reveal the lovely hidden places, the jewelled lakes and singing trout streams, the National Parks that are the heritage of every American.

Millions will go by Greyhound — because Greyhound will, in coming days, offer a finer type of highway travel than this old world has ever known. That will include luxurious new-type coaches, better terminal and post-house facilities, new expense-paid tours that will make travel more carefree than ever before.

NEW SUPER-COACHES LIKE THIS *are more than a dream ... they are shaping up right now in practical models that will be even further refined and improved for post-war travel.*

GREYHOUND

This is NEW MEXICO
THE LAND OF ENCHANTMENT

Yesteryear it was the land of primitive man, of conquering *Conquistadore*, of lonely prospector and hardy pioneer. Today it's a land redolent with romance and color...a land of cattle and mines and thriving towns, of timbered mountain areas and great solitudes and vast distances. Here, you'll find picturesque Indian *pueblos* where you'll thrill to the throbbing rhythm of age-old ceremonial dances...you'll long remember the lingering traces of Spanish culture and a robust Old West...you'll want to visit its many scenic and historic sites including eight National Monuments and Carlsbad Caverns National Park. Here, too, by your own choosing, your vacation can be different—restful or gay, exciting or quiet...but most important of all, you'll discover peace and beauty in this Land of Enchantment, and once you have shared it you'll never forget it!

WILLARD ANDREWS

NEW MEXICO STATE TOURIST BUREAU
Room 1201, State Capitol • Santa Fe, New Mexico
Please send free: ☐ New booklet "Land of Enchantment,"
☐ Official Highway Map, ☐ New Mexico "Recreation Map."

NAME . . . .
STREET . . . .
CITY . . . . ZONE . . . . STATE . . . . .

Mail This Coupon Today AND WE'LL
SEND YOU OUR FREE BOOKLET AND MAPS, PRONTO

YOUR VACATION WILL BE

Easy to Take

—when you take it by GREYHOUND

EASY TO TAKE! These three little words seem to sum up vacation trips by Greyhound—and here are the reasons why . . .

It's *Easy to Find* the right schedules—Greyhound buses leave so frequently, at such convenient hours. • It's *Easy to Reach* the choicest vacation places, since Greyhound serves all 48 States, Canada, Mexican border cities. • It's *Easy to Relax* in deeply-cushioned, recliner-type chairs.

Easy on the Eyes are the highway beauty spots, seen best by Greyhound . . . and *Easy to Like* are the congenial, cosmopolitan people who travel by bus. • *Easy to Buy* are Greyhound tickets, offering great big savings on almost any trip . . . *Easy to Plan* is your outing, with the help of a friendly Greyhound agent. Phone or call on him—and soon!

GAY SHORE RESORTS

GREAT SOUTHWEST

ATLANTIC COAST

NATIONAL PARKS

NORTHERN LAKES

Only by

GREYHOUND

YOU MEET THE *REAL* AMERICA

"[A]N INTEGRAL PART OF MY DREAM
WAS TO SHOW THE COUNTRIES
MOST EXPOSED TO COMMUNISM
THE OTHER SIDE OF THE COIN—
THE FRUITS OF THE FREE WORLD."
— CONRAD HILTON

1950

«JE RÊVAIS DE MONTRER
AUX PAYS LES PLUS
EXPOSÉS AU COMMUNISME
L'AUTRE FACE DE
LA MÉDAILLE, LES FRUITS
DU MONDE LIBRE. »
– CONRAD HILTON

„EIN INTEGRALER TEIL
MEINES TRAUMES WAR
ES, DEN AM MEISTEN
DEM KOMMUNISMUS
EXPONIERTEN LÄNDERN
DIE ANDERE SEITE DER
MEDAILLE ZU ZEIGEN:
DIE FRÜCHTE DER
FREIEN WELT."
– CONRAD HILTON

-1959

PAX AMERICANA AND THE COLD WAR

In Istanbul, Cairo, Berlin, and Athens, Hiltons were open, airy, and accessible—the essence of American modernism thrust into the center of an alien city.

AT THE HEIGHT OF THE COLD WAR, IN THE 1950S, CONRAD HILTON SAW HIS HOTELS AS THE VANGUARD OF AMERICAN VALUES — and the U.S. government did, too. A federal agency, the Economic Cooperation Administration, used Hilton hotels as a major selling point for U.S. soft power and influence. With this help from Washington, and foreign governments, Hilton hotels were built in major Cold War capitals — where the West faced off against the Soviet Bloc.

Hilton wanted his hotels to epitomize America, to "show the countries most exposed to Communism the other side of the coin — the fruits of the free world." In Istanbul, Cairo, Berlin, and Athens, his hotels were open, airy, and accessible — the essence of American modernism thrust into the center of an alien city, as Annabel Jane Wharton writes in her smart book, *Building the Cold War*. But Hilton was not only building hotels, he was buying them. In 1954, he acquired the entire Statler hotel chain for $111 million, the largest price paid for a real-estate venture since the Louisiana Purchase.

While standardized American values rubbed up against the "other" in Hiltons around the globe, the architect Morris Lapidus was shaking up Miami Beach. His modern baroque design for the 1954 Fontainebleau Hotel was loved by celebrities and the public but loathed by critics, who deemed the $13 million hotel and its "Staircase to Nowhere" far too gaudy.

Flashiness was the exception, not the rule, as a desire for standardization took hold across the nation. In 1952, the first Holiday Inn, offering inexpensive, reliable, family accommodations, opened in Memphis, Tennessee. In five years, Kemmons Wilson's franchises formed a chain of clean, family-friendly motels. By 1959, there were 100, all essentially replicas of the original. Meanwhile, the first

Howard Johnson's Motor Lodge opened in Savannah, Georgia, in 1954. This chain was built around the popular restaurants, featuring an appealing — and standardized — menu. These and other motels thrived as America's roadways developed in the postwar era. In 1956, President Dwight Eisenhower signed the Interstate Highway Act, the largest public works project yet known to mankind.

Air travel also hit new heights when the first commercial jet liner took off on May 2, 1952. The Jet Set era began with BOAC's service from London to Johannesburg, flying 480 miles per hour, compared to 180 mph on the DC-3.

But travel did not have to be peripatetic. Golfing vacations were in vogue. In 1951, former pro golfer Johnny Dawson and other investors bought the Thunderbird Dude Ranch in Rancho Mirage, California. They turned it into Palm Springs's first 18-hole golf course and development. Bing Crosby, Jimmy Van Heusen, and Phil Harris were charter members.

On screen, the incomparable Marilyn Monroe assured travel's allure in films that virtually bookended the decade. First, as Lorelei Lee, a gold-digging showgirl bound for Europe on a liner in *Gentlemen Prefer Blondes* (1953), Monroe stole the picture singing "Diamonds Are a Girl's Best Friend." Then, in Billy Wilder's classic *Some Like It Hot* (1959) — set in "Florida" at San Diego's Hotel del Coronado — Monroe's version of "I'm through with Love" stole America's heart.

◄◄ United Air Lines, 1952   ► Insurance by North America, 1957

1952   **1952**   **1953**

First Holiday Inn, offering inexpensive, standardized family accommodations, opens in Memphis, Tennessee

Eröffnung des ersten Holiday Inn als preiswerte, solide Familienherberge in Memphis, Tennessee

Ouverture du premier Holiday Inn offrant un hébergement familial bon marché à Memphis, Tennessee

From Here to Eternity, set on military base in Hawaii, features starry cast — Montgomery Clift, Deborah Kerr, and Burt Lancaster

Der in Hawaii spielende Film *Verdammt in alle Ewigkeit* zeigt Montgomery Clift, Deborah Kerr und Burt Lancaster

Tant Qu'il Y Aura des Hommes est tourné sur une base militaire de Hawaï avec des stars (Montgomery Clift, Deborah Kerr, Burt Lancaster)

Air Canada first airline to use computer reservation system with remote terminals

Air Canada als erste Fluglinie mit computerisiertem Reservierungssystem und Fernterminals

Air Canada devient la première compagnie aérienne à utiliser un système de réservation informatique avec terminaux distants

Tomorrowland at Disneyland. Over on Main Street U. S. A., CAREFREE CORNER is the official Information Center maintained by INA and their independent agents

A new world of happiness

see a family so thrilled! They're finding
ll about space from the Space Man himself.
this is only one of Disneyland's exciting
res. There are plenty more. Everywhere
alt Disney's Magic Kingdom there is the
carefree sense of being lifted above worries.

his Disneyland 'magic of happiness' can
joyed all year 'round. The forward-looking
le of the North America Companies (INA)

have developed a new Family Accident & Sickness policy that helps families keep carefree.
It's a *package policy* like the famous INA Home-
owners and Tenants policies that add so much
to the protection of homes. It is full-scale protection for a family and its members.

INA's new Family Security Program against
accident and sickness is unique. It is really FOUR
policies in ONE. And so flexible that you can

make it your entire program or select just the
portions needed to fill out the insurance you
now have. Here is protection for the new world
of happiness that healthy young families are
building for themselves! Ask your INA agent
about it.   *   *   *

Insurance Company of North America • Indemnity Insur-
ance Company of North America • Philadelphia Fire and
Marine Insurance Company • Life Insurance Company of
North America • Philadelphia

INSURANCE BY NORTH AMERICA

PAX AMERICANA
UND DER KALTE KRIEG

Die Hiltons waren offen, luftig und leicht erreichbar,
sei es in Istanbul, Kairo, Berlin oder Athen –
die Essenz des amerikanischen Modernismus,
mitten in eine fremde Stadt hineingeworfen.

AUF DEM HÖHEPUNKT DES KALTEN KRIEGS SAH CONRAD HILTON IN SEINEN HOTELS DIE SPEERSPITZE DER AMERIKANISCHEN WERTE – und die US-Regierung ebenfalls. Eine Bundesagentur, die Economic Cooperation Administration, bediente sich der Hilton-Hotels, um anderen den sanften Einfluss der USA schmackhaft zu machen. Mit Unterstützung durch Washington und ausländische Regierungen entstanden Hilton-Hotels in den wichtigen Kapitalen des Kalten Krieges – dort, wo der Westen dem Sowjetblock gegenüberstand.

Für Hilton sollten seine Hotels ein Symbol Amerikas sein, um „den Ländern, die dem Kommunismus am stärksten ausgesetzt sind, die andere Seite der Medaille zu zeigen – die Früchte der freien Welt". Seine Hotels waren offen und luftig, sei es in Istanbul, Kairo, Berlin oder Athen – die Essenz des amerikanischen Modernismus, mitten in eine fremde Stadt hineingeworfen, wie Annabel Jane Wharton in ihrem Buch *Building the Cold War* schreibt. Doch Hilton baute nicht nur Hotels, er kaufte sie auch. Für 111 Mio. $ erwarb er 1954 sämtliche Statler-Hotels – auf diesem Sektor die höchste je gezahlte Summe seit dem Kauf von Louisiana im Jahr 1803.

Währenddessen räumte der Architekt Morris Lapidus in Miami Beach auf. Sein moderner Barockentwurf von 1954 für das Fontainebleau Hotel wurde von Prominenten wie auch der Öffentlichkeit gut aufgenommen, doch von Kritikern verabscheut, die das 13 Mio. $ teure Hotel und seine „Treppe ins Nichts" als viel zu schrill empfanden.

Doch eine solche Aufdringlichkeit war nicht die Regel, denn man begann, landesweit verbindliche Standards anzustreben. In Memphis, Tennessee, eröffnete 1952 das erste Holiday Inn als preis-

MAIN LINE OF SUPPLY!

ONE of our country's most important military assets is the fleet of General Motors Diesel locomotive units now in service on the main lines of America's railroads. Railroad demand for this power has increased with the national emergency.

Although General Motors Diesels comprise less than one-sixth of the nation's locomotives, they are hauling 33% of the total freight ton-miles on U. S. railroads today.

As compared to steam engines, Diesels average 64% more ton-miles of work per hour.

They average three times as many hours per day!

Diesels haul longer trains on faster schedules—and require far less time out for maintenance, servicing and refueling. With Diesel power, every train carries more tonnage —reducing traffic congestion on

the rails and speeding up release of cars for return loads.

All this has been proved by 16 years of General Motors Diesel performance in main-line service. So urgent is the demand for these modern locomotives, we are now building General Motors Diesels as rapidly as our facilities and materials permit—a program that assures American railroads a power task-force without equal for the rapid transportation of food, fuel and munitions.

ELECTRO-MOTIVE DIVISION
GENERAL MOTORS · LA GRANGE, ILLINOIS
Home of the Diesel Locomotive

◄◄ TWA, 1953   General Motors Diesels, 1953

werte Familienherberge. Innerhalb von fünf Jahren führte Kemmons Wilsons Franchiseprojekt zu einer Kette von sauberen Motels. 1959 waren es bereits 100, im Wesentlichen schlichte Nachbildungen des Originals. Die erste Howard Johnson's Motor Lodge wurde 1954 in Savannah, Georgia, eröffnet. Hieraus sollte eine ganze Kette rund um die populären Restaurants mit ihrer attraktiven – und standardisierten – Speisekarte entstehen. Während man das Fernstraßennetz in der Nachkriegsära auszubauen begann, folgten noch viele weitere Motels. Präsident Dwight Eisenhower unterzeichnete 1956 mit dem Interstate Highway Act das weiträumigste öffentliche Bauvorhaben aller Zeiten.

Auch mit den Flugreisen ging es steil nach oben, als sich am 2. Mai 1952 der erste kommerzielle Linienjet in die Lüfte schwang. Die Jetsetära begann mit dem Linienflug der BOAC von London nach Johannesburg – mit 770 km/h, verglichen mit

1953

Kiwi Sir Edmund Hillary and Nepali Tenzing Norgay first to reach summit of Mt. Everest, Earth's tallest mountain

Erstbesteigung des Mount Everest, höchster Berg der Welt, durch den Neuseeländer Sir Edmund Hillary und den Sherpa Tenzing Norgay

L'alpiniste kiwi Sir Edmund Hillary et le Népalais Tenzing Norgay sont les premiers à atteindre le sommet du Mont Everest

1954

First Howard Johnson's motor lodge opens in Savannah, Georgia

Eröffnung der ersten Howard Johnson's Motor Lodge in Savannah, Georgia

Ouverture du premier motel Howard Johnson à Savannah, Géorgie

1956

Airline travel in America hits 55 million passengers that year

Neuer Rekord mit 55 Millionen Flugreisenden in den USA

Le voyage aérien aux États-Unis atteint le pic des 55 millions de passagers den 290 km/h der DC-3. Reisen musste nun aber nicht unbedingt Rastlosigkeit bedeuten. Auch Golfreisen waren gefragt. Zusammen mit anderen Investoren erwarb der frühere Profigolfer Johnny Dawson 1951 die Thunderbird Dude Ranch in Rancho Mirage, Kalifornien. So entstand Palm Springs' erster Golfplatz mit 18 Löchern.

Auf der Leinwand unterstrich Marilyn Monroe den Reiz des Reisens mit Filmen, die das Jahrzehnt praktisch einrahmten. Zunächst in *Gentlemen Prefer Blondes* (*Blondinen bevorzugt*, 1953) als Lorelei Lee, ein aufs Geld versessenes Showgirl auf einem Schiff nach Europa. Und in Billy Wilders Klassiker *Some Like It Hot* (*Manche mögen's heiß*, 1959), dessen Florida-Szenen im Hotel del Coronado unweit von San Diego (Kalifornien) gedreht wurden, gewann Monroes Version von „I'm Through With Love" die Herzen der Amerikaner.

New Mexico, 1955

1956

Brigitte Bardot's posing in bikini popularizes style for beachgoers in Europe, then America

Brigitte Bardot macht den Bikini als Strand-outfit zunächst in Europa und dann auch in den USA salonfähig

L'apparition de Brigitte Bardot en bikini lance cette mode auprès des amateurs de plage en Europe, puis en Amérique

1956

Architect Morris Lapidus's glamorous Fontainebleau hotel sparks renaissance in Miami Beach, Florida

Das glamouröse Fontainebleau Hotel des Architekten Morris Lapidus verhilft Miami Beach, Florida, zu einer Renaissance

Rayonnant de glamour, l'hôtel Fontainebleau de l'architecte Morris Lapidus annonce la renaissance de Miami Beach, Floride

1957

"Just say the words, and we'll beat the birds down to Acapulco Bay," Frank Sinatra sings in "Come Fly with Me"

In „Come Fly With Me" meint Frank Sinatra, es bedürfe nur der richtigen Worte, und schon sei man schneller als die Vögel in Acapulco

« Just say the words, and we'll beat the birds down to Acapulco Bay », chante Frank Sinatra dans « Come Fly With Me »

LA PAX AMERICANA ET LA GUERRE FROIDE

À Istanbul, au Caire, à Berlin et à Athènes,
les structures des hôtels Hilton étaient ouvertes,
légères et accessibles – l'emblème par excellence
de la poussée du modernisme américain au
cœur d'une ville étrangère.

EN PLEINE GUERRE FROIDE, DANS LES ANNÉES 1950, CONRAD HILTON CONSIDÉRAIT SES HÔTELS COMME L'AVANT-GARDE DES VALEURS AMÉRICAINES – et le gouvernement américain vit dans les hôtels Hilton un argument commercial majeur pour le « soft power » des États-Unis. Avec l'aide de Washington et des gouvernements étrangers, les hôtels Hilton s'installèrent dans les grandes capitales de la Guerre Froide, là où l'Occident affrontait le Bloc soviétique.

Hilton voulait que ses hôtels symbolisent l'Amérique pour « montrer aux pays les plus exposés au communisme l'autre face de la médaille, les fruits du monde libre ». À Istanbul, au Caire, à Berlin et à Athènes, les structures de ses hôtels étaient ouvertes, légères et accessibles – l'emblème par excellence de la poussée du modernisme américain au cœur d'une ville étrangère, comme l'explique Annabel Jane Wharton dans son remarquable livre *Building the Cold War*. Hilton ne se contentait pas de construire des hôtels, il en achetait aussi. En 1954, il racheta toute la chaîne hôtelière Statler pour 111 millions de dollars, le prix le plus élevé jamais payé pour un projet immobilier depuis la Vente de Louisiane par Napoléon en 1803.

Pendant ce temps, l'architecte Morris Lapidus révolutionnait Miami Beach. En 1954, son design baroque moderne pour le Fontainebleau Hotel enchanta les célébrités et le public, mais fut méprisé par les critiques qui trouvaient cet hôtel de 13 millions de dollars et son « escalier pour nulle part » de très mauvais goût. Cette extravagance était l'exception et non la règle car un désir de standardisation s'emparait de tout le pays. En 1952, le premier Holiday Inn proposa des options d'hébergement bon marché et solides aux familles à Memphis dans le Tennessee. Cinq ans plus tard, les franchises de

Kemmons Wilson formaient une chaîne de motels bien tenus et à l'ambiance familiale. En 1959, on en comptait déjà 100, autant de répliques quasi identiques à l'original. De même, le premier Howard Johnson's Motor Lodge ouvrit à Savannah, Géorgie, en 1954. Cette chaîne fut développée comme une extension des restaurants éponymes à succès qui proposaient un menu alléchant – et standardisé. De tels motels poussèrent comme des champignons au fur et à mesure du développement du réseau routier américain. En 1956, le Président Eisenhower signa l'Interstate Highway Act, le plus grand projet de travaux publics de tous les temps.

Le voyage aérien atteignit aussi de nouveaux sommets quand le premier avion de ligne commerciale prit son envol le 2 mai 1952. L'ère de la jet-set s'ouvrit grâce à la liaison assurée par la compagnie BOAC entre Londres et Johannesburg, avec un appareil lancé à 770 kilomètres à l'heure, contre seulement 290 pour le DC-3.

On pouvait aussi voyager sur un mode sédentaire. Les séjours de golf étaient en vogue. En 1951, l'ancien golfeur professionnel Johnny Dawson et d'autres investisseurs achetèrent le Thunderbird Dude Ranch à Rancho Mirage, Californie. Ils en firent le premier parcours 18 trous et country club de Palm Springs. Bing Crosby, Jimmy Van Heusen et Phil Harris comptaient parmi ses membres fondateurs.

Au cinéma, Marilyn Monroe fit la promotion du voyage dans les films qu'elle tourna dans les années 1950 : dans *Les Hommes préfèrent les blondes* (1953), dans lequel elle incarne Lorelei Lee, danseuse qui voyage à bord d'un paquebot, ainsi que dans *Certains l'aiment chaud* (1959), qui se déroule en « Floride », à l'hôtel del Coronado de San Diego.

◄◄ Western Air Lines, ca. 1950   ► Hotel Nacional de Cuba, 1953

1958

1959

1959

American Express, whose traveler's checks have toured with American tourists since 1891, debuts charge card

American Express, dessen Travellerschecks die Amerikaner seit 1891 begleiten, präsentiert die erste Kundenkreditkarte

American Express, dont les « traveller's checks » voyagent avec les touristes américains depuis 1891, lance sa carte de paiement

Cairo Hilton opens with gala attended by President Gamal Abdel Nasser; site of all important local events for two decades

Eröffnung des Kairoer Hilton in Anwesenheit von Präsident Gamal Abdel Nasser; für 20 Jahre Schauplatz wichtiger lokaler Events

L'hôtel Hilton du Caire, qui ouvrit en présence du Président Nasser, fut un site majeur pendant vingt ans

Cary Grant pursued in white-knuckle chase down Mt. Rushmore, in Alfred Hitchcock's *North by Northwest*

Cary Grant sucht im packenden Finale von Alfred Hitchcocks *Der unsichtbare Dritte* Zuflucht auf dem Mount Rushmore

Dans *La Mort aux trousses* d'Alfred Hitchcock, Cary Grant est victime d'une course-poursuite haletante devant le Mont Rushmore

Hotel
Nacional de Cuba
HAVANA

A Kirkeby Hotel

IN CHICAGO IT'S THE

SHERATON
HOTEL

IN BALTIMORE IT'S THE **SHERATON -BELVEDERE**

SHERATON *the proudest name in* HOTELS

◄ Sheraton Hotels, 1954   Sheraton-Belvedere, 1954

Explore colorful, cosmopolitan San Francisco and Hollywood. Or simply loaf in the sun along beautiful Pacific shores, enjoying the extra time TWA gives you.

Your camera lens captures unbelievable colors in the glorious Southwest, where outdoor fun reigns in the wide-open spaces of dude ranches and resorts.

For wonderful fishing, fly TWA to Chicago and head North to the pine-forested lake country. There's camping, resort life, golfing, swimming and sailing.

Look for the new, the old, the smart and unique in New York — served by more than 25 TWA flights daily. It's a vacation full of memorable sights and experiences.

New England holds a treasure of Americana, cool salt breezes at Cape Cod sand dunes and sparkling lakes nestled in the mountains.

Where in the world <u>can</u> you go on just 2 weeks' vacation?

Here's an easy way to measure your own new horizons along the HIGH ways of TWA.

You pick the places you'd *like* **to go,** then check the TWA time-map below.* Possibilities are TWA can save you so much travel time you actually *can* go . . . even with limited vacation time off! And TWA fares are surprisingly easy on your budget.

So forget the old, usual vacation haunts. This year, follow the TWA highway to the Great Southwest, to the east or west coast; to the mountains; to the seashores; to the Golden Gate or the Grand Canyon or the canyons of New York. You pick it—you measure it—you can make it, easily, probably in mere hours from where you are right now!

But perhaps your eyes are on the Old World . . . way, way overseas. How far is it by TWA? Look at the map again and see what a vast distance one single day's flight can cover. Yes, you *can* go to Paris on a two weeks' vacation. You can go to Switzerland; to Rome; to Cairo; to Lisbon; to Madrid. You can take your pick of these and many other famed holiday centers and resort lands along TWA's direct world routes and *still keep well within the practical time limits of a short vacation!*

If *you* have been dreaming about a certain trip, don't put it off this year due to a short vacation. Plan to use the speed of Skyliner travel to bridge the distance and make that dream come true. Your travel agent will be glad to help with all the answers to your trip questions. Or call TWA.

All flying times shown are approximate. Check your travel agent or TWA for exact schedules.

Ireland is a season of color- and fun-filled events . . . from and fine racing to the famous se Show in August.

For leisurely sight-seeing, try the quiet lanes of provincial France. For gaiety and sidewalk cafes—there's nothing like Paris! 16 TWA flights weekly from the U. S.

Like luxurious living? Then take a 300-mph TWA Skyliner to the Mediterranean area. You'll find the finest hotels and smart casinos on the world-famous Riviera.

Motoring offers rich rewards in the Swiss Alps, where breath-taking new scenes await you at every turn. And car rentals are reasonable in Europe.

Magnificent monuments and ancient art masterpieces are everywhere in Rome, scene of the Holy Year observances. Less than a day from the U. S. by TWA.

of the pleasure on your vacation will be the few pleasant hours ute, when you travel by world-proved 300-mph TWA Skyliner. on as you board, the thoughtful TWA hostess sees that you're ortably settled in a deep, reclining seat. She'll bring you maga-, playing cards, writing material . . . serve you delicious hot meals n it's time to eat. As you relax and rest, your dependable Sky-speeds you to your destination in *hours* instead of days.

Across the U.S. and overseas . . .
you can depend on

TWA
TRANS WORLD AIRLINE
U.S.A. · EUROPE · AFRICA · ASIA

Ship almost anything anywhere by TWA Air Cargo—fast, dependable, low-cost! For mail and small packages, use air mail and air parcel post.

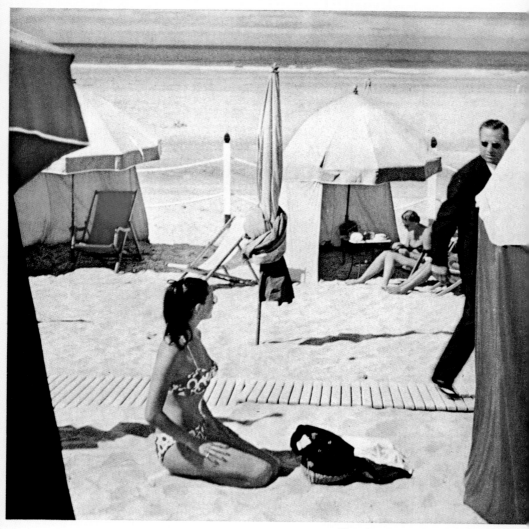

Your fastest way to tropic sun — fly DC-7

Whatever your reason for getting there faster...

Nothing beats the DC-7 — world's fastest airliner

You go up to *50 mph faster* in the new DC-7 than in any other airliner—its top speed is 410! You fly in luxury, too, with scores of new comforts, new conveniences.

Next time, be sure to go by DC-7. See why twice as many people fly Douglas as all other airplanes *combined.*

DC *means* DOUGLAS

◄◄ TWA, 1950

Douglas, 1956

The Douglas DC-7, first flown in 1953, was the last word in piston engines before the jet arrived. But its speed was heralded, since it allowed passengers to fly nonstop across the country in eight hours. Flying was indeed for pleasure.

Bevor die Jets aufkamen, verkörperte die ab 1953 verkehrende Douglas DC-7 die letzte Maschine mit Kolbenmotor. Doch ihre Geschwindigkeit kündete bereits von einer neuen Ära, denn nun konnte man in nur acht Stunden nonstop von einer Küste zur anderen gelangen. Und Fliegen machte wirklich Spaß.

Quand le Douglas DC-7 prit son envol en 1953, il représentait le nec plus ultra des appareils à moteurs à pistons, avant l'arrivée de l'avion à réaction. Il présageait toutefois sa vitesse, puisqu'il permettait aux passagers de traverser le pays sans escale en huit heures. Le voyage en avion devenait enfin un plaisir.

► Northwest Airlines, 1955

Sunny Hawaii...exotic foods...lazy days...silver surf

Hawaii—where it's always springtime—is as near as tomorrow when you fly Northwest. And what a way to go to Hawaii! Before you know it you're wrapped in golden sunshine lazing on a breeze-kissed beach. You fly in Royal Aloha Service luxury aboard fast DC-6B's with two-abreast seating and exclusive Twin-Screen Radar. You're treated to complimentary champagne . . . delicious hot meals . . . beverage service is available. All at low, low tourist fares. And you can take advantage of Northwest's lowest-cost Fly Now—Pay Later plan. Only 10% down. So stop dreaming, start planning today! See your travel agent or call

NORTHWEST *Orient* AIRLINES

32 years of superior Airmanship

Fly NWA's Royal Aloha Service with complimentary champagne. For more information mail the coupon today.

HAWAII INFORMATION SERVICE
NORTHWEST ORIENT AIRLINES
St. Paul 1, Minnesota

Send me your illustrated Hawaii Guide Book describing where to go and what to see in *all* the islands of Hawaii. Enclosed is 25¢.

Name_____

Street_____

City_____ Zone____ State____

Hilton and Statler Hotels select Rent-a-Car for their guests

These 28 distinguished hotels will deliver you a fine, new car from Avis ... or reserve one for you when you reserve your room.

For they know the discriminating traveler wants the freedom and comfort of a personal car wherever he stays ... on business or pleasure. And they know that Avis provides cars you are proud to drive ... new models, sparkling clean, fully insured and serviced.

It's easy to reserve an Avis car. Call any Avis Office or Hilton-Statler—or ask your plane or train ticket agent. You can reserve a car almost anywhere in the world at Avis' 800 offices. They honor credit cards from Avis, Hilton-Statler, and many others.

Next time you travel have a new Avis car available wherever you go ... for as long as you need it. And ask about the convenient "Rent it here—leave it there" service.

AWAY OR AT HOME...
A CAR OF YOUR OWN

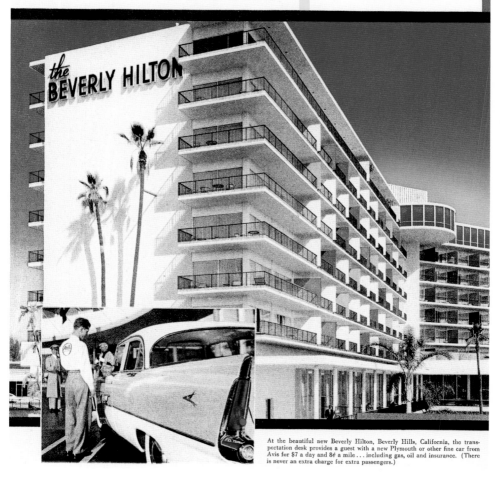

At the beautiful new Beverly Hilton, Beverly Hills, California, the transportation desk provides a guest with a new Plymouth or other fine car from Avis for $7 a day and 8¢ a mile ... including gas, oil and insurance. (There is never an extra charge for extra passengers.)

Avis, 1956

When the Beverly Hilton Hotel opened in 1955, it was labeled "The Motel in Cinemascope" by *Architectural Forum*. In a city based on the car, the Beverly Hilton was in the best possible location, where Wilshire and Santa Monica boulevards meet. In 1954, Conrad Hilton had bought the entire Statler Hotel chain.

Die Zeitschrift *Architectural Forum* bezeichnete das 1955 eröffnete Beverly Hilton Hotel als „Das Motel in Cinemascope". Das am Schnittpunkt des Wilshire und des Santa Monica Boulevard platzierte Beverly Hilton war wie geschaffen für eine Stadt, in der das Auto unverzichtbar war. Conrad Hilton hatte 1954 sämtliche Statler-Hotels erworben.

La revue *Architectural Forum* qualifia le Beverly Hilton Hotel de « motel en cinémascope » lors de son ouverture en 1955. Dans une ville dépendante de l'automobile, le Beverly Hilton se trouvait au meilleur endroit possible, au croisement de Wilshire et Santa Monica Boulevard. En 1954 Conrad Hilton, avait racheté toute la chaîne hôtelière Statler.

▶ Hertz, 1957

Hertz rents the kind of cars you like to drive!

What's your pleasure? A Cadillac, maybe? Hertz rents Cadillacs. Hertz rents big Buicks and Oldsmobiles, too. Thousands of new Chevrolets and other fine cars. Station wagons, convertibles, sports cars. Take your pick at most Hertz offices.

They're all in A-1 condition, expertly maintained, more dependable, cleaner cars. More with power steering. That's The Hertz Idea. You'll get the kind of car you like to drive at

over 1,350 Hertz offices in more than 900 cities —world-wide. That's *more* offices by far where you can *rent* a car. *More* cities by far where you can *leave* a car. *More* locations where you can make a *reservation* for a car!

Just show your driver's license and proper identification. The national average rate for a new Powerglide Chevrolet Bel Air is only $7.85 a day plus 8 cents a mile. And that includes the cost of all the gasoline and oil you use en

route . . . and proper insurance. In addition to the Hertz charge card, we honor all air, rail, Diners' Club and hotel credit cards.

To be sure of a car at your destination—anywhere—use Hertz' more efficient reservation service. Call your local Hertz office for fast, courteous service. We're listed under "Hertz" in *alphabetical* phone books everywhere! Hertz Rent A Car, 218 South Wabash Avenue, Chicago 4, Illinois.

More people by far...use

HERTZ
Rent a car

"Rent it here...Leave it there" Now, nation-wide at no extra charge! (on rentals of $26.00 or more).

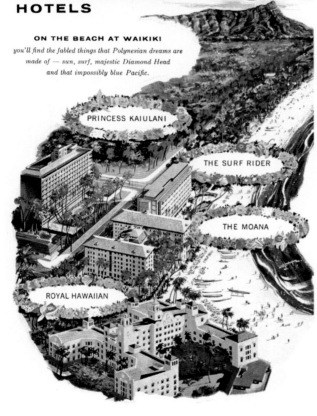

NOW IN **HAWAII**

SHERATON

HOTELS

ON THE BEACH AT WAIKIKI

you'll find the fabled things that Polynesian dreams are made of — sun, surf, majestic Diamond Head and that impossibly blue Pacific.

PRINCESS KAIULANI

THE SURF RIDER

THE MOANA

ROYAL HAWAIIAN

Sheraton Hotels, 1959

▶ Rand McNally, 1956

CROSSING*

By Philip Booth

Stop, look, listen
as gate stripes
swing down,
count the cars
hauling distance
upgrade through town:
warning whistle,
bell clang,
engine eating steam,
engineer waving,
a fast-freight dream;
B. & M. boxcar,
boxcar again,
Frisco gondola,
eight-nine-ten,
Erie and Wabash,
Seaboard, U.P.,
Pennsy tank car,
twenty-two, three,
Phoebe Snow, B.&O.,
thirty-four, five,
Santa Fe cattle
shipped alive,
red cars, yellow cars,
orange cars, black,
Youngstown steel
down to Mobile
on Rock Island track,
fifty-nine, sixty,
hoppers of coke,
Anaconda copper,
hotbox smoke,
eighty-eight,
red-ball freight,
Rio Grande,
Nickel Plate,
Hiawatha,
Lackawanna,
rolling fast
and loose.
ninety-seven,
coal car,
boxcar,
CABOOSE!

*There's poetry at every whistle stop. Rand McNally is proud of its
100 year history of printing maps, tickets, and timetables for buslines,
airlines, railroads, and highway travel — the lifelines of America.*

1856   1956

RAND McNALLY

100th Anniversary

PUBLISHERS · PRINTERS · MAP MAKERS · CHICAGO · NEW YORK · NASHVILLE · SAN FRANCISCO · WASHINGTON

THE NEWEST HOTEL IN CAIRO...MODERN AS A *TWA JETSTREAM**

Nile Hilton

⊛JETSTREAM IS A SERVICE MARK OWNED EXCLUSIVELY BY TWA

CAIRO—Another Hilton Hotel! New and beautiful as the mighty TWA JETSTREAM, longest-range airliner in the world today. The magnificent, 400-room Nile Hilton, on the banks of the majestic Nile, overlooks the Pyramids, the old Citadel and the city of Cairo with its mosques, museums and his-toric monuments. Completely air-conditioned, it is an ideal year-round meeting place for world travelers. Surrounded by symbols of ancient civilization and Pharaonic splendor, guests will enjoy every modern comfort, convenience and famous Hilton hospitality. And, TWA will fly you direct to Cairo.

RESERVATIONS: *See your Travel Agent or call New York, LOngacre 3-6900 • Chicago, FInancial 6-2772 • San Francisco, YUkon 3-0576 • Miami, FRanklin 9-3427 • Pittsburgh, COurt 1-5600 • Toronto, EMpire 2-3771 • London, Whitehall 3061 or any Hilton Hotel.* **CARTE BLANCHE**—*The Hilton All-Purpose Credit Card — Your Finest Credit Credential.*

Hilton Hotels

EXECUTIVE
OFFICES
THE CONRAD HILTON
CHICAGO 5, ILLINOIS

Conrad N. Hilton, President

Hilton Hotels, 1959

Hilton Hotels, 1959   ▶▶ Santa Fe Railway, 1951

Be carefree, be comfortable and enjoy a
New World

Standard in Travel

The new Santa Fe

Super Chief

Advanced ideas for your travel luxury...new cradled smoothness in the ride...daily between Chicago and Los Angeles

From the flanges on the wheels to the tip of the Pleasure Dome, the Super Chief is new—entirely new.

To give you the smoothest ride of your life on rails, this new Super Chief glides on cushioned springs . . . revises any ideas you ever had about any train.

The keynote is comfort.

You find it in the distinctive Turquoise Room in the lounge car—a delightful place to relax, enjoy a cocktail or entertain your friends at dinner—the first time such a room has been provided on any train.

You find it in the Pleasure Dome—"top of the Super, next to the stars"—that brings you an unobstructed view of wonderful southwestern scenery.

You find it in the new dining cars where Fred Harvey chefs present new and exciting menus.

Accommodations in this beautiful all-room train are designed to pamper you every mile of the way. "Push-button" radio or music in your room when you *want* it . . . beds you just can't help sleeping in . . . charming apartments by day.

From the engineers who glide you across this great country to the porter who answers your bell, this is the train of thoughtful service.

For your next trip between Chicago and Los Angeles say "Super Chief." Now, more than ever, it is America's train of trains. Just consult your local ticket agent.

SANTA FE SYSTEM LINES
Serving the West and Southwest

Santa Fe

BURR TILLSTROM, KUKLA AND OLLIE, *whimsical, lovable stars of NBC television trade their five nights a week spotlight for days of sunlight on their recent Mediterranean holiday aboard the great new Sun-Liner Independence.*

Every voyage ~~~ a Gay Cruise...

When you sail the Sun-Lane to Europe, it's not just a trip from one port to another but an exciting voyage that touches upon the loveliest lands of the Mediterranean. And liberal stop-over privileges make all of these garden spots yours to sample if you're in a hurry, or to linger in if you wish.

On the great new Sun-Liners of American Export Lines, you enjoy "Modern American Living at Sea"...a gay, friendly, carefree informality amid every comfort and service that American ingenuity can provide.

Even the weather on the Sun-Lane conspires to lift your spirits. Fall, winter and spring average 87 per cent rain-free days, and through the summer the gentle trade winds cool your smooth path to a perfect 71 degrees average. When you enter the Continent from the sunny, southern side you'll find much of the best of Europe all around you . . . the rest of Europe just hours away.

SEE YOUR TRAVEL AGENT OR **AMERICAN EXPORT LINES** 39 BROADWAY, N. Y. 6, N. Y.

INDEPENDENCE · CONSTITUTION ☆ EXETER · EXCALIBUR · EXOCHORDA · EXCAMBION
GIBRALTAR, CANNES, GENOA, NAPLES ☆ FRANCE, ITALY, EGYPT, LEBANON, SYRIA, TURKEY, GREECE, SPAIN

American Export Lines, 1952

Getting there is half the *fun!*

AUTUMN is ideal for your visit to Europe . . . when Britain
and the Continent are at their sparkling, uncrowded best . . . and ideal, too,
for a gay, relaxing ocean voyage! When you go Cunard, each day at sea
and each brilliant, enchanted evening is a glorious new adventure shared with interesting companions
amid all the comforts of a great seaside resort. You'll delight in the bright conviviality, the thoughtful,
attentive service for which Cunard is famous . . . and the marvelous food,
prepared for your sea-sharpened appetite by internationally trained chefs.
See your travel agent about Cunard's lower "Thrift Season" rates.

Write for Cunard's attractive new brochure "Gracious Living at its Best."

Swimming Pool in the Queen Mary

No wonder more people prefer CUNARD

From New York: QUEEN ELIZABETH • QUEEN MARY • MAURETANIA • CARONIA • BRITANNIC • MEDIA • PARTHIA
From Canada: FRANCONIA • SCYTHIA • SAMARIA • ASCANIA

Cunard, 1953

THE CHARMING SETTING for your luxury flight overseas is the smart interior of your Air France Constellation. Limited number of "sky-lounger" chairs provide the most spacious accommodations in air travel for your individual comfort. You are served in the inimitable French manner by friendly English-speaking stewards and hostess.

Fly in Luxury UNEXCELLED IN AIR TRAVEL
—AT NO EXTRA COST! Fly Air France!

VETERAN PILOTS—many of whom have logged more than a million miles in the air— fly the new-type AIR FRANCE Constellations. Seasoned world-travelers know and respect the world-famed AIR FRANCE reputation for regularity and dependability. They know, too, that AIR FRANCE offers the ultimate in gracious living aloft—luxury *unequalled* in air travel. Gourmet cuisine, prepared by masters of the art of French cooking. Champagne, too, or a vintage wine...a liqueur after dinner, of course. Your entire trip by AIR FRANCE is an adventure in living as *only* the French know how!

"THE PARISIAN"—Luxury trans-Atlantic air travel—an experience in gracious living. Departures from New York, Boston, and Montreal to Paris, Frankfurt, Berlin, Rome.

"THE PARISIAN SPECIAL"—The world-famous ultra-de-luxe AIR FRANCE flight—non-stop overnight from New York to Paris. Ten dollars additional fare.

NEW TOURIST SERVICE. New York-Paris round-trip $522 April 1-October 31. $453 November 1-March 31. New Type constellations. Meals obtained at moderate prices.

AIR FRANCE
THE LUXURY WORLD-WIDE AIRLINE

What airline gives you *Red Carpet* Service?

United Air Lines

It's "Red Carpet" luxury all the way...

aboard United's special nonstop DC-7s!

Inviting lounge, superlative service...

de luxe meals and refreshments!

Games, kits, scores of travel items...

many other "extras" at no extra cost!

On United's "Red Carpet" flights you enjoy brilliant new service on DC-7s, the world's fastest airliners. Everything is special — from the red carpet itself, air travel's warmest welcome mat, to the extra-fast way your luggage is delivered to you on arrival. Choose "Red Carpet" Service — coast-to-coast and on other special nonstop flights. And for extra savings, fly half-fare Family Plan — now Monday noon through Thursday noon. Call or write United or your Authorized Travel Agent.

There's a **difference**

UNITED AIR LINES

when you travel in the Mainliner® Manner

Air France, 1952   United Air Lines, 1956

The Douglas DC-8 in flight, newest bearer of the most respected name in aviation

Look up to the DC-8 ... world's _newest_ jetliner!

Into the skies—from the Northern Lights to the Southern Cross—flies the Douglas DC-8. And with this flight, travel by air reaches a new high level of performance and comfort.

In the still, blue stratosphere, the miles tick away on the wings of this most modern of passenger planes. The earth's masses of land and water, awesome as they are, yield to the murmuring power of the DC-8 jet engines. Cradled in peace and luxury, you now can reach the world's farthest corners in less time than it takes the sun to go full circle.

But speed alone is not what distinguishes Douglas from all other names in aviation. The DC-8—like each of its world-famous predecessors—takes to the skies a family tradition of experience, dependability and comfort unrivalled in the annals of flight. It is this—and more—which makes passengers and pilots look up to Douglas . . . reveals, in part, why more people and more airlines fly Douglas than all other airplanes combined.

Your own personal introduction to the jet age is not far off. Like so many others, you will experience it in the nonpareil of the upper air, the fabulous . . .

DOUGLAS DC-8 JETLINER

Built by the most respected name in aviation

These famous airlines already have purchased the DC-8: ALITALIA-Linee Aeree Italiane · DELTA AIR LINES · EASTERN AIR LINES · JAPAN AIR LINES · KLM ROYAL DUTCH AIR LINES · NATIONAL AIRLINES · OLYMPIC AIRWAYS · PANAGRA · PANAIR DO BRASIL · PAN AMERICAN WORLD AIRWAYS · SCANDINAVIAN AIRLINES SYSTEM · SWISSAIR · TRANS-CANADA AIR LINES · TRANS CARIBBEAN AIRWAYS · TRANSPORTS AÉRIENS INTERCONTINENTAUX · UNION AÉROMARITIME DE TRANSPORT · UNITED AIR LINES

Douglas, 1958

It is hard to have a Jet Set without a jet. The Douglas DC-8 jetliner took off in 1958, in direct competition with the Boeing 707. Passengers "getting away from it all" considered jet flight an enthralling experience.

Jetset ohne Jet wäre ein Unding. Der Linienjet Douglas DC-8 schwang sich 1958 in die Lüfte, in direkter Konkurrenz zur Boeing 707. Fluggäste, die einfach mal alles hinter sich lassen wollten, zeigten sich überaus angetan.

Sans jet, pas de jet-set. L'avion à réaction Douglas DC-8 décolla en 1958, en concurrence directe avec le Boeing 707. Les passagers en quête d'évasion trouvaient qu'il n'y avait rien de plus excitant que de voyager en jet.

▶ Scandinavian Airlines System, 1954

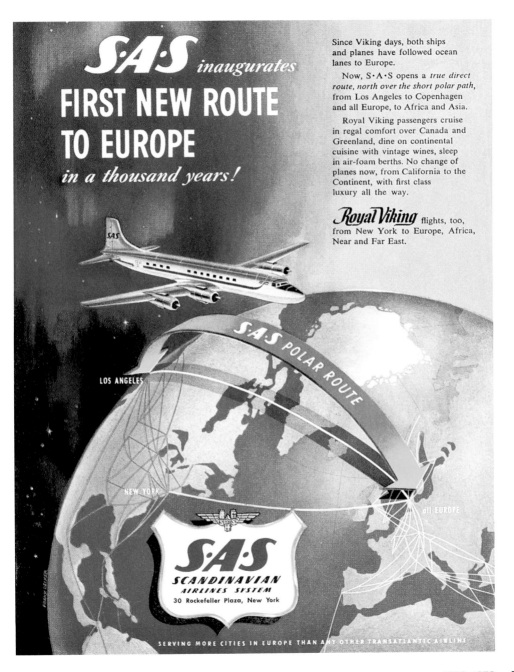

S·A·S *inaugurates*

FIRST NEW ROUTE TO EUROPE

in a thousand years!

Since Viking days, both ships and planes have followed ocean lanes to Europe.

Now, S·A·S opens a *true direct route, north over the short polar path*, from Los Angeles to Copenhagen and all Europe, to Africa and Asia.

Royal Viking passengers cruise in regal comfort over Canada and Greenland, dine on continental cuisine with vintage wines, sleep in air-foam berths. No change of planes now, from California to the Continent, with first class luxury all the way.

Royal Viking flights, too, from New York to Europe, Africa, Near and Far East.

LOS ANGELES

NEW YORK

all EUROPE

S·A·S POLAR ROUTE

S·A·S
SCANDINAVIAN
AIRLINES SYSTEM
30 Rockefeller Plaza, New York

SERVING MORE CITIES IN EUROPE THAN ANY OTHER TRANSATLANTIC AIRLINE

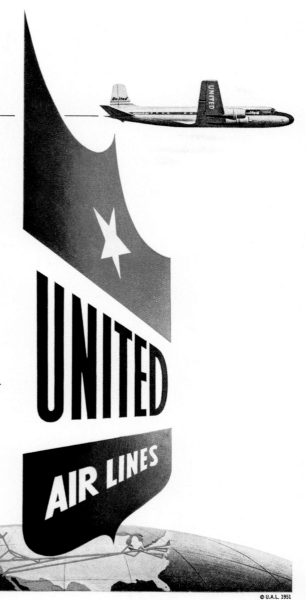

United Air Lines is the
only airline linking the East,
the Middle West, all major
Pacific Coast cities and Hawaii.
Wherever you travel,
fly United's Main Line Airway—
truly the Nation's
No. 1 Coast-to-Coast Airline.

© U.A.L. 1951

United Air Lines, 1951   ▸ Capital Air Lines, 1953   ▸▸ Scandinavian Airlines System, 1958

The other 50 weeks are richer if you spend 2 ab...
so start planning your foreign vacation by Clippe...

*L*ive a lot...go abroad on *even* a 2-week vacation

Ever stop to think that your vacation lasts *you* a whole year? You look forward to it. You take it. You look back on it. So no matter when your vacation comes around, it should provide the lift that carries you through the year. That's why Pan American—the first choice of experienced travelers—will *never* let you down!

No place on earth is over 40 hours from your home on the wings of Pan Am's Flying Clippers*. As a matter of fact, many of the most glamorous places to which Pan American flies are only overnight. Indeed, in less time than it takes to drive 200 miles you can fly by Clipper to a foreign land from many parts of the U.S.A.

If your budget's tight, there are many ways to loosen it: Pan Am's Family Fare savings, thrifty tourist-fare *Rainbow* service, excursion fares, cost-inclusive *Pan Am Holidays* . . . all available on Pan Am's World-Wide Plan, Go Now—Pay Later: only 10% down.

Next year follow your heart, not the crowds. You're off to a flying start with a copy of *New Horizons*—the book that's put wings on the dreams of half a million world travelers. Call your Travel Agent or one of Pan Am's 53 offices in the U.S. and Canada. *TRADE-MARKS, REG. U.S. PAT. OFF.*

YOUR VACATION PLANNER
Send for your copy of *New Horizons**—Pan Am's 576-page, best selling world-wide travel guide. Mail $1 to Pan American, Dept. 170, Box 1111, New York 17, N.Y.

WORLD'S MOST EXPERIENCED AIRL...

◄ Pan Am, 1957

American Airlines, 1956

Acapulco was a key Jet Set hub during the 1950s. Hollywood mingled with European aristocrats and American plutocrats in the hills above Acapulco Bay. The sybaritic Las Brisas Hotel, where each casita has its own private swimming pool, became the place to be when it opened in 1957.

Acapulco war in den 1950er-Jahren ein beliebter Treffpunkt des Jetset. Auf den Hügeln über der Bucht von Acapulco gaben sich Hollywoodstars, europäische Aristokraten und amerikanische Plutokraten ein Stelldichein. Das verschwenderische, 1957 eröffnete Las Brisas Hotel, wo jede Casita einen privaten Pool besaß, wurde zum absoluten Muss.

Pendant les années 1950, Acapulco était un rendez-vous incontournable pour la jet-set. Hollywood frayait avec l'aristocratie euro-péenne et les plutocrates américains sur les collines de la Baie d'Acapulco. L'ultra luxueux Las Brisas Hotel, où chaque bungalow possédait sa propre piscine privée, devint le must dès son ouverture en 1957.

►► Convair, 1958

880

...of unquestioned luxury... the Convai

ight-eighty

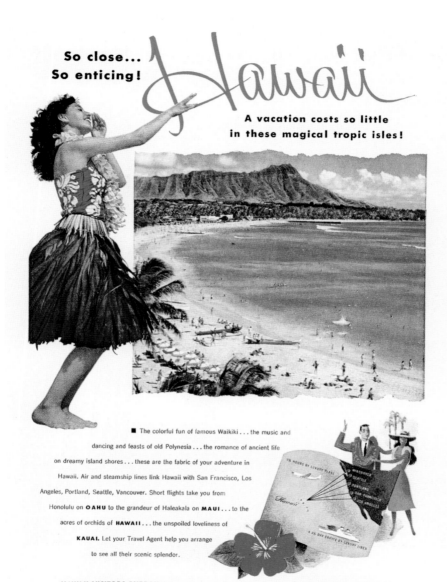

So close...
So enticing!

Hawaii

**A vacation costs so little
in these magical tropic isles!**

■ The colorful fun of famous Waikiki . . . the music and
dancing and feasts of old Polynesia . . . the romance of ancient life
on dreamy island shores . . . these are the fabric of your adventure in
Hawaii. Air and steamship lines link Hawaii with San Francisco, Los
Angeles, Portland, Seattle, Vancouver. Short flights take you from
Honolulu on **OAHU** to the grandeur of Haleakala on **MAUI** . . . to the
acres of orchids of **HAWAII** . . . the unspoiled loveliness of
KAUAI. Let your Travel Agent help you arrange
to see all their scenic splendor.

HAWAII VISITORS BUREAU A non-profit organization maintained for your service by **THE PEOPLE OF HAWAII**

Hawaii Visitors Bureau, 1950 ▶ Intercontinental Hotels, 1959

how to work up an appetite
for what's cooking in Caracas

Pirates had to eat, too, but they never had it so good as modern-day guests of the Hotel Tamanaco in Caracas, Venezuela, on the Ancient Spanish Main.

Whether you're licking your chops at the "groaning board" or "loafing it up" beside the sun-drenched swimming pool, you'll find yourself heir to the best of two worlds: the adventure of foreign travel, the comfort of American care.

From the food to the accommodations and entertainment, American attention to detail tempers Latin imagination. For that is what an Intercontinental vacation holds for you: service and efficiency blended with traditions of hospitality that are centuries old.

So if you've been looking for a vacation spot that's tailor-made for good times and good eating, the Hotel Tamanaco is your kind of place. Even without pirates, it's the most exciting place in Caracas.

Phone your travel agent or write Intercontinental Hotels, Chrysler Bldg., New York 17, N.Y. (If you prefer, call STillwell 6-5858 in New York.)

egant service — that's just one specialty of the house at the fabulous Hotel Tamanaco in Caracas, Venezuela

This is Florida—Sunshine, U.S.A.—where everything you do and every place you go are filled with glorious adventure.

This year take it *all* in—the brilliance of Florida's palm-fringed beaches and sun-warmed surf; the tingling excitement of landing that first, or *hundred*-and-first, big-game fish; the thrill of driving one down the middle of velvet-green fairway. This year discover for yourself the splendor of Florida's scenic landmarks; the glamour of its renowned spectator events; the romance of its nights under the stars. And this year see with your own eyes why so many millions agree, there's no place like Florida for sunny pleasure, healthful relaxation, and sheer good living.

Plan it today—your sparkling Winter with Sunshine in Florida—the vacation adventure you'll remember a lifetime.

Florida

MAIL THIS COUPON TODAY

STATE OF FLORIDA,
2201 COMMISSION BUILDING, TALLAHASSEE.

Please send at once new, free 48-page booklet in full color: "Florida, the Sunshine State."

Name_____

Street and No._____

City_____ Zone____State_____

◄ American President Lines, 1951   State of Florida, 1950

The lovely new *Andrea Doria*

These men have built a ship…

What gives a ship that thing called personality? From where come those qualities of warmth and friendliness? How do you take the coldness out of steel? How do you breathe life into glass and tile? You won't find the answer in blueprints. You can't do it with money or calloused hands. You build such a ship with your heart.

Into every detail of this lovely vessel have gone the skill and pride of the greatest artisans of Italy. Every mural, every tapestry, every rug and chair…each exquisite bit of glassware and every glowing tile is the work of craftsmen. Yes, a ship is built of many hearts. This is the tradition of Italy. This is the *Andrea Doria*.

The completely air conditioned *Andrea Doria* enters transatlantic service to New York in January. *Special West Indies Cruise January 30 . . . 17 glorious days.*

Italian Line

"ITALIA" — Società di Navigazione — Genova

See your Travel Agent or
AMERICAN EXPORT LINES (General Agents)
39 Broadway, New York 6, N. Y.

ANDREA DORIA express service on the "Sunny Southern Route" • 6 days to GIBRALTAR • 8 days to NAPLES • 9 days to CANNES and GENOA
SATURNIA • VULCANIA to LISBON • GIBRALTAR • BARCELONA • PALERMO • NAPLES • CANNES • GENOA

Italian Line, 1952

The Italian Line brought in the influential Gio Ponti to redesign the interiors of its ships, SS *Conte Biancamano* and *Conte Grande*, as well as the *Giulio Cesare*, *Africa*, and *Oceana*. He reenvisioned this fleet as a sleekly modern "manifestation of the arts" of Italy. Ponti favored anodized-gold aluminum, which he seemed to use wherever possible. He talked about it as the best possible material—extremely light and aesthetically pleasing. Ponti also designed the interiors of the ill-fated SS *Andrea Doria*, the Italian Line's biggest and swiftest ship. In 1956, it collided with another vessel and sank the next day.

Die Italian Line engagierte den einflussreichen Architekten Gio Ponti für den Neuentwurf der Interieurs ihrer Schiffe, SS *Conte Biancamano* und *Conte Grande* ebenso wie *Giulio Cesare*, *Africa* und *Oceana*. Ponti verwendete Goldeloxal, wo immer möglich, für ihn war es das bestmögliche Material – extrem leicht und zugleich gefällig. Ebenso entwarf er das Interieur der unglückseligen *Andrea Doria*, des wohl flottesten und größten Schiffs der Italian Line. Es kollidierte 1956 mit einem anderen Schiff und sank am Tag darauf.

La Società di Navigazione italienne demanda à l'influent Gio Ponti de réaménager les intérieurs de ses navires, le *Conte Biancamano* et le *Conte Grande*, ainsi que le *Giulio Cesare*, l'*Africa* et l'*Oceana*. Il reconçut la flotte avec une modernité épurée, à l'image d'une « manifestation des arts » de l'Italie. Ponti privilégiait l'aluminium anodisé doré dès qu'il le pouvait. Il en parlait comme du meilleur des matériaux, à la fois extrêmement léger et esthétique. Il conçut aussi les intérieurs de l'infortuné *Andrea Doria*, considéré comme le paquebot le plus grand et le plus rapide de la compagnie italienne. En 1956, il heurta un autre bateau et coula le lendemain.

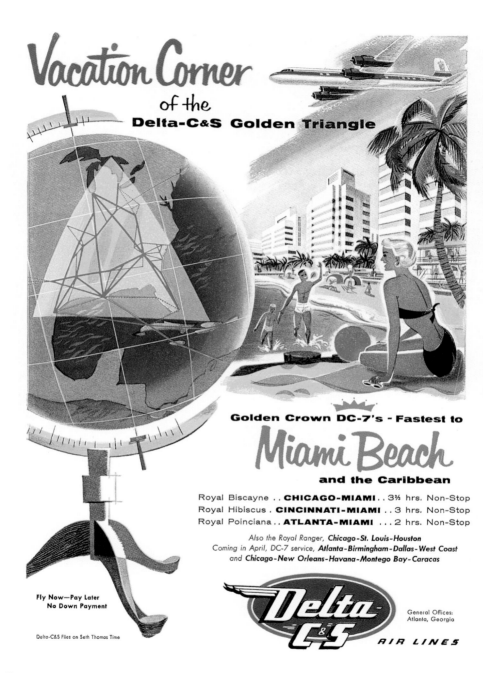

Vacation Corner
of the
Delta-C&S Golden Triangle

Golden Crown DC-7's - Fastest to

Miami Beach
and the Caribbean

Royal Biscayne .. **CHICAGO-MIAMI** .. 3½ hrs. Non-Stop
Royal Hibiscus . **CINCINNATI-MIAMI** .. 3 hrs. Non-Stop
Royal Poinciana .. **ATLANTA-MIAMI** ... 2 hrs. Non-Stop

Also the Royal Ranger, Chicago-St. Louis-Houston
Coming in April, DC-7 service, Atlanta-Birmingham-Dallas-West Coast
and Chicago-New Orleans-Havana-Montego Bay-Caracas

Fly Now—Pay Later
No Down Payment

Delta-C&S Flies on Seth Thomas Time

Delta-C&S

General Offices:
Atlanta, Georgia

AIR LINES

◄ Delta-C&S Air Lines, 1955

Delta-C&S Air Lines, 1954

Morris Lapidus's Fontainebleau Hotel, a medley
of fabulous French baroque, breathed new
life into the tired Miami Beach scene when
it opened in 1954. The next year, Lapidus
designed the flamboyant Eden Roc Hotel, an
Italian fantasy and business rival, right beside it.
The sands sizzled.

Morris Lapidus' 1954 eröffnetes Fontainebleau
Hotel, ein Mix aus französischen Barockfanta-
sien, hauchte der ermatteten Szene von Miami
Beach neues Leben ein. Im Jahr darauf entwarf
Lapidus das extravagante Eden Roc Hotel, eine
italienische Fantasie und Konkurrentin in unmit-
telbarer Nachbarschaft. Der Sand brodelte.

À son ouverture en 1954, le Fontainebleau
Hotel de Morris Lapidus, pot-pourri fabuleux
de baroque français insuffla une vie nouvelle
à un Miami Beach fatigué. L'année suivante,
Lapidus conçut son concurrent juste à côté,
le flamboyant Eden Roc Hotel au style italien
fantaisiste. Leurs plages ne désemplissaient pas.

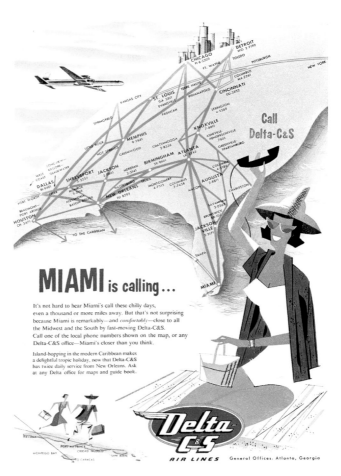

MIAMI is calling ...

It's not hard to hear Miami's call these chilly days,
even a thousand or more miles away. But that's not surprising
because Miami is remarkably—and *comfortably*—close to all
the Midwest and the South by fast-moving Delta-C&S.
Call one of the local phone numbers shown on the map, or any
Delta-C&S office—Miami's closer than you think.

Island-hopping in the modern Caribbean makes
a delightful tropic holiday, now that Delta-C&S
has twice daily service from New Orleans. Ask
at any Delta office for maps and guide book.

Delta-C&S AIR LINES General Offices: Atlanta, Georgia

Getting there is half the fun!

For more than a century the name Cunard
has been the hallmark of transatlantic
travel luxury . . . relaxation . . . gaiety.
Your first day aboard will show you why
more travelers choose Cunard than any other lin
See your local travel agent.

GO *CUNARD*

◄ Cunard, 1956

Las Vegas, 1952

Las Vegas emerged as a sophisticated, and decadent, getaway. In 1950, the Desert Inn opened on the Strip. Its celebrated "crystal showroom" nightclub featured a slew of big names, including a memorable series of shows with Frank Sinatra and the entire Rat Pack when they were shooting *Ocean's Eleven* there at decade's end.

Las Vegas entwickelte sich zu einem durchgeplanten – und dekadenten – Zufluchtsort. In dem als „kristallener Schauraum" gefeierten Nachtclub des 1950 am Strip eröffneten Desert Inn ließen sich einige große Namen blicken, und es gab eine Reihe denkwürdiger Auftritte von Frank Sinatra und seinem Rat Pack während der Dreharbeiten von *Ocean's Eleven* (*Frankie und seine Spießgesellen*) gegen Ende des Jahrzehnts.

Las Vegas apparut d'abord comme une destination sophistiquée et décadente. En 1950, le Desert Inn ouvrit sur le Strip. Sa célèbre salle de spectacles, le « crystal showroom », accueillit une cohorte de grands noms, notamment une série de représentations mémorables avec Frank Sinatra et tout le Rat Pack pendant le tournage de *L'Inconnu de Las Vegas* à la fin de la décennie.

►► American Airlines, 1954

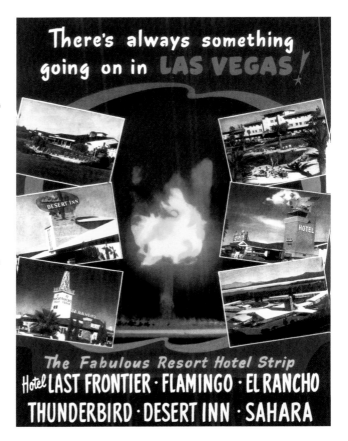

American's New DC-7 Leads

In 1954 YOU'LL FLY THE MOST MODERN FLEET OF TRANSPORT AIRCRAFT IN THE WORLD ON THE ROUTE OF THE FLAGSHIPS

In 1954 American's new DC-7 is leading the finest Flagship Fleet in history. It includes such outstanding passenger carriers as the popular inter-city Convair and the famous long range DC-6 and DC-6B Flagships as well as the DC-6A, the biggest, fastest cargo plane in operation today.

American's magnificent new Turbo Compound DC-7 Flagship is the *first* plane especially designed for NONSTOP transcontinental travel and the *only* aircraft capable of nonstop coast-to-coast service under 8 hours.

This means that American now offers the fastest service between New York and Los Angeles and New York and San Francisco. The addition of the DC-7 also enables American to greatly expand its nonstop service between major cities on its 10,800 miles of routes.

So welcome aboard the Flagship Fleet for '54. Welcome *to* the most modern fleet of transport aircraft in the world. And welcome *from* American's 17,000 trained personnel whose friendly attentive service has long set the standard for air transportation.

AMERICAN AIRLINES INC.

America's Leading Airline

e Finest Flagship Fleet Ever

Step aboard at New York and step out at Rio de Janeiro in 20⅔ hours ... fly on to Buenos Aires in 6⅓ hours. This is a deluxe all-sleeper service with double-decked "Strato" Clippers.

The best vacations begin with Samsonite Luggage

Take a tip from the Dick Powells!
Vacation by *Air-Conditioned* Scenicruiser

Greyhound, 1956   ▶ Santa Fe Railway, 1957

ONE MILLION

passengers have now flown the Boeing 707 jetliner!

BOEING 707 and 720

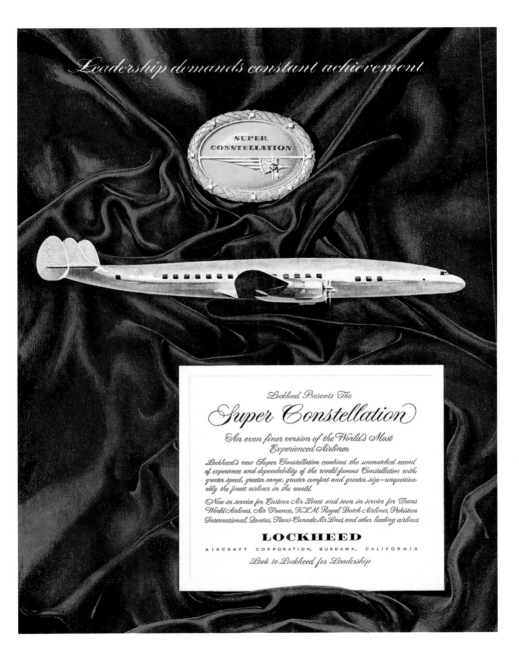

Leadership demands constant achievement

SUPER CONSTELLATION

Lockheed Presents The

Super Constellation

An even finer version of the World's Most Experienced Airliner

Lockheed's new Super Constellation combines the unmatched record of experience and dependability of the world-famous Constellation with greater speed, greater range, greater comfort and greater size—unquestionably the finest airliner in the world.

Now in service for Eastern Air Lines and soon in service for Trans World Airlines, Air France, K.L.M. Royal Dutch Airlines, Pakistan International, Qantas, Trans-Canada Air Lines and other leading airlines

LOCKHEED

AIRCRAFT CORPORATION, BURBANK, CALIFORNIA

Look to Lockheed for Leadership

◄ Boeing, 1959   Lockheed, 1951

YOURS: EXTRA CARE AT NO EXTRA FARE!

Fly United Air Lines for Red Carpet* Service on the luxurious DC-7, nonstop coast to coast, along the West Coast and to Hawaii. It's extra care for you all the way—the finest service, with luxuries that will delight you. Memorable meals and tempting delicacies, smart lounge, pleasant, thoughtful stewardesses—add up to extra care at the regular First Class fare!

YOU GET EXTRA CARE AT THE REGULAR FARE ON UNITED, THE RADAR AIRLINE

Untied Airlines, 1958

IN SAN FRANCISCO MAINTENANCE BASE

UNITED AIR LINES

WHITE PLANES represent United Mainliners in the air, YELLOW PLANES Mainliners on the ground awaiting passengers, in reserve, or undergoing daily maintenance.

© U.A.L. 1952

At 5:59 p.m. on United's Main Line Airway

This is a picture of one minute in a day of United Air Lines — 5:59 p. m., Central Standard Time, to be exact. Here you see United's 13,250-mile Main Line Airway in action — the only airline linking the East, the Middle West, all major Pacific Coast cities and Hawaii.

At this moment, over 2000 passengers are aloft in United Air Lines Mainliners, along with about 100,000 pounds of air mail, express, and freight.

Multiplying this scene to span the year 1952, Mainliner travel will amount to nearly 2½ billion

passenger-miles — more than enough to pick up every man, woman, and child in Boston, Mass., and carry them all to San Francisco!

The frequency, precision, and regularity with which United Air Lines operates have placed it among the nation's foremost transportation systems. And among the most *economical* too — for Mainliner travel often costs less than first-class rail plus lower berth today! For reservations call or write United or an Authorized Travel Agent.

PASSENGERS • MAIL • EXPRESS • FREIGHT • AIR PARCEL POST

UNITED AIR LINES

ONE OF THE SCHEDULED AIRLINES OF THE U.S.

United Airlines, 1952

Don made the Trip
—TOO LATE AGAIN

John made the Sale
— HE TOOK THE PLANE

America's Leading Airline **AMERICAN AIRLINES** INC.

American Airlines, 1952   ▶ TWA, 1958   ▶▶ Douglas, 1959

ON TIME!

TWA Captain Thomas Lynch brings in Flight 4

We're proud of our clock-watchers at TWA!

It takes *team* work to send the mighty Jetstreams* winging to their destinations all over the world, departing *on schedule,* arriving *on time!* And it takes a *big* team of clock-watchers to do it—maintenance men, weather analysts, flight dispatchers, operating crews. TWA is proud of them. You'll understand why . . . when, after the smoothest, most luxurious flight you've ever had . . . *your* TWA plane taxis in *on time!* For reservations, telephone your travel agent or nearest TWA office today.

FLY THE FINEST . . . FLY TWA TRANS WORLD AIRLINES

✱Jetstream is a service mark owned exclusively by TWA.

"WE TRAVEL, SOME OF US FOR-
EVER, TO SEEK OTHER STATES,
OTHER LIVES, OTHER SOULS."
– ANAÏS NIN

„WIR REISEN, EINIGE VON
UNS EWIG, UM ZU SUCHEN,
ANDERE STAATEN, ANDERE
LEBEN, ANDERE SEELEN."
– ANAÏS NIN

1960

« NOUS VOYAGEONS, PARFOIS ÉTERNELLEMENT, POUR TROUVER D'AUTRES ÉTATS, D'AUTRES VIES, D'AUTRES ÂMES. » – ANAÏS NIN

1969

JET SET AT FULL THROTTLE

Modern travel was going to bring everyone closer together, and airplanes would be the vehicle of choice.

MAY 25, 1961, PRESIDENT JOHN F. KENNEDY DECLARED TO THE NATION, AND THE WORLD: "WE CHOOSE TO GO TO THE MOON." The charismatic president vowed that Americans would stand on the moon by decade's end. Technology was viewed as a powerful and positive force. Anything was possible. The 1964 New York World's Fair joyously proclaimed, "It's a Small World after All," and its 51 million visitors agreed. Modern travel was going to bring everyone closer together—and jets were the vehicle of choice.

This heady optimism was epitomized in Eero Saarinen's swooping TWA Terminal at Idlewild—later John F. Kennedy—Airport. Air travel never looked as alluring and glamorous as in that 1963 structure. Movie audiences savored the élan of the first James Bond movie, *Dr. No* (1962), which hopscotched across the globe—a sexy travelogue disguised as a spy thriller. And Federico Fellini's acclaimed *La Dolce Vita* (1960) was punctuated by the celebrity arrivals at the Rome airport.

Braniff International Airways hired advertising whiz Mary Wells, whose remarkable "End of the Plain Plane" campaign in 1965 enlisted the Jet Set's favorite fashion designer, Emilio Pucci, to create futuristic stewardess uniforms with layers, bold patterns, and plastic "space" helmets. She brought in Alexander Girard to revamp the planes, waiting areas, check-in counters, and ticket offices. He saturated every surface with strong colors, inside and out.

But air travel was no longer just for the wealthy. It was increasingly essential to business executives. Eastern Airlines, seeing this, introduced its Air Shuttle service between New York and Washington, D.C., in 1961. Passengers needed no reservations, had no hard ticketing, and had guaranteed seating on hourly flights. In 1967, United Air Lines launched a sparkling TV campaign featuring a chorus line of wives singing to their businessmen husbands, "Take Me Along."

By 1965, with the introduction of the Boeing 707 jet, air travel upshifted into mass ridership: The annual U.S. air passenger count hit 100 million, doubled from 1958. Boeing's 737 became the most ordered and most produced jet in history — ultimately more than 1,250 of them were airborne at any time, with one departing or landing somewhere every five seconds on average.

As airlines further democratized travel, once-exclusive locales welcomed a panoply of guests. In Hawaii, tourism revenue reached $161 million in 1960, for the first time bringing in more money than the island's leading staples, pineapples and sugar. Elvis Presley compounded the tropical allure with his 1961 hit movie *Blue Hawaii*. The appeal of sun and surf also made a cult hit of *The Endless Summer* (1966), in which two surfers travel the globe in search of the perfect wave. Yet even as travelers sought a sultry tropical paradise, they expected to get there quickly. Ocean liners had lost their mystique. In 1967, Cunard Lines announced that the *Queen Mary* and *Queen Elizabeth* had each lost $1.8 million that year and the company wanted to send them to the scrap heap.

◄◄ Italian Line, 1960   ► Ken-L-Products, 1960

1960 | **1960** | **1961**

Adventures and misadventures of college students on spring break in Florida come to screen in *Where the Boys Are*

Der Streifen *Dazu gehören zwei* handelt von den Abenteuern und Missgeschicken einiger Collegestudenten während der Ferien in Florida

Where the boys are conte les aventures et mésaventures des étudiants passant leurs vacances de Pâques en Floride

Paul Williams–designed futuristic Theme Building opens as restaurant at Los Angeles International Airport

Eröffnung des von Paul Williams entworfenen futuristischen Restaurants auf dem internationalen Flughafen von Los Angeles

Le « Theme Building » futuriste de Paul Williams ouvre en tant que restaurant à l'aéroport international de Los Angeles

Work begins on Albert Frey's Palm Springs Aerial Tramway, largest double reversible passenger tramway in world

Baubeginn von Albert Freys Palm Springs Aerial Tramway, der längsten Luftseilbahn der Welt

Début des travaux du Palm Springs Aerial Tramway, le plus grand téléphérique à double sens du monde

DER JETSET GIBT VOLLGAS

Moderne Verkehrsmittel sollten die Menschen näher zueinanderbringen, und das Flugzeug war das Gefährt der Wahl.

AM 25. MAI 1961 ERKLÄRTE PRÄSIDENT JOHN F. KENNEDY DER GANZEN WELT: „WIR WOLLEN ZUM MOND." Er versprach, dass Amerikaner am Ende der Dekade auf dem Mond stehen würden. Technologie galt als ein starkes, positiv besetztes Instrument. Nichts war unmöglich. Die New Yorker Weltausstellung 1964 verkündete freudig: „Eigentlich ist die Welt doch klein", und die 51 Millionen Besucher stimmten zu. Moderne Verkehrsmittel sollten die Menschen näher zueinanderbringen – und der Jet war das Gefährt der Wahl.

Sinnbild dieses berauschenden Optimismus war Eero Saarinens flügelartiger TWA-Terminal des Idlewild (später John F. Kennedy) Airport. Flugreisen besaßen nirgendwo sonst einen derartigen Reiz und Glamour wie in diesem Gebäude aus dem Jahr 1963. Das Kinopublikum ließ sich vom ersten Bond-Film *Dr. No* (*James Bond jagt Dr. No*, 1962) mit seinen zahlreichen Schauplätzen mitreißen, ein Reisebericht mit Sex-Appeal im Gewand eines Spionagethrillers. Und in Fellinis gefeiertem *La Dolce Vita* (*Das süße Leben*, 1960), einem Blick auf die Hautevolee der Via Veneto, trudelten die Berühmtheiten auf dem Flughafen von Rom nur so ein.

Braniff International Airways wandte sich an die Top-Werberin Mary Wells, bei deren bemerkenswerter Kampagne „End of the Plain Plane" Emilio Pucci, der vom Jetset bevorzugte Modeschöpfer, für die Stewardessen futuristische Uniformen kreierte – mit kühnen Mustern und „Astronautenhelmen" aus Plastik. Alexander Girard fiel die Aufgabe zu, die Maschinen, Wartezonen, Empfangsschalter und Ticketbüros aufzumöbeln. Hierzu tauchte er sämtliche Flächen in kräftige Farben, innen wie außen.

Doch Flugreisen waren nun nicht länger nur den Reichen vorbehalten. Für Geschäftsleute wurden sie zunehmend unverzichtbar. So startete Eastern Airlines 1961 einen Shuttleservice zwischen New York und Washington, D.C. – eine echte Revolution. Nun brauchte man nicht mehr zu reservieren und hatte auf den stündlichen Flügen garantiert einen Sitzplatz. Während die Geschäftsreisen rapide zunahmen, lancierte United Air Lines 1967 einen TV-Spot mit Hausfrauen als Revuegirls, die ihre geschäftlich verreisenden Männer singend baten, sie doch mitzunehmen („Take Me Along").

Dank Einführung der Boeing 707 waren die Flugreisen 1965 zum Massenmarkt geworden: Die Vereinigten Staaten zählten nun jedes Jahr 100 Millionen Flugpassagiere, doppelt so viele wie 1958. Die Boeing 737 wurde zum meistproduzierten Jet aller Zeiten – heute befinden sich jederzeit mehr als 1250 Maschinen in der Luft, und durchschnittlich alle fünf Sekunden startet oder landet eine irgendwo auf der Welt.

◄◄ Pan Am, 1964   Samsonite, 1963

1962

American Airlines and IBM partner to release Sabre, first airline electronic booking system

American Airlines und IBM präsentieren mit Sabre das erste elektronische Flugbuchungssystem

Partenariat entre American Airlines et IBM pour le lancement de Sabre, premier système de réservation électronique pour compagnies aériennes

1963

Opening of Mandarin Hotel's flagship in Hong Kong

Eröffnung des Mandarin Oriental, des Flaggschiffs der gleichnamigen Hotelkette, in Hongkong

Ouverture du fleuron des hôtels Mandarin à Hong Kong

1963

Pan Am flight bags reach iconic status

Pan-Am-Taschen werden zum Statussymbol

Les sacs de voyage Pan Am deviennent de vrais objets culte

Während Flugreisen für immer mehr Menschen erschwinglich wurden, fanden sich die unterschiedlichsten Gäste an den einstmals exklusiven Ferienorten ein. In Hawaii erzielte man 1960 mit dem Tourismus erstaunliche 161 Mio. $, erstmals mehr als mit den beiden Haupterzeugnissen Ananas und Rohrzucker. Mit *Blue Hawaii* (*Blaues Hawaii*, 1961) leistete Elvis Presley einen nicht unbedeutenden Beitrag. Die Verlockungen von Sonne und Wellen machten *The Endless Summer* (1966), in dem zwei Surfer auf der Suche nach der perfekten Welle um die Welt reisen, zum Kultfilm. Aber auch jene, die ein sinnliches Tropenparadies ansteuerten, wollten schnell hinkommen. Die Linienschiffe hatten ihren einstigen Nimbus eingebüßt. Cunard Lines gab bekannt, dass die *Queen Mary* und die *Queen Elizabeth* 1967 Verluste von je 1,8 Mio. $ eingefahren hatten. Die Ozeanriesen drohten auf dem Schrotthaufen zu landen.

Seattle World's Fair, 1962

1964

First ride of Japanese bullet train, Tokaido Shinkansen

Jungfernfahrt des japanischen Hochgeschwindigkeitszugs Tokaido Shinkansen

Lancement du Tokaido Shinkansen, train à grande vitesse japonais

1967

United Air Lines ad campaign features wives singing to businessmen husbands, "Take Me Along"

Werbekampagne von United Air Lines mit Frauen, die ihre viel fliegenden Männer singend bitten, sie doch mitzunehmen

La campagne publicitaire de United Air Lines présente des femmes chantant « Emmène-moi avec toi » à leurs maris hommes d'affaires

1967

U.S. air carriers begin announcing future Concorde flights to the general public; most will not materialize

US-Fluggesellschaften versprechen künftige Concorde-Flüge für alle – was weitgehend unerfüllt bleibt

Les compagnies aériennes américaines annoncent des vols en Concorde pour le grand public ; la plupart n'aboutiront jamais

LA JET-SET À PLEINS GAZ

Le voyage moderne allait rapprocher le monde entier, avec l'avion comme véhicule de prédilection.

LE 25 MAI 1961, LE PRÉSIDENT JOHN F. KENNEDY DÉCLARA À LA NATION ET AU MONDE ENTIER: «NOUS CHOISISSONS D'ALLER SUR LA LUNE». Le charismatique chef d'État promit que les Américains iraient sur la Lune avant la fin de la décennie. On considérait la technologie comme une grande force très positive. Tout devenait possible. En 1964, la Foire Internationale de New York proclama joyeusement «Le Monde est petit». Le voyage moderne allait rapprocher le monde entier, avec l'avion comme véhicule de prédilection.

Cet optimisme enivrant fut symbolisé par le terminal en forme d'oiseau stylisé conçu par Eero Saarinen pour la TWA à l'aéroport d'Idlewild, rebaptisé plus tard Kennedy Airport. Dans cette structure de 1963, voyager en avion n'avait jamais semblé plus glamour. Le public des cinémas se délecta de l'impétuosité d'un nouveau personnage globe-trotter dans *James Bond 007 contre Dr. No* (1962), véritable catalogue touristique sexy déguisé en film d'espionnage. Les spectateurs adorèrent aussi *La Dolce Vita* (1960) de Federico Fellini, un film sur l'élite sophistiquée de la Via Veneto, dont l'histoire était ponctuée par l'arrivée de célébrités à l'aéroport de Rome.

Braniff International Airways fit appel au génie publicitaire de Mary Wells Lawrence. En 1965, sa campagne «End of the Plain Plane» bénéficia des talents d'Emilio Pucci, le couturier favori de la jet-set, qui créa des uniformes futuristes pour les hôtesses, assortis de superpositions, de motifs audacieux et de casques «spatiaux» en plastique. Mary Wells collabora avec Alexander Girard pour relooker les avions, les salles d'embarquement, les comptoirs d'enregistrement et de vente de billets. Il satura de couleurs vives toutes les surfaces, à l'intérieur comme à l'extérieur.

Le voyage aérien n'était cependant plus réservé aux plus riches ou aux plus ambitieux. Les hommes d'affaires ne pouvaient désormais quasiment plus s'en passer. Eastern Airlines flaira le bon filon et lança en 1961 une ligne effectuant la navette entre New York et Washington qui révolutionna le voyage aérien. Les passagers n'avaient pas besoin de réservations ni de billets, et se voyaient garantir un siège sur les vols horaires. Face à la croissance rapide des voyages d'affaires, United Air Lines diffusa en 1967 une brillante campagne télévisée présentant une troupe de femmes en train de chanter « Emmène-moi avec toi » à leurs businessmen d'époux.

Avec l'arrivée du Boeing 707 en 1965, le nombre annuel de passagers aux États-Unis atteignit les 100 millions, soit le double du chiffre de 1958. Le Boeing 737 devint l'avion le plus produit de l'histoire aéronautique, à tel point qu'on en comptait plus de 1250 en vol simultané, avec un décollage ou un atterrissage toutes les cinq secondes dans le monde.

Des destinations autrefois exclusives accueillaient désormais toutes sortes de touristes. En 1960, les revenus du tourisme à Hawaï atteignirent les 161 millions de dollars, rapportant pour la première fois plus que les ananas et le sucre, principales ressources de l'île. Elvis Presley imposa le style tropical en 1961 dans *Sous le ciel bleu de Hawaï*. L'attrait du soleil et du surf transforma aussi en film culte le documentaire *The Endless Summer* (1966), qui suit deux surfeurs parcourant le monde en quête de la vague parfaite. Les voyageurs tenaient à se rendre rapidement dans les paradis tropicaux. Les paquebots avaient perdu de leur mystique. En 1967, la Cunard Line annonça que le *Queen Mary* et le *Queen Elizabeth* avaient chacun perdu 1,8 million de dollars cette année-là. Les majestueux navires s'apprêtaient à finir au rebut.

◄◄ TWA, 1963   ► American Airlines, 1960

1967

Opening of Hyatt Regency Atlanta, John Portman's influential hotel design based on multistory atrium

Eröffnung des Hyatt Regency Atlanta mit mehrstöckigem Atrium, ein revolutionäres Hoteldesign von John Portman

Ouverture du Hyatt Regency d'Atlanta, avec un design révolutionnaire de John Portman reposant sur un atrium de plusieurs étages

1969

In *If It's Tuesday, this Must Be Belgium*, an American tour group visits seven countries in 18 days

In *If It's Tuesday, This Must Be Belgium* absolviert eine Reisegruppe aus den USA sieben Länder in 18 Tagen

« Si on est mardi, c'est qu'on est en Belgique » : les touristes américains peuvent visiter sept pays en 18 jours

1969

In *Easy Rider*, a pair of bikers (Peter Fonda and Dennis Hopper) travel across country in search of America

In *Easy Rider* machen sich zwei Biker (Peter Fonda und Dennis Hopper) auf die Suche nach Amerika

Dans *Easy Rider*, deux motards (Peter Fonda et Dennis Hopper) traversent le pays en quête de l'Amérique

AMERICAN AIRLI
STEWARDESS
COLLEGE

Our weekend special
Lower fares in effect to May 31st

The long weekend seafari on ss United States is one of the most luxurious specials going. It goes to Europe about every two weeks. And from now to May 31st the fares are lower but fun runs high. When you sail with us you'll relax through 4½ days of gracious living. Once aboard you'll choose wines from the largest wine cellar afloat. Enjoy memorable dinners. Dance all night. Our Meyer Davis tempos have a way of coaxing the most reluctant. Take in a pre-release movie. Perhaps you'd like to play bridge, an excellent way to meet the kind of people you enjoy. Set your own pace—be as lazy or as lively as you like.

SAFETY INFORMATION. The ss United States, world's fastest ship, meets International Safety Standards for new ships developed in 1960.

s.s. UNITED STATES!
Top Resort between New York and Europe

For information and reservations call your Travel Agent or United States Lines, One Broadway, New York, N.Y. 10004.

◄◄ TWA, 1967

SS *United States*, 1968

The SS *United States* took the Blue Riband for fastest transatlantic crossing in 1952 and remained one of the most desirable ships that decade. But by the '60s, ocean liners struggled in a Jet Set world—where speed mattered most. Here, low fares are promised. Grand liners, like Cunard's *Queen Mary*, lost money every year.

Die SS *United States* eroberte 1952 das Blaue Band für die schnellste Atlantiküberquerung und blieb in der gesamten Dekade eines der gefragtesten Schiffe. Inzwischen aber hatten die Linienschiffe zu kämpfen – in einer vom Jetset bestimmten Welt, der es vor allem ums Tempo ging. Diese Anzeige lockt mit niedrigen Preisen. Ozeanriesen wie die *Queen Mary* von Cunard schrieben indes Jahr für Jahr rote Zahlen.

Le paquebot *United States* remporta le Ruban Bleu en 1952 pour la traversée la plus rapide de l'Atlantique et demeura l'un des navires les plus demandés au cours de la décennie. Dans les années 1960, la jet-set délaissa pourtant les paquebots car elle recherchait avant tout la vitesse. Cette publicité promet des tarifs bas. Même les plus beaux bateaux, comme le *Queen Mary* de la compagnie Cunard, perdaient de l'argent chaque année.

► Panagra, 1961

THE ONLY JET SERVICE 'ROUND SOUTH AMERICA

Only with Pan American and Panagra can you enjoy speedy Jet service down both coasts of South America. Go one way, return the other with the U.S. airline system that has 33 years of experience in Latin America.

No other airline system offers such a variety of Jet routes in South America from so many gateways in the U.S.A.

Choose first-class or low-fare service. From New York, down the West Coast of South America fly daily Jet without change of plane over the routes of National, Pan American and Panagra. On the East Coast, fly Pan Am Jet all the way.

Many preplanned *Pan Am Holidays* give you full benefit of favorable exchange rates in South American republics. They include Jet flights, fine hotels, sightseeing! Rates are surprisingly low. Free folder gives you full details. You will also enjoy the 128-page book, "How to Get the Most out of Your Trip to South America." For either or both write to Pan American, Dept. 152, Box 1111, New York 17. (Enclose 25¢ for the book.) See your Travel Agent or your nearest Pan American office.

PANAGRA · PAN AMERICAN

LET YOURSELF GOoooooo MEXICO

WESTERN AIRLINES

FRIENDLY ★ AMIGO FLIGHTS

WESTERN AIRLINES

FARES SO LOW YOU CAN'T SAY NO...

144.50 ROUND TRIP

EXCURSION FARE TAX FREE

WESTERN AIRLINES

AMIGO FLIGHTS

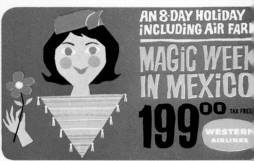

AN 8-DAY HOLIDAY INCLUDING AIR FARE

MAGIC WEEK IN MEXICO

199.00 TAX FREE

WESTERN AIRLINES

Saludos Amigos! Here's the biggest foreign travel bargain ever! Western's Amigo Flights on swift Jet/Powered Electra II's put you in Mexico City and return for just $144.50. That's right. It's round-trip —and it's tax-free. You'll like the bright Mexican atmosphere you'll find aboard, and the festive Mexican snacks. We think you'll like our night-flight schedule, too—because it saves you a night's hotel bill in the bargain, puts more pesos in your fun-purse.

Want even more fun on a budget? Take Western's "Magic Week in Mexico." 8 full days in Mexico City, Taxco, and Acapulco, for just $199.00, including round-trip air fare, hotels, sightseeing.

If you want to see Mexico in really high style, fly Western's 720B Fan/Jet Fiesta Flight. Nothing faster or finer. Just ask your Travel Agent. Get all the details on Western's wonderful vacations to Mexico now, and let yourself go—Mexico!

Fares shown above are from Los Angeles or San Diego. From San Francisco, round-trip excursion fare is $167.36; "Magic Week in Mexico" is $221.86.

WESTERN AIRLINES

◄ Western Airlines, 1963

► Sabena, 1961

►► Hilton Hotels, 1964

Conrad Hilton expanded his empire by offering a standardized level of accommodations. He saw his international hotels as islands of America in exotic foreign lands. Hilton described them as emissaries for American values—transparent, welcoming, and modern. U.S. travelers liked them because they felt familiar.

Conrad Hilton baute sein Imperium aus, indem er einen genau festgelegten Hotelstandard anbot. Er betrachtete seine internationalen Hotels als amerikanische Inseln in exotischen fremden Ländern, als Botschafter der amerikanischen Werte – transparent, einladend und modern. Auf Amerikaner wirkten sie sehr vertraut und dadurch angenehm.

Conrad Hilton étendit son empire en proposant un niveau d'hôtellerie standardisé. Il considérait ses hôtels internationaux – transparents, accueillants, modernes – comme des ambassadeurs des valeurs américaines, des îlots d'Amérique au milieu de pays étrangers et exotiques. Les voyageurs américains les appréciaient car ils s'y sentaient comme chez eux.

Why do well-traveled people travel Sabena? "Flight-seeing" via helicopter is only part of it. People who know Europe know Sabena shows it off best: with the world's only 3-speed fleet of Boeing "Intercontinental" jets, *Caravelle "Continental" jets and Sikorsky helicopters; with a special savoir-faire that extends to and through Europe, Africa and the Middle East. Next trip ... fly Sabena. Le service Belgique–c'est magnifique!

*(soon)
Ask your Travel Agent to book you Sabena all the way... or simply call Sabena Belgian World Airlines. More than 200 offices in the principal cities of the world

The new Hilton Hotels: in San Francisco, Washington, D

San Francisco. Next trip to the Golden Gate, take in the breathtaking new 18-floor San Francisco Hilton. If you're driving you'll be delighted to find you can drive your car *upstairs*, along a unique interior ramp which leads to the first seven guest floors. And on the upper floors: swimming pool, tropical gardens, four floors of cabaña rooms overlooking the p the delights of resorting right in San Francisco's business, shoppi entertainment district. Next to Airport Bus Terminal and just two from Union Square. Free parking for registered guests. Opening N

nolulu, Mayaguez, Guadalajara, Tel Aviv.

Mayaguez, Puerto Rico. Overlooking Puerto Rico's third largest city from a beautifully-landscaped 25-acre hilltop site is the new Mayaguez Hilton. Here you can swim in the fresh water pool, play tennis, romp on nearby beaches. The deep sea fishing is some of the best in the world, too. Ample facilities here for meetings and conventions—for those of a mind to mix business with pleasure. Opening spring, 1964.

gton, D.C. The 1240-room Washington Hilton will esort living to the city's convenient downtown em-area. For your relaxation: tennis courts, Olympic-wimming pool, gardens, children's wading pool, four restaurants. For business and diplomatic functions: gton's finest ballroom seating 4300, plus 36 other meeting and dining rooms. Opens early 1965.

Guadalajara, Mexico. Amid the centuries-old fiestas and colorful bullfights of Mexico's second city—just one hour by air from Mexico City—stands the new Guadalajara Hilton. You'll enjoy air-conditioned comfort in all of the hotel's 250 rooms, superb Mexican and international cuisine, exciting local color, year-round swimming in the hotel pool and 12-month springtime climate. Opening spring, 1964.

Honolulu. With Diamond Head to the west and ad to the east, facing a white, coral-free beach, in ed area, is the magnificent new Kahala Hilton, just It offers sailing, surfing, golf, tennis or just plain in the sun. Dine in the Maile Lanai beside a lagoon, nally on the Hala Terrace near the swimming pool. ooners invited? Encouraged is the word.

Tel Aviv. Right on the edge of the Mediterranean, close to Tel Aviv's business and shopping center, near its theatres and night life, is the dramatic new 403-room Tel Aviv Hilton. Every Hilton comfort is being planned for this new hotel, opening in the spring of 1965—from individually air-conditioned rooms and suites with balconies to a salt water swimming pool.

Rome.
And you thought Irish only flew to Ireland.

You didn't know that Rome is an Irish city! So are twenty-four other European cities outside the Emerald Isle. On your way, going or coming, we can arrange a splendid vacation bargain...Ireland itself, for no extra air fare! Ask your Travel Agent.

OFFICES IN: New York, Boston, Chicago, Cleveland, Dallas, Detroit, Washington, D.C., Los Angeles, Philadelphia, San Francisco, Montreal, Toronto, Vancouver.

IRISH
AER LINGUS
IRISH INTERNATIONAL AIRLINES

◄ Irish Aer Lingus, 1969

The Plaza, 1967

The Plaza, celebrated as one of world's best hotels since opening in 1907, was perhaps most famous in the mid-1960s. Truman Capote gave his famous masked Black and White Ball there in 1966, and everyone who was anyone went. This ad demonstrates the Plaza's chic panache in that era.

The Plaza, seit seiner Eröffnung im Jahr 1907 als eines der weltbesten Hotels gefeiert, stand vielleicht Mitte der 1960er-Jahre auf dem Gipfel seines Ansehens. Truman Capote gab hier 1966 seinen berühmten Maskenball „Black and White", und jeder, der etwas darstellte, ging hin. Diese Anzeige zeugt vom Chic des Plaza in jener Ära.

Le Plaza, encensé comme l'un des meilleurs hôtels du monde depuis son ouverture en 1907, atteignit sans doute l'apogée de sa gloire au milieu des années 1960. En 1966, Truman Capote y donna son fameux Bal masqué en Noir et Blanc qui vit danser tout le bottin mondain. Cette publicité démontre le grand chic et le panache du Plaza à cette époque.

When you come to New York this summer, catch a great show. The Plaza.

Stay where it's liveliest on the eve of your crossing. Till the children arrive from camp. While you take in the Broadway hits that you missed.
Midnight ambience afterglows the Oak Room. The tom-tom throbs in Trader Vic's. Cupid mit schlag sweetens the Palm Court evenings. And the Persian Room stars come out between dances.
That's the great thing about The Plaza. It turns on in the summer. Like the air-conditioning.

THE PLAZA
HOTEL CORPORATION OF AMERICA

Don't turn off the vacation fun when the sun goes down

Aren't vacations all about escaping routine? And monotony? Shouldn't each day be filled with excitement? And surprise? And anticipation? And happiness and fun?

Well, your vacation fun can follow you right into a Best Western Motel. Because the only monotonous feature about us is excellence... hard-earned, rigidly enforced excellence that's your assurance of superb accommodations in 800 cities coast to coast.

From then on, Best Western is a world of 1043 different surprises. Maybe tonight it's a Mediterranean setting that starts you dreaming . . . tomorrow night you go Western Style, pardner . . . the next night you luxuriate in a French Provincial atmosphere.

Whatever the mood, it's fun. Whether it's fine food, or swimming, or recreational facilities, or children's play areas, your Best Western host serves it in a way that makes every Best Western night a happy and memorable experience.

Join the 27 million individualists who'll go Best Western this year. Contact any Best Western Motel and make a free advance reservation for your first night on the road. Or send coupon for our new 1968 Travel Guide.

Be an Individualist! Go where new experiences await you every night.

THE BEST Western MOTELS

FREE! 1968 TRAVEL GUIDE... complete information on 1043 individually-owned motels that make Best Western the world's largest network of fine motels.
Best Western, 2910 Sky Harbor Blvd., Phoenix, Arizona 85034

Name_____
Address_____
City/State/Zip_____

Best Western, 1968

► Air New Zealand, 1967

►► TWA, 1964

Fly the Flight Fantastic

AIR NEW ZEALAND's 27 years' experience brings to perfection a blend of South Seas decor and service called the Flight Fantastic. The Flight Fantastic features exquisite cabin decor, Polynesian dishes and fabulous drinks prepared by Don the Beachcomber. The Flight Fantastic's wide choice of destinations includes both gateways to the South Pacific — Hawaii and Tahiti.* Stop over in both. Go one way, return the other. See magnificent New Zealand and make it home base for all your Down Under tours that will make this the trip of a lifetime. AIR NEW ZEALAND's DC-8 Five Star Jets leave from Los Angeles twice a week for New Zealand and Australia via Honolulu; once a week via Tahiti. All are evening departures. For full details see your travel agent, AIR NEW ZEALAND, or our General Sales Agents, BOAC. For free colorful literature, write AIR NEW ZEALAND, Dept. H6, 510 West Sixth Street, Los Angeles, California 90014.

AIR NEW ZEALAND ➤

THE AIRLINE THAT KNOWS THE SOUTH PACIFIC BEST.

WITH QANTAS AND BOAC OFFERS 16 FLIGHTS WEEKLY DIRECT FROM THE UNITED STATES TO THE SOUTH PACIFIC.

Los Angeles, Honolulu, Auckland, Wellington, Christchurch, Sydney, Melbourne, Brisbane, Fiji, New Caledonia, Norfolk Island, Samoa, Singapore, Hong Kong.* Tahiti service begins late 1967.

ALITALIA'S ITALY

"Take me along"

Or how to turn your husband's next business trip into a swinging time for both of you.

How long has it been since you danced together?

Explored a city together?

Or been alone together?

United will show you the way.

With our "Take Me Along" fare, that saves you up to ⅓ of a wife's fare.

With our credit card, that lets you charge it.

We'll even give you side-by-side seating. Naturally.

What's more, you can get reduced hotel and car rental rates on the weekend in most cities. So you can stay over and stretch your trip.

Sound good?

Say "Take Me Along" tonight.

Then dust off your suitcase, and call United or your Travel Agent.

"But, Don, we can't dance on the plane!"

fly the friendly skies of United.

Try the lyrics below on your husband.
They're from the Broadway Musical "Take Me Along."

"*Take me a-long, if you love-a-me. Take me a-long, if you love-a-me. Take me a-long with you.*

My heart will ride, sweet and glo-ri-ous, high a-bove the throng, if you will take me a-long with you."

United Air Lines, 1967

As more businessmen traveled, United Air Lines produced a sparkling campaign about wives traveling along. The effervescent TV ad featured a chorus line of wives, in Pop Art–colored chorine costumes, imploring their husbands to "Take Me Along." Michael Cimino, who later won an Oscar for the Vietnam War movie *The Deer Hunter*, was the unlikely director.

Im Zuge zunehmender Geschäftsreisen brachte United Air Lines einen prickelnden Fernsehspot über mitreisende Ehefrauen, die – in poppige Revuekostüme gekleidet – ihre Männer im Chor anflehen, sie doch mitzunehmen („Take Me Along"). Regie führte niemand anderes als Michael Cimino, der später für den Spielfilm *The Deer Hunter* (*Die durch die Hölle gehen*) den Oscar gewann.

Comme les hommes d'affaires voyageaient toujours plus, United Air Lines diffusa une brillante campagne mettant en scène les épouses qui les accompagnaient. Un spot TV pétillant présentait une troupe de femmes vêtues de costumes aux couleurs Pop Art en train de chanter « Emmène-moi avec toi ». Michael Cimino, plus tard oscarisé pour son film sur la guerre du Vietnam *Voyage au bout de l'Enfer*, en était le réalisateur.

▶ United Air Lines, 1967

Our Song.
(To be sung to your husband before his next business trip.)

Take Me Along

From the Broadway musical "Take Me Along."

"Take me a - long if you love - a - me. Take me a - long if you love - a - me.

Take me a - long with you——. My heart will ride, sweet 'n glo-ri-ous

high a-bove the throng if you will Take me a - long with you——."

And this'll sound like music to his ears, too!
United's "Take Me Along" fare will save up to one-third of a wife's fare both ways.
We'll let you charge it with our credit card.
We'll give you side-by-side seating.
And what's more, you can even get reduced hotel and car rental rates on the weekend in most cities.
So you can stay over and stretch your trip.
Why not try our song?
It's really a pretty sound idea.
First Step: Call United or your Travel Agent.

fly the friendly skies of United.

"Dave, they're playing our song."

The former Miss Butterfingers.

Two months ago Sheri Woodruff couldn't even balance a cup of coffee.

But she was friendly, intelligent, and attractive. And wanted more than anything else to be a great stewardess.

So we put her to the test. (We take only one out of thirty applicants.) Five and a half weeks at United's Stewardess School.

We taught Sheri how to serve a gourmet dinner, how to soothe a first-flyer, how to apply everything from make-up to first-aid. Along with courses like aviation principles and geography.

Today she can warm a baby's formula with one hand and pour four cups of coffee with the other.

But more than that.

She's still the same Sheri Woodruff. Friendly, intelligent, attractive. And wants more than anything else to be a great stewardess.

She is.

"This is what I call a balanced meal."

fly the friendly skies of United.

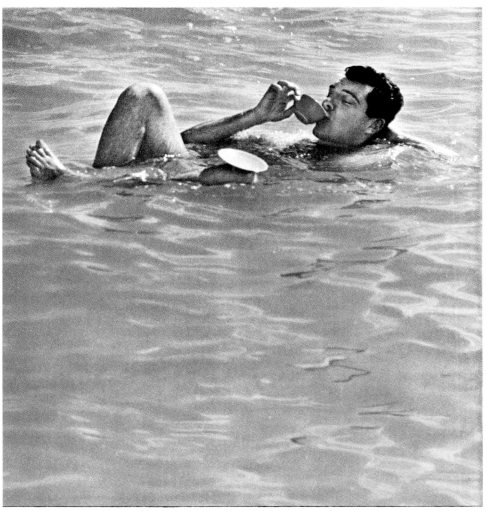

High tea on the Dead Sea.

Israel's Dead Sea is the lowest spot on earth.

You go down 1,292 feet through a moonscape to get there. Cups and saucers float on it. So do bridge tables. And so do you: You pop right to the top.

You can float clear to Sodom, if you like.

Nearby, in Beersheba, there's a newer source of water: a swimming pool in the land of Abraham.

Everywhere in Israel, the Bible is part of the scenery.

You can skin dive at Ashkelon, at the beach where Samson met Delilah. At the Sea of Galilee, you can watch fishermen toss nets for St. Peter's fish as they did 2,000 years ago.

Afterwards, you can visit a kibbutz with a concert hall and a banana plantation, enjoy St. Peter's fish for dinner and pay the bill with your Diners' Club card.

Where else in the world?

THE NEW

707 ★ ASTROJET*

AMERICAN AIRLINES OPENS *JET AGE: STAGE II*, introducing the world's most advanced, most dependable jetliner in daily transcontinental passenger service. ■ American's fleet of Astrojets will bring you a new standard in jet performance by the airline that's *first choice of experienced travelers.* ■ The 707 Astrojet easily outperforms all other airliners. Its more powerful Jet-Fan engines represent the most significant advance in commercial aviation since the development of the original jet engine. ■ Powered by these new Jet-Fan engines, American's 707 Astrojet has the thrust for quicker take-off, using far less runway than the best of standard jets. You'll enjoy a wonderful sense of confidence as you experience the Astrojet's exceptional rate of climb—as you relax on the jet that cruises smoothly, easily, within the transonic range at speeds unsurpassed by any jetliner in the world ■ In keeping with a 25-year tradition of leadership, American is proud to be first in bringing you this new dimension in jet travel—this historic new era in air transportation.

AMERICAN AIRLINES
America's Leading Airline

*Service mark of American Airlines, Inc.

Funny. You don't look like a French restaurant.

Ah, but don't let our disguise fool you.

Any time you're on a Pan Am®Jet Clipper,® you're dining out with *Maxim's of Paris.* The same *Maxim's* you'll find along Rue Royale in Paris.

The same *Maxim's* that dreams up the finest international menu that ever got off the ground.

Plan to fly First-Class President Special. Or Rainbow Economy. Either way, you can go just about anywhere in the world.

And you'll know you're flying the very best there is: the world's most experienced airline.

Ask a Pan Am Travel Agent to make your reservations. And make it dinner for two.

Pan Am makes the going great.

World's most
experienced airline.

◄ Pan Am, 1968

Convair, 1960

This jet with exclusively first-class seating seems
to be taking a page from the early deluxe "flyer"
service on trains in the early part of the century.
It was increasingly common for businessmen
to bring their wives along on a work trip—and
extend stays a few extra days for a quick
getaway.

Dieser exklusive Business-Class-Jet macht
offenbar Anleihen bei den luxuriösen „Flyer"-
Schnellzügen aus der Frühzeit des Jahrhunderts. Immer mehr Geschäftsleute nahmen ihre
Ehefrauen mit auf die Dienstreise – um für eine
kurze Auszeit ein paar Tage anzuhängen.

Cet appareil configuré entièrement en classe
affaires semble s'inspirer des premiers voyages
de luxe proposés par les compagnies ferroviaires au début du siècle. Il était de plus en plus
courant que les hommes d'affaires emmènent
leurs femmes avec eux lors de leurs déplace-
ments professionnels, et qu'ils prolongent leur
séjour par une petite escapade à deux.

Lockheed JetStar, 1961   ▸ McDonnell Douglas, 1969   ▸▸ TWA, 1962

Boeing, 1962

This Boeing ad looks remarkably like the logo of The Four Seasons, the sophisticated boîte in the legendary Seagram Building in New York. The restaurant served as an elite clubhouse for Jet Set plutocrats, including Madison Avenue panjandrums, who nursed old fashioneds in the Mies van der Rohe–Philip Johnson–designed bar.

Diese Anzeige von Boeing ähnelt auffallend dem Logo des Nobelrestaurants The Four Seasons im legendären Seagram Building in New York, einem elitären Clubhaus schwerreicher Jetsetter – wie der Bonzen der Madison Avenue –, die in der von Mies van der Rohe und Philip Johnson entworfenen Bar ihre Old-Fashioned-Cocktails schlürften.

Cette publicité Boeing rappelle vraiment le logo du restaurant The Four Seasons, rendez-vous chic installé dans le légendaire immeuble Seagram de New York. Ce restaurant faisait office de club pour les plutocrates de la jet-set, gros bonnets de Madison Avenue y compris, qui venaient biberonner leurs « old fashioneds » dans le bar conçu par Mies van der Rohe et Philip Johnson.

▶ Trailways, 1962

WHEN YOU GO BY BUS . . RIDE WITH US. Enjoy the modern comforts of highway travel without the bother of traffic and fatigue . . . And for the finest of travel pleasures, join a TRAILWAYS ESCORTED TOUR or let us plan a fun packed INDIVIDUAL TOUR for you and your family. Beautiful color vacation folders will be sent to you upon request. Trailways offers you . . . "The Easiest Travel on Earth."

TRAILWAYS

1012 14th Street, N. W., Washington, D. C.

SPECIAL SERVICES

Charterbus ★ Package Express ★ Study Groups ★ Five Star Luxury Service

SEATTLE WORLD'S FAIR 1962

It's April 21, 1962, in Seattle...World's Fair time! The curtain's going up on the 21st Century...and on the most exciting preview ever seen. This is Seattle's spectacular Space-Age World's Fair, where the epic of man's journey into the next 100 years will unfold for you. What's ahead? How will man live? What will he see? Look at cities in the year 2000, see homes whose walls are jets of air, where cordless appliances work for you, cars ride without wheels, TV wrist telephones speed everyday communications. Time and distance will disappear in the gigantic, pillar-less Coliseum Century 21 jutting eleven stories up from the heart of the fair. You'll soar past the moon into outer galaxies—no space suit, no gravity, in the $9 million complex of the United States Science Pavilion. You will discover the secrets of the future in these six gleaming buildings rising above lighted fountains and courtyard pools. But it's not all the story of man's great tomorrows. Much of this $80 million show will be a glittering world of today. Dine atop the towering 60-story Space Needle which revolves to view Mt. Rainier, the Olympic and Cascade Ranges. Stroll Boulevards of the World filled with the sights and sounds of foreign lands. Thrill to the Monorail as it whisks you the mile from downtown Seattle in 95 seconds.

Expo 67, 1967

Expo 67 was the century's most successful world's fair, with more than 50 million visitors. "Man and His World" focused on housing. Popular exhibits included the U.S. pavilion, a geodesic dome by Buckminster Fuller, and Habitat 67, a landmark housing complex. But most popular was the Soviet Union pavilion, which drew 13 million visitors.

Mit über 50 Millionen Besuchern war die Expo 67 die erfolgreichste Weltausstellung des Jahrhunderts. Das Wohnen stand im Mittelpunkt von „Der Mensch und seine Welt". Besonderen Zulauf fanden der US-Pavillon in Form einer geodätischen Kuppel von Buckminster Fuller sowie Habitat 67, ein bahnbrechender Wohnhauskomplex. Absoluter Publikumsmagnet war jedoch der Pavillon der Sowjetunion mit 13 Millionen Besuchern.

Avec plus de 50 millions de visiteurs, l'Expo 67 fut l'exposition internationale qui remporta le plus de succès au XXᵉ siècle. Avec pour thème « Terre des Hommes », elle s'intéressait au logement. Parmi les pavillons plébiscités figuraient celui des Américains, un dôme géodésique de Buckminster Fuller, et Habitat 67, un complexe d'habitation révolutionnaire, mais le pavillon le plus visité fut celui de l'Union soviétique, qui attira 13 millions de personnes.

Look what the Russians are building, just 40 miles from the U.S.A.

As an American, you should look into it.

The U.S.S.R. hopes you will. You're invited to step in, and take a look at life in the Soviet Union. Meet the people, see what they do for a living in Vladivostok or Minsk, and how they have fun.

What kind of ideas do the Russians have, about education, medicine, housing, industrial development, space exploration? You'll find out here. In the great Lunar Hall, they'll treat you to an eerie expedition to the moon. On the way, you'll discover what the feeling of weightlessness is like (just how is their secret).

And on the lighter side of things, you can see what the Moscow miss is wearing, at a fashion parade. Browse through nearby stores that sell the identical items you'd find in shops in Leningrad or Kiev. Drop into the 600-seat cinema and watch a Russian movie. And wind up in one of

the restaurants, where you can take your pick of specialties from every part of the country. (Incidentally, they've ordered 20 tons of sturgeon, eight tons of caviar and 28,000 litres of vodka, just for starters.)

The place to come for this fascinating experience is the U.S.S.R. Pavilion at Expo 67, Montreal, Canada. It's just across the way from the giant U.S.A. Pavilion — another world of wonders. And a few steps away, the French, British, Italians, Japanese, Canadians — more than two thirds of all the nations on earth — spread before you the best of their arts and culture. The latest in science and technology. Their past, present and future.

In all, some 70 governments have spent hundreds of millions of dollars to make Expo 67 the greatest world exhibition of them all, and the first of its kind on this continent. It opens on April 28th, for six wonderful months only. You'll find it the experience of a lifetime.

Start planning now. Expo 67 admission tickets at reduced advance prices save you up to 29%, are on sale at banks, department stores, American Express offices, and wherever you see the Expo 67 sign.

Accommodations in Montreal? No need to worry. LOGEXPO, the official accommodation bureau, guarantees you a place to stay, at government controlled prices. Reserve now — just write, mentioning dates, type of accommodations preferred, and the number in your party, to LOGEXPO, Expo 67, Harbor City, Montreal, Quebec, Canada. Or see your travel agent.

Or write for free Expo 67 vacation planning information to Expo 67 Information Services, 150 Kent St., Ottawa, Ont. Canada.

MONTRÉAL, CANADA
The Universal and International Exhibition of 1967
Montreal, Canada/APRIL 28-OCTOBER 27, 1967

HOLIDAY / MARCH

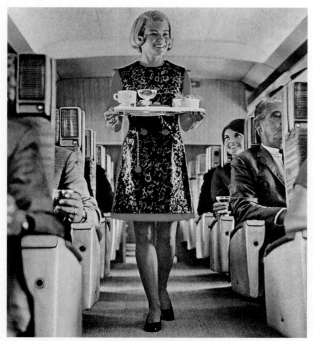

No floor show
just a working girl working

This is for real. No model. No put-on smiles. Her name is Carol Koberlein. But it could be Virginia White. Or Linda Epping. Or any one of the other 1724 stewardesses who work for Delta. In her new chic outfit, she looks like anything

but a stewardess working. But work she does. Hard, too. And you hardly know it. Even when she spreads Delta's new eight-course, 1200-mile first-class meal before you. Or a Tourist meal that seems anything but economical. Next

trip, come see our working girls work. It's no floor show. But it's funny how you get to feel like a leading man. Delta Air Lines, Inc., General Offices, Atlanta Airport, Atlanta, Ga. 30320 ≙DELTA

Delta is ready when you are!

Delta Air Lines, 1966

▶ American Airlines, 1968

▶▶ Braniff, 1966

Mary Wells's campaign for Braniff International Airways aimed to show that travel on this airline was unlike any other—special even for jaded business travelers. She brought in the influential designer Alexander Girard, known for his chic, important restaurants, and he saturated the jets with strong colors—inside and out.

Mary Wells Kampagne für Braniff International wollte zeigen, dass diese Fluglinie etwas ganz Besonderes bot – sogar für übersättigte Vielflieger. Alexander Girard, der für seine schicken Restaurantausstattungen berühmte Designer, tunkte die Jets in kräftige Farben – innen wie außen.

La campagne conçue par Mary Wells pour Braniff International visait à prouver que cette compagnie aérienne n'avait rien à voir avec les autres, même pour les voyageurs d'affaires les plus blasés. Elle collabora avec l'influent designer Alexander Girard, réputé pour son travail de décoration dans les grands restaurants, qui satura les avions de couleurs vives à l'intérieur comme à l'extérieur.

Think of her as your mother.

She only wants what's best for you.
A cool drink. A good dinner. A soft pillow and a warm blanket.
This is not just maternal instinct. It's the result of the longest
Stewardess training in the industry.
Training in service, not just a beauty course.
Service, after all, is what makes professional travellers prefer American.
And makes new travellers want to keep on flying with us.
So we see that every passenger gets the same professional treatment.
That's the American Way.

Fly the American Way
American Airlines

The end of the plain plane, explained.

It's obvious that our airplanes look—well—different than other airplanes.

Not so obvious, perhaps, is why we made them look different.

You see, all airplanes look pretty much the same. And it was this monotonous *sameness* that we were trying to get away from.

(Oooooh, how those 3-hour plane rides can bore you. Especially if you're a guy who travels for his living.)

Painting our airplanes different colors was a step in the other direction.

We also changed the fabrics on the seats, the uniforms our hostesses wear, our passenger loun

food service.
he list goes on and on.
fact, we've made 17,543 changes in our airline
r. (This includes the small ones, like the
er satisfying change we made in the package that
s the sugar for your coffee.)
nce no other airline has ever gone to so much

trouble before, you may still not understand
why *we* did.
   But even if you can't understand it, you can relax
and enjoy it.

Braniff International
United States Mexico South America

Andy Warhol and Sonny Liston fly on Braniff. (When you got it-flaunt it.)

We see them a lot, and they always enjoy themselves. They like our vigor, and they like our verve. Good. That's why we paint our planes different colors and make the interiors so plush. That's why we pick the sharpest girls we can find and dress them in Pucci's.

And that's why the whole airline harps on service, service, service. Make every drink ice cold. Serve every meal piping hot. Bring them a magazine. Fling them a pillow. Get them there on time. And guess what. It works. They keep coming back. They keep asking their Travel Agent: "Does Braniff fly there too?" Put me on it.

Braniff International Airways, 1967 ► British Overseas Airways Corporation, 1962

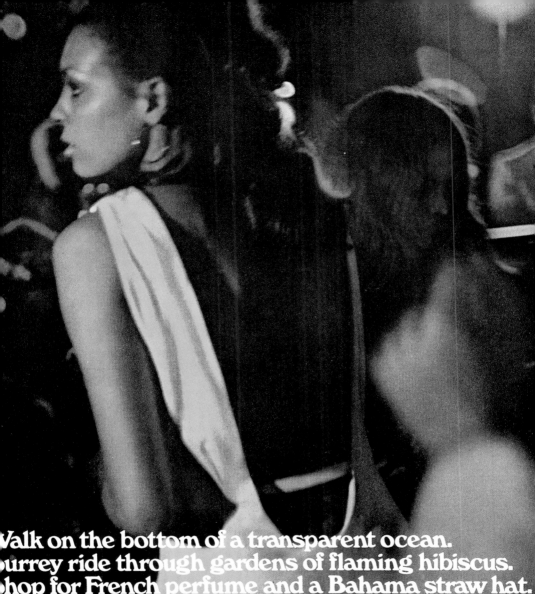

Walk on the bottom of a transparent ocean.
Surrey ride through gardens of flaming hibiscus.
Shop for French perfume and a Bahama straw hat.
Or close a place down and go wake the sun up.

If all the things you can do in the world, you can do more of them in the

BAHAMAS
Nassau · Freeport · 700 Out Islands

Now shining in the Las Vegas sky, the newest, most brilliant star—a unique, self-contained resort in the middle of the glitter and glamor of the Strip. So fantastic that it out-dazzles Las Vegas itself.

This star they call
THE DESERT INN.

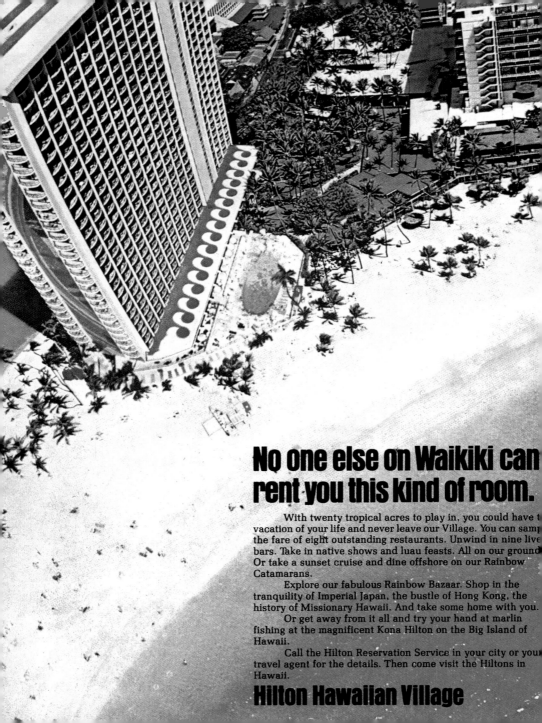

Big settings.
Big time. Big value.

Big Sunsets. Those typical glowing sunsets south of the equator are as big as the scenes they colour. For anyone who has visited South Africa there is the memory of evening after evening of glorious sunsets.
Big Variety. For every evening, great reddened settings of mountains, river valleys, umbrella-treed game reserves and surf-washed coastlines in contrast with modern city skylines. Every day brings its new, exciting attractions.
Big Value. With such an incredible variety of things to see and do, there is one other great attraction – the low cost. Exciting

game touring from as little as $9,46 per night. Hotels with all the comforts from $8,60 per night to $20,64 and upwards for 5-star status. Discover that there is still a place

on earth where a plate-sized grilling steak costs under $3,44, in fact, where even the cost of travel, entertainment or almost anything one can buy in a shop just hasn't caught up with the rest of the world.

Big Welcome. Yet one of the best things in South Africa is free – the traditional warm hospitality. Ask the many who come.

South African Tourist Corporation
New York: Rockefeller Center, 610 Fifth Avenue, New York 10020.
Los Angeles: Suite 721, 9465 Wilshire Boulevard, Beverly Hills, California 90212. **Toronto:** Suite 1001, 20 Eglinton Avenue West, Toronto M4R 1K8.
Also at: Chicago, London, Frankfurt, Amsterdam, Paris, Milan, Zürich, Sydney, Salisbury, Tokyo, Buenos Aires and Pretoria.
S/1

Please send me full colour literature to plan my South African tour.

Name_____

Address_____

South Africa.
A world tour in one country.

KMP 4132/e

Million-miler Capt. Shin (2nd from the left) and airline personnel offer you a unique blend of American efficiency and Korean hospitality.

We fly with an American accent.

Sure, the crew looks Korean. But step aboard and the feeling is wonderfully American.

Because flying Korean Air Lines is a lot like flying an American airline. That's a Korean custom you'll truly appreciate.

It means that our planes are built in America. A luxurious fleet of wide-bodied 747's and DC-10's.

It means that Korean crews that fly them, fly them American. With a majority of the pilots and navigators licensed by the Federal Aviation Authority. And every wide-bodied jet captain a 15 year veteran. A skilled million-miler.

It means that our lovely stewardesses speak American. Pampering you in the style to which you'd love to be accustomed.

And it means no surprises. We want your flight with us to be as comfortable, secure and pleasant as we can make it.

So we give you superb American efficiency, combined with superb Korean service. A custom we take wherever we go, and wherever you go with us.

At Korean Air Lines, we do cherish the unique, the exciting, the exotic.

But only on the ground. Not in the air.

And that's an accent we know you'll understand.

FLY KOREAN

Korean Air Lines, 1977   ▶ Host International Restaurant, 1976

The only international restaurant in Los Angeles with its own airport.

You've seen it a hundred times.

The Theme Building at Los Angeles International Airport. You might know there's a restaurant inside. You might not know there's a superb restaurant inside. With convenient, complimentary valet parking outside.

Let us tempt you to try it:

Our dinner menu contains sumptuous appetizers, soups, salads, entrees and beverages from twenty-two countries. Prepared by continental chefs from carefully collected and tested international recipes. All served in the classic French manner by a captain and internationally-costumed waitresses.

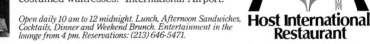

To complement your meal, you will find a bountiful selection of fine imported and domestic wines.

Our rich Columbian coffee brews slowly at your table while you dine. For an encore, our dessert menu offers a tempting array of world-renowned pastries, ice cream and flaming crepes.

The beautiful harp, piano and violin music you hear throughout the restaurant is live. And the unique view from your table is a continuous airshow provided by 36 airlines.

Next time you're looking for an unusually elegant dining experience at moderate prices, don't look in the usual places.

Look for our place right in the center of Los Angeles International Airport.

Open daily 10 am to 12 midnight. Lunch, Afternoon Sandwiches, Cocktails, Dinner and Weekend Brunch. Entertainment in the lounge from 4 pm. Reservations: (213) 646-5471.

Host International Restaurant

JAL made it to the top by helping tourists <u>know</u> the Orient instead of merely looking at it.

On JAL's Happi Holidays tours of the Orient, you see a world where the sights aren't merely variations of the sights back home. Where wonders are commonplace. Where splendor is taken for granted.

Even more important, JAL's Orient is a place where you gather memories of the people you've met as well as the sights you've seen.

These are the reasons why more people tour the Orient with JAL than with any other airline.

Come to JAL's Orient. See your travel agent or send us the coupon to-day. And come <u>this</u> year, not next year or the year after. As an old Japanese proverb says, "Time flies like an arrow." Another suggests, "The day you decide to do a thing is the best day to do it."

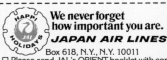

We never forget how important you are.

JAPAN AIR LINES

Box 618, N.Y., N.Y. 10011

☐ Please send JAL's ORIENT booklet with com tour listings and ORIENT TOUR BUYING GUID

Name_____

Address_____ City_____

State_____ Zip_____ Tel.___

My Travel Agent_____K

NS 05

Now.
Japan's most beautiful gardens blossom aboard the world's most spacious jet.

Starting this summer, during EXPO '70, the first of eight JAL 747 jets will cross the Pacific. Outside it will be the biggest commercial airliner ever developed. Inside it will feature the most extraordinary decor ever created.

For each section of this spacious jet will have one of our country's most beautiful features: the Japanese Garden.

First Class will have the elegant Garden of Wisteria with an upstairs lounge called Teahouse of the Sky.

In Economy, you can choose from one of three unique sections: the Gardens of Wild Orange, Pine or Maple. Each has decor all its own and individualized service. More comfort, too. Thanks to wider seats and stand-up headroom everywhere.

There will be wide screen movies, stereo entertainment and the finest of international beverages and cuisine.

Best of all, there will be more of what legends are made of – our lovely hostesses in kimono who will pamper you throughout your flight. And introduce you to the subtle delights of Japanese comfort and hospitality.

Your travel agent is now accepting reservations for our maiden flight. Be one of the first to reserve a seat in the garden of your choice on our new 747 Garden Jet.

JAPAN AIR LINES 747 Garden Jet

◄ Japan Air Lines, 1978

Japan Air Lines, 1970

In the 1970s, *mass* began to overwhelm *class* in air travel. Bigger planes, packed with more people, filled the skies. The exclusivity and glamour of flying was becoming a thing of the past. This ad focuses on Japan Air Lines' serene and courteous service, but that was growing harder to deliver.

In den 1970er-Jahren siegte bei den Flugreisen allmählich *Masse* über *Klasse*. Immer größere, mit immer mehr Menschen vollgestopfte Flugzeuge bevölkerten den Himmel. Exklusivität und Glamour des Fliegens waren bald dahin. Die Anzeige betont den entspannt heiteren Service von Japan Air Lines, doch der ließ sich zunehmend schwerer erbringen.

Dans les années 1970, la *masse* commença à surpasser la *classe* en matière de voyage aérien. De plus gros avions encore plus bondés emplissaient le ciel. Le luxe et le glamour du voyage en avion appartenaient désormais au passé. Cette publicité se concentre sur le service discret et courtois de Japan Air Lines, mais il était de plus en plus difficile d'assurer de telles prestations.

Cooks Travel Cheques, 1970

Club Méditerranée, 1973

The sybaritic enticements of a Club Med are clear. These resorts offered an all-inclusive stay, where everything was part of the package—a sort of stationary cruise. The clubs had been developed for a singles scene, but family-oriented resorts also flourished in the '70s. Parents could have a vacation while their children were occupied elsewhere.

Ein Club Med geizt nicht mit seinen Reizen. Sein All-inclusive-Angebot enthält praktisch alles und bietet so etwas wie eine ortsfeste Kreuzfahrt. Die Clubs waren eigentlich für Singles geschaffen worden, doch in den 1970er-Jahren florierten auch die familienorientierten Resorts. Hier konnten die Eltern Urlaub machen, während man sich anderswo um ihre Kinder kümmerte.

Les charmes sybaritiques du Club Med sont clairs. Ses clubs proposaient des séjours où tout était inclus dans le forfait, comme dans une sorte de croisière stationnaire. Les clubs avaient été conçus pour une clientèle de célibataires, mais les complexes destinés aux familles explosèrent aussi dans les années 1970. Les parents pouvaient profiter de leurs vacances sans avoir leurs enfants dans les pattes.

► British Overseas Airways Corporation, 1971

We enjoy flying from Los Angeles to visit our kissing cousins down under. So will you.

Every time one of our BOAC VC10s takes off from Los Angeles on its direct flight to Sydney or Melbourne, Australia, it's like visiting family.

Perhaps that's why so many passengers tell us they enjoy our service across the South Pacific so much. Enjoy the comfort of really being looked after. The courtesy of being waited on. Even the old-fashioned delight of having someone say please and thank you.

But we mustn't take all the credit for making a lengthy trip pass so pleasantly. Our VC10 jets are a joy to fly. With a roomier economy seat than any comparable jet. Overhead lockers to keep your hand luggage out of your lap. And a blissfully peaceful cabin, thanks to four powerful rear-mounted engines that leave all the noise behind.

So be our guest next time you visit our Australian family "out west." For reservations and details of our many and varied tours of the Pacific see our Travel Agents in and around Los Angeles. Or call us. British Overseas Airways Corporation, 1901 Ave. of the Stars, Los Angeles, California 90067. Tel: 272-8866.

➤ BOAC takes good care of you.

British Overseas Airways Corporation

HIGHWAY TRAVEL

$ 000 ⁹⁹ $ 000 ⁹⁹
VENTA TOTAL   VENTA TOTAL

More Mileage for your dollar in MEXICO

MEXICAN GOVERNMENT DEPARTMENT OF TOURISM
National Tourism Council
625 North Michigan Ave. Chicago III., 60611
3106 Wilshire Blvd. Los Angeles, Cal.
630 Fifth Ave. New York, N. Y. 10020
Av. Juárez No. 92. México 1, D. F.

◄ Mexican Government Tourist Office, 1979   Mexican Government Department of Tourism, 1972

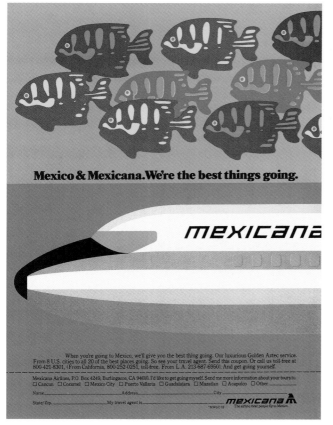

Mexico & Mexicana. We're the best things going.

mexicana

When you're going to Mexico, we'll give you the best thing going. Our luxurious Golden Aztec service. From 8 U.S. cities to all 20 of the best places going. So see your travel agent. Send this coupon. Or call us toll-free at 800-421-8301, (From California, 800-252-0251, toll-free. From L.A. 213-687-6950). And get going yourself.

Mexicana Airlines, P.O. Box 4249, Burlingame, CA 94010. I'd like to get going myself. Send me more information about your tours to:
☐ Cancun ☐ Cozumel ☐ Mexico City ☐ Puerto Vallarta ☐ Guadalajara ☐ Mazatlan ☐ Acapulco ☐ Other _____

Name _____ Address _____ City _____
State/Zip _____ My travel agent is _____
*NWGC16   *mexicana*
The airline most people fly to Mexico

Mexicana, 1972

This Mexicana Airline ad may talk of Aztec service, but the design is dramatically contemporary. The colors are acid-trippy, with the pop of Pop Art. This stylish design signals the sophistication of the multilayered Mexican culture that awaits travelers who go there.

Auch wenn in dieser Anzeige der Fluglinie Mexicana von aztekischem Service die Rede sein mag, ist sie doch überaus modern gestaltet. Ihre modernen Farben zeugen vom Schwung der Pop-Art. Das raffinierte Design gibt einen Vorgeschmack auf das Raffinement der vielschichtigen mexikanischen Kultur, die den Reisenden erwartet.

Cette publicité de Mexicana Airline évoque peut-être le passé aztèque du pays, mais son design est absolument contemporain. Les couleurs acidulées possèdent tout le pep du Pop Art. Ce design élégant annonce la complexité de la culture mexicaine attendant les voyageurs.

▸ Mexicana, 1979

MEXICO &
MEXICANA

"I'm a Brazil nut."
—Marlene Dietrich

Says Miss Dietrich: "Brazil isn't a country. It's a poem." In Brazil, you find the most beautiful baroque churches in the Western Hemisphere and the world's most startling modern architecture. You experience the pandemonium of a Rio soccer game and the perfect peace of jungle rivers where the only sounds are birds. Brazil is yesterday — colonial towns that have remained in the 17th century. And it's Brasilia, a surrealist's dream. But mostly it's people who move like dancers, talk like songs, and smile like friends. Travelers don't simply like Brazil, they go mad for the place.

You can spend seven nights in Rio for as little as $630, including roundtrip airfare, first class hotel, full Brazilian breakfasts, transfer services and sightseeing tours. See your travel agent.*

For this beautiful 112 page booklet on Brazil call 800-447-4700 (toll free).
In Illinois call 800-322-4400.
In Canada write: Brazilian Travel Offer, Box 3900, Peoria, Ill. 61614.

Ⓔ EMBRATUR/BRAZILIAN TOURISM AUTHORITY

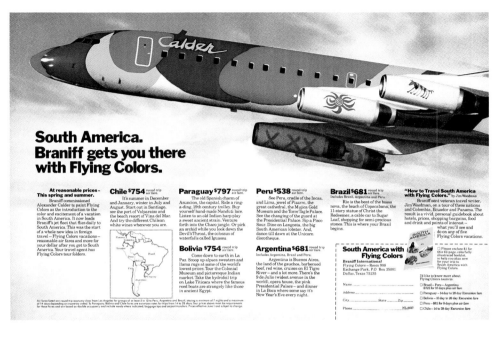

◄ Brazilian Tourism Authority, 1979

Braniff, 1974

Advertising legend Mary Wells, as part of her continuing campaign to show Braniff International as unique, brought in the artist Alexander Calder. He used one of the company's jets as a canvas. "Flying Colors" became an international sensation. Calder's bright colors also connected strongly with Latin America, where Braniff flew regularly.

Für ihre Dauerkampagne, die Einzigartigkeit von Braniff International herauszustellen, konnte Mary Wells den Künstler Alexander Calder gewinnen. Er nutzte einen der Jets gleichsam als Leinwand, und seine „Flying Colors" wurden zur internationalen Sensation. Calders leuchtende Farben verweisen zudem deutlich auf Lateinamerika, das von Braniff regelmäßig angeflogen wurde.

Dans le cadre de sa campagne présentant Braniff International comme une compagnie unique en son genre, la légende de la publicité Mary Wells fit appel à l'artiste Alexander Calder. Il utilisa l'un des avions de la compagnie comme une toile. « Flying Colors » fit sensation dans le monde entier. Les couleurs vives de Calder créaient aussi un lien fort avec l'Amérique Latine, régulièrement desservie par Braniff.

SCANDINAVIA. SHE'S MORE THAN YOU DREAMED.

NORWAY: Ancient Viking Ships. Majestic Fjords. A park that's a sculpture museum. Picturesque open air markets. Scenic railroad trips through the mountains. Unique Stave Churches. Unrivaled deep-sea and fresh water fishing.

DENMARK: Hans Christian Andersen Fairytale Villages. Hamlet's Castle. Tivoli Gardens. The Little Mermaid. The Royal Palace. Bicycling, Sailing, Swimming, Life-seeing.

SWEDEN: Skansen, the outdoor live folk museum. The beautiful ride through the Gota Canal. Stockholm and its 30,000 Islands. Lappland's picturesque people, unchanged in centuries. Dance Festivals under the Midnight Sun. Underground gourmet restaurants centuries old.

Scandinavian Tourist Board, 1974   ▶ Air New Zealand, 1970

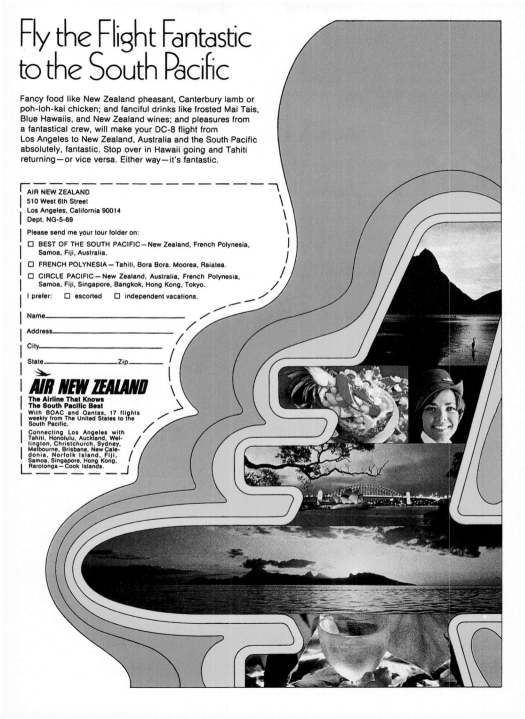

Fly the Flight Fantastic to the South Pacific

Fancy food like New Zealand pheasant, Canterbury lamb or poh-loh-kai chicken; and fanciful drinks like frosted Mai Tais, Blue Hawaiis, and New Zealand wines; and pleasures from a fantastical crew, will make your DC-8 flight from Los Angeles to New Zealand, Australia and the South Pacific absolutely, fantastic. Stop over in Hawaii going and Tahiti returning—or vice versa. Either way—it's fantastic.

AIR NEW ZEALAND
510 West 6th Street
Los Angeles, California 90014
Dept. NG-5-69

Please send me your tour folder on:

☐ BEST OF THE SOUTH PACIFIC—New Zealand, French Polynesia, Samoa, Fiji, Australia.

☐ FRENCH POLYNESIA—Tahiti, Bora Bora. Moorea, Raiatea.

☐ CIRCLE PACIFIC—New Zealand, Australia, French Polynesia, Samoa, Fiji, Singapore, Bangkok, Hong Kong, Tokyo.

I prefer: ☐ escorted ☐ independent vacations.

Name_____

Address_____

City_____

State_____Zip_____

AIR NEW ZEALAND

**The Airline That Knows
The South Pacific Best**
With BOAC and Qantas, 17 flights weekly from The United States to the South Pacific.

Connecting Los Angeles with Tahiti, Honolulu, Auckland, Wellington, Christchurch, Sydney, Melbourne, Brisbane, New Caledonia, Norfolk Island, Fiji, Samoa, Singapore, Hong Kong, Rarotonga—Cook Islands.

Memphis is ready for take-off. Come soar with us. You'll like our style, because we're looking for the same thing you are: expansion. What's more, the very assets that make us look good are the ones that will mean profit and growth for your company in Memphis.

Memphis has big-city production capabilities: manpower, land, low utility rates, location, and fine transportation facilities. Big-city office space, too. And we offer all this without big-city problems. As Memphis grows bigger, it grows better —carefully maintaining a friendly, relaxed way of life.

If you'd like the best of two worlds for your people, write on your company letterhead to **Dan Dale,** Director of Industrial Development, Memphis Light, Gas and Water, Box 388C, or **Ralph U. Thomas,** Mgr., Economic Development Dept., Memphis Area Chamber of Commerce, Box 224R, Memphis, Tennessee 38101.

MEMPHIS

CITY OF MANAGEABLE SIZE

Disneyland Hotel, 1970

When Disneyland opened in 1955, construction had proven so costly that Walt Disney arranged for a developer to build the Disneyland Hotel. To finally gain control, the Walt Disney Company bought the developer's entire company in 1989. When Disney World opened, Disney owned and operated 23 of the 35 resorts and hotels there.

Als Disneyland 1955 eröffnet wurde, hatte man bereits so viel Geld ausgegeben, dass Walt Disney den Bau des Disneyland Hotel aus der Hand gab. Um die Kontrolle zu gewinnen, erwarb die Walt Disney Company 1989 gleich die gesamte Firma des Bauunternehmers. Als Disney World seine Pforten öffnete, besaß und betrieb Disney 23 der 35 dortigen Resorts und Hotels.

Quand Disneyland ouvrit en 1955, les travaux s'avérèrent si onéreux que Walt Disney demanda à un promoteur immobilier de construire le Disneyland Hotel. Pour en reprendre le contrôle, Walt Disney Company racheta l'entreprise du promoteur en 1989. À l'ouverture de Disney World, Disney possédait et gérait 23 de ses 35 hôtels et clubs de vacances.

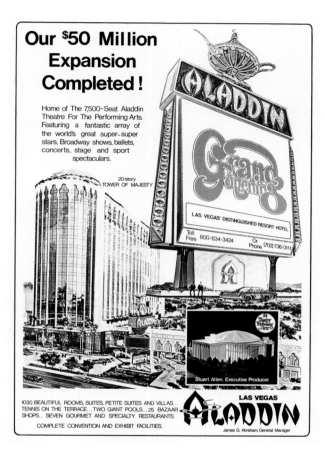

Our $50 Million Expansion Completed!

Home of The 7,500-Seat Aladdin Theatre For The Performing Arts. Featuring a fantastic array of the world's great super-super stars, Broadway shows, ballets, concerts, stage and sport spectaculars.

20-story TOWER OF MAJESTY

LAS VEGAS' DISTINGUISHED RESORT HOTEL

Grand Opening

Toll Free 800-634-3424 Or Phone (702) 736-0111

Stuart Allen, Executive Producer

1030 BEAUTIFUL ROOMS, SUITES, PETITE SUITES AND VILLAS... TENNIS ON THE TERRACE... TWO GIANT POOLS... 25 BAZAAR SHOPS... SEVEN GOURMET AND SPECIALTY RESTAURANTS.

COMPLETE CONVENTION AND EXHIBIT FACILITIES.

LAS VEGAS ALADDIN

James G. Abraham, General Manager

Aladdin Hotel, 1976

The Aladdin Hotel, one of the first big casinos on the Strip, had a string of owners, often later revealed as mob-related. The re-opening party this time featured Neil Diamond, reportedly paid $750,000 for two shows. By 1979, one of these new owners was indicted in a million-dollar kickback scam. The hotel was again up for sale.

Das Aladdin Hotel, eines der ersten großen Kasinos auf dem Strip, hatte mehrere, oft nicht ganz lupenreine Eigentümer. Star dieser Wiedereröffnungsparty war Neil Diamond, der für zwei Auftritte angeblich 750 000 $ kassierte. Einer der neuen Eigentümer wurde 1979 im Rahmen eines millionenschweren Provisionsbetrugs angeklagt. Und das Hotel stand erneut zum Verkauf.

L'hôtel Aladdin, l'un des premiers grands casinos du Strip, avait de nombreux propriétaires qui s'avéraient souvent liés à la Mafia. Cette fois, sa soirée de réouverture accueillit Neil Diamond : on dit qu'il aurait touché 750 000 dollars pour deux représentations. En 1979, l'un des nouveaux propriétaires fut inculpé dans une affaire de pots de vin de plusieurs millions de dollars. L'hôtel fut mis en vente une fois de plus.

▶ Hilton Hotels, 1979

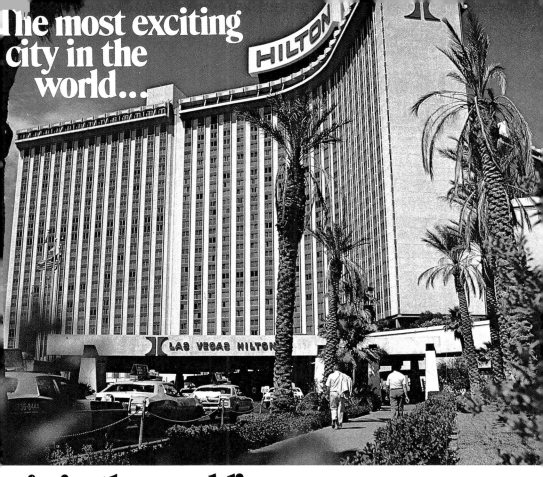

The most exciting city in the world...

...is in the world's most exciting city !!

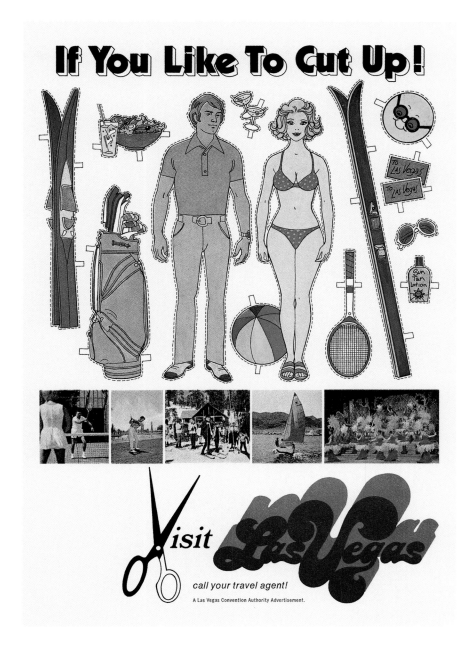

Las Vegas Convention Authority, 1973 ▶ Las Vegas Convention Authority (Bob Peack), 1973

LAS VEGAS

We tackle 24 out of 26 N.F.L. teams.

fly the friendly skies of United.

"You Can't Win Them All."

◄ United Air Lines, 1972

►► American Airlines, 1971

The '70s opened with the first flight of the Boeing 747. This two-level jumbo jet is two times the size of a 707. The ad compared its first-class section to an ocean liner, but air travel time to Europe was a fraction of what it was on a ship. Mass-market travel had taken off – literally.

Die Siebziger starteten mit dem ersten Flug der Boeing 747 alias Jumbojet. Dieses Großraumflugzeug war zweimal so groß wie die 707. Auch wenn die Anzeige den Komfort der ersten Klasse mit dem eines Linienschiffs vergleicht, benötigte man für einen Flug nach Europa doch nur noch einen Bruchteil der Zeit. Und mit den Pauschalreisen ging es steil nach oben – wortwörtlich.

Les années 1970 s'ouvrirent sur le premier envol du Boeing 747. Ce « jumbo jet » à deux niveaux est deux fois plus gros que le 707. La publicité comparait sa première classe à celle d'un paquebot, même si on pouvait rejoindre l'Europe infiniment plus vite qu'en bateau. Le tourisme de masse avait littéralement décollé.

► Hertz, 1976

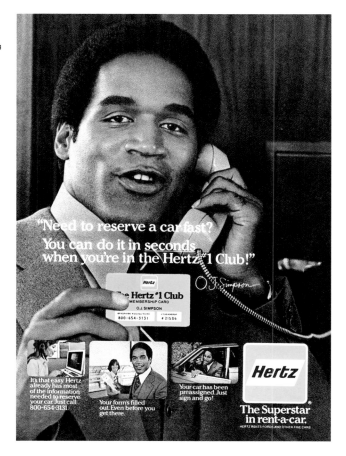

American Airlines
The plane with

Coach Lounge.

No matter where you've been in the world, you've never gone in comfort like this. From our spacious new Coach Lounge, with its stand-up bar, all through the plane and up the stairs, to our totally redesigned first class lounge. It's a new standard in flying comfort. The American Airlines 747 LuxuryLiner. First of all, in coach, there's a lounge bigger than most living rooms.

It's a place where you can mingle, make new friends, have a snack, have some fun. Enjoy being sociable, or just enjoy the space. No other airline has anything like it. And back down the aisle at your seat, we've rearranged the rows. So besides getting **more leg room and sitting room,** you'll have more getting up room when you try out the lounge. If you're flying first class, why not call ahead

New 747 LuxuryLiner no competition.

First Class Lounge.

and **reserve a table for four.**
You can wine and dine with
friends, do a little business,
or maybe play some bridge.
And a floor above is our beautiful
new first class lounge.
A plush, intimate spot where
you can socialize over after-
dinner liqueurs or champagne.
And for everybody on transcontinental flights,

there's an added service. Flagship Service.
Featuring Polynesian food. Special warming
wagons to keep your food piping hot.
And pretty new outfits for our stewardesses.
So if you like going places to see things,
this new airplane is something to see.
Every one of our 747s is now a LuxuryLiner.
And all of the extra comforts won't cost
you an extra cent.
For reservations call us or your Travel Agent.

American Airlines 747 LuxuryLiner

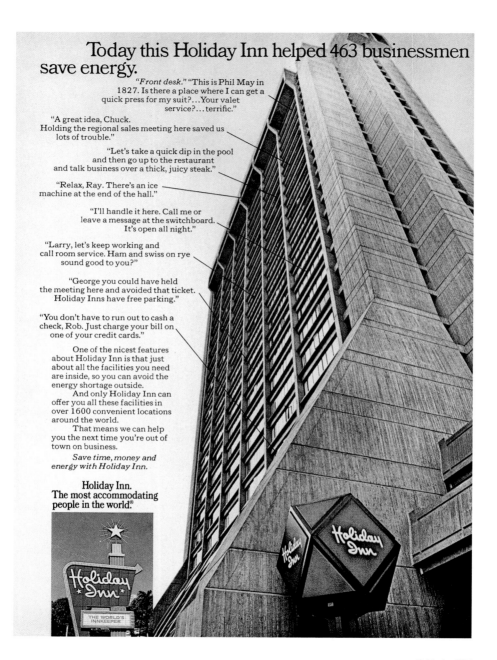

Today this Holiday Inn helped 463 businessmen save energy.

"Front desk." "This is Phil May in 1827. Is there a place where I can get a quick press for my suit?...Your valet service?...terrific."

"A great idea, Chuck. Holding the regional sales meeting here saved us lots of trouble."

"Let's take a quick dip in the pool and then go up to the restaurant and talk business over a thick, juicy steak."

"Relax, Ray. There's an ice machine at the end of the hall."

"I'll handle it here. Call me or leave a message at the switchboard. It's open all night."

"Larry, let's keep working and call room service. Ham and swiss on rye sound good to you?"

"George you could have held the meeting here and avoided that ticket. Holiday Inns have free parking."

"You don't have to run out to cash a check, Rob. Just charge your bill on one of your credit cards."

One of the nicest features about Holiday Inn is that just about all the facilities you need are inside, so you can avoid the energy shortage outside.

And only Holiday Inn can offer you all these facilities in over 1600 convenient locations around the world.

That means we can help you the next time you're out of town on business.

Save time, money and energy with Holiday Inn.

Holiday Inn.
The most accommodating people in the world.®

THE WORLD'S INNKEEPER

Holiday Inn, 1974

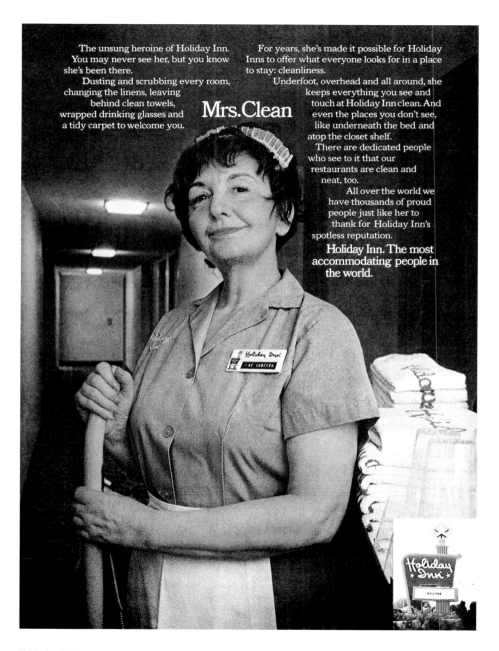

The unsung heroine of Holiday Inn. You may never see her, but you know she's been there.

Dusting and scrubbing every room, changing the linens, leaving behind clean towels, wrapped drinking glasses and a tidy carpet to welcome you.

For years, she's made it possible for Holiday Inns to offer what everyone looks for in a place to stay: cleanliness.

Underfoot, overhead and all around, she keeps everything you see and touch at Holiday Inn clean. And even the places you don't see, like underneath the bed and atop the closet shelf.

There are dedicated people who see to it that our restaurants are clean and neat, too.

All over the world we have thousands of proud people just like her to thank for Holiday Inn's spotless reputation.

Mrs. Clean

Holiday Inn. The most accommodating people in the world.

Holiday Inn, 1972

In Chicago, Hyatt's a 700-foot column of Oriental kites rising through spanning bridges and hanging gardens. In Atlanta, Hyatt's glass bubble elevators glide through a park 24 stories tall.

In Knoxville, Hyatt's an Aztec pyramid. In Toronto, a tower of shimmering glass.

Hyatt's got butler service in San Francisco. A lounge that orbits Houston. The largest swimming pool in Acapulco.

And the toll free number gets you information and reservations at any Hyatt Hotel. Call your Travel Agent. Or Hyatt. And get it all.

HYATT HOTE

800-228-9000 Gets You Hyatt

Hyatt Hotels, 1972

In 1967, Hyatt opened the world's first atrium hotel, changing the look of the hospitality industry. The architect John Portman structured the building around a dramatic multi-story atrium. The view down from the sleek glass elevators was jaw-dropping. The chain flourished throughout the '70s—nationally and internationally.

Als Hyatt 1967 das weltweit erste Atrium-Hotel eröffnete, war ein neuer Look geschaffen. Der Architekt John Portman machte ein imposantes, mehrgeschossiges Foyer zum Mittelpunkt des Gebäudes, und die eleganten gläsernen Aufzüge boten einen einfach phänomenalen Blick hinab. Die Hotelkette florierte während der gesamten 1970er-Jahre, national wie international.

En 1967, Hyatt ouvrit le premier « hôtel atrium » du monde et transforma le visage de l'industrie hôtelière. L'architecte John Portman structura l'édifice autour d'un atrium spectaculaire de plusieurs étages. La vue depuis les ascenseurs en verre était à couper le souffle. La chaîne prospéra tout au long des années 1970, aux États-Unis comme à l'étranger.

▶ Hyatt Hotels, 1975

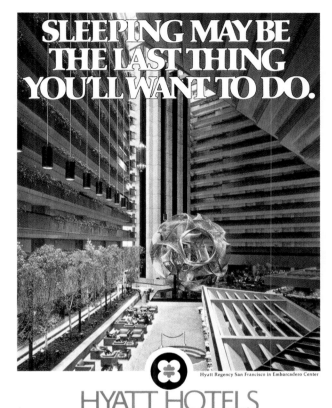

SLEEPING MAY BE THE LAST THING YOU'LL WANT TO DO.

Hyatt Regency San Francisco in Embarcadero Center

HYATT HOTELS
800-228-9000 gets you 57 Hyatt Hotels world wide. Toll free.

"THE JOURNEY IS THE DESTINATION."
– DAN ELDON

« LE VOYAGE EST LA
DESTINATION. »
– DAN ELDON

„DIE REISE IST DAS ZIEL."
– DAN ELDON

1980

1999

JOINING THE CROWD

*Mass travel encouraged exclusivity at the high
end, and boutique hotels became all the rage.*

**THE 1978 AIRLINE DEREGULATION ACT ENDED ALL RESTRICTIONS ON ROUTES ON
JANUARY 1, 1982.** That year, domestic airfare regulation ended. Long-established airlines faced
strong competition from nimble new rivals with less-powerful unions. It was telling that the decade
opened with *Airplane!*, a zany spoof of every airline disaster movie ever made. Meanwhile, a new
sort of airline, People Express, no-frills and low-cost, began service out of Newark Airport. At the
opposite end of the spectrum, Richard Branson's luxury-obsessed Virgin Atlantic Airways began
flying between Newark and London's Gatwick in 1984, and was profitable that first year. It was the
once-flourishing air carriers that had trouble. For example, Braniff International Airways closed up in
1982. Ultimately nine major airlines folded.

During this same period, a new kind of hotel emerged: the intimate yet stylish boutique hotel.
Guests could choose their brand of bottled water, even the pillow they would sleep on. It began when
Ian Schrager and Steve Rubell, the former owners of New York nightclub Studio 54, opened Morgans
Hotel in New York in 1984. It was so chic, no apostrophe was needed. This Andrée Putman-designed
hotel changed the rules of the hospitality industry. They followed up with a bigger success, the
Royalton, in 1988. Every detail here was planned by Philippe Starck. The cool, dark lobby became the
hottest cocktail lounge in New York.

But the wealthy were, as usual, on to the next thing. If grand hotels felt musty and boutique
hotels chichi, then ultra-exclusive eco-conscious enclaves like the Aman Resorts appeared. These
small, sumptuous hotels emphasized natural surroundings. Amanpuri, the flagship, opened in
Phuket, Thailand, in 1988.

Las Vegas responded by becoming family friendly. More than 14.2 million visitors came to the gambling capital in the first 11 months of 1986 alone. Hotels there were now supersized. In 1989, the visionary gaming impresario Steve Wynn opened the Mirage, the largest private hotel in the world, with 3,303 guest rooms. The cost: a half-billion dollars. It was fully booked.

Las Vegas was, in a sense, offering all-inclusive vacations. Its hotels served a guest's every need, like a cruise ship. As people's daily lives grew busier, they clearly wanted every detail taken care of—so vacations really could be vacations. No wonder, then, that the number of cruise passengers to the Caribbean more than doubled between 1980 and 1990—growing to 7.8 million from 3.8 million.

Aside from that, in the '80s speed mattered. While air travel boomed, it was not only about bargain airlines. The private jet was increasingly common, a kind of family car for the superrich.

AT A CENTURY'S END, NOSTALGIA IS OFTEN THE FASHION. So filmmakers probably thought it was a good idea to remake *Sabrina*, the 1954 Audrey Hepburn confection about a charming chauffeur's daughter and two wealthy, if very different, brothers. In the 1995 version, it is bizarre that the brother who is a powerful businessman makes a big deal out of going to Paris. After all, he owns a private jet and lives in New York, where commercial jets take off for Paris from three local airports virtually every hour. It's odd that he *hasn't* been to *Paris*.

By the 1990s, getting on an airplane was like boarding a bus—if less enjoyable. Travel was quick and superconvenient. In 1994, after decades of planning, high-speed trains finally started running through the Channel Tunnel. The project cost doubled from its original estimate to £9.5 billion. But trains now took two hours 15 minutes between Paris and London.

Mass travel encouraged exclusivity at the high end, and boutique hotels became even more the rage. Ian Schrager opened the Paramount in New York in 1990; headed south for a $20-million makeover of the Delano, a 1947 Miami Beach streamline moderne hotel, in 1995; then out to Los Angeles to revamp the Mondrian on the Sunset Strip, in 1996. Boutique hotels even caught on in

1980

1982

1982

Airplane! spoofs every airport disaster movie ever made

Airplane! nimmt jeden je gedrehten Flugkatastrophenfilm auf die Schippe

Y a-t-il un Pilote dans L'Avion ? parodie tous les films de catastrophe aérienne jamais tournés

The Go-Go's release hit single "Vacation"

The Go-Go's präsentieren ihre Hitsingle „Vacation" (Urlaub)

Les Go-Go's sortent le tube « Vacation »

Braniff International Airways closes shop

Braniff International Airways schließt die Pforten

La compagnie Braniff International Airways dépose le bilan

Paris, the city of the grandest hotels. In 1991, the Costes brothers opened Hôtel Costes, and it became one of the City of Light's brightest spots.

Still, mass-market travel kept growing. In 1999, less expensive versions of boutique hotels appeared. The Starwood chain, owner of St. Regis hotels, launched W, while Andre Balazs, who owned high-end hostelries like the Chateau Marmont on the Sunset Strip, opened the first Standard. JetBlue Airways, with its budget fares, was announced the same year.

And travel transformed Las Vegas, as the age demographics shifted downward. Las Vegas was the fastest-growing city in America, particularly for retirees. But the city's median age plummeted after Peter Morton opened the Hard Rock Hotel & Casino in 1995. Younger visitors used it as their beachhead.

Modern art and architecture also influenced travel patterns. Art cognoscenti turned San Sebastian, Spain, into a travel Mecca when Frank Gehry's stunning Guggenheim Museum opened in nearby Bilbao in 1997. In 1996, Thermal Baths opened in the sleepy Swiss hamlet of Vals. The design by Peter Zumthor, who later won a Pritzker Prize, garnered attention—and a waiting list. Major art exhibitions, like those in Venice, Italy, and Kassel, Germany; as well as big art fairs in Basel, Switzerland, and Miami were Stations of the Cross for devoted art followers.

It seemed almost a metaphor when Pamela Harriman, the U.S. ambassador to France, died during her morning swim at the Ritz in Paris in 1997. Pamela Digby Churchill Hayward Harriman had traveled far. A former English debutante, she married multimillionaire diplomat W. Averell Harriman, who controlled the Union Pacific Railroad and had built Sun Valley, the first U.S. ski resort. The belle of many an Atlantic crossing, whose charm had attracted a string of wealthy and powerful beaus, Pamela Harriman had morphed into a Jet Set power player. Yet she died at the Ritz, the grande dame of grand hotels, which had opened before the 20th century, in 1898. In a way, this could be viewed as more than the death of one person. Harriman's death marked the passing of an entire way of life—and travel.

◄◄ United Air Lines, 1985

1984

1984

1984

With air travel now mainstream, airlines begin to design more subdued, business-like cabins

Flugreisen gehören inzwischen zum Alltag, und so greift man zu eher verhaltenen, geschäftsmäßigen Interieurs

Face à la démocratisation du voyage en avion, les compagnies aériennes conçoivent des cabines plus neutres

Virgin Atlantic Airways begins service between Newark and Gatwick and is profitable in first year

Virgin Atlantic Airways beginnt mit der Strecke Newark–Gatwick und macht bereits im ersten Jahr Gewinn

Virgin Atlantic Airways commence à assurer la liaison entre Newark et Gatwick et devient rentable dès la première année

First Embassy Suites hotel opens, Overland Park, Kansas; chain targets businessmen by making every room a suite

Overland Park in Kansas, erstes Embassy Suites Hotel mit ausschließlich Suiten, soll Geschäftsleute ansprechen

Ouverture du premier hôtel Embassy Suites à Overland Park, Kansas : la chaîne attire les hommes d'affaires en proposant des suites

BAD IN DER MENGE

Pauschalreisen förderten die Exklusivität
des Topsegments, und Boutiquehotels waren
der letzte Schrei.

MIT INKRAFTTRETEN DES AIRLINE DEREGULATION ACT VON 1978 AM 1. JANUAR 1982 FIELEN SÄMTLICHE EINSCHRÄNKUNGEN BEZÜGLICH DER FLUGPREISE, -ROUTEN UND -PLÄNE WEG. Neue flexible Fluglinien mit weniger gewerkschaftlichem Einfluss wurden den etablierten Airlines zur ernst zu nehmenden Konkurrenz. Eingeläutet wurde die Dekade bezeichnenderweise mit *Airplane!* (*Die unglaubliche Reise in einem verrückten Flugzeug*, 1980), einer irrwitzigen Persiflage auf sämtliche je gedrehten Flugzeugkatastrophenfilme. Auf dem Flughafen von Newark, New Jersey, nahm unterdessen mit People Express eine neuartige Fluglinie ohne Schnickschnack und mit niedrigen Preisen den Betrieb auf. Am anderen Ende des Spektrums begann die von Luxus angetriebene Virgin Atlantic Airways von Richard Branson 1984 mit Flügen von Newark nach London-Gatwick und war gleich im ersten Jahr profitabel. Probleme hatten indes die einstmals florierenden Fluglinien. So musste Braniff International Airways 1982 dichtmachen. Letztlich überlebten neun größere Fluglinien nicht.

Derweil entwickelte sich eine neue Art von Herberge: das intime und doch stilvolle Boutiquehotel. Als Gast konnte man die Tafelwassermarke und sogar die Art des Kopfkissens selbst auswählen. Alles begann 1984, als Ian Schrager und Steve Rubell, einstige Eigentümer des New Yorker Nachtclubs Studio 54, das Morgans Hotel in New York eröffneten. Es war so schick, dass man sogar auf den Apostroph im Namen verzichten konnte. Dieses von Andrée Putman designte Hotel sollte die Regeln der Beherbergungsindustrie verändern. Schrager und Rubell ließen 1988 mit dem Royalton einen noch größeren Hit folgen, der bis ins letzte Detail die Handschrift von Philippe Starck trug und dessen coole, dunkle Lobby zur heißesten Cocktaillounge von New York wurde.

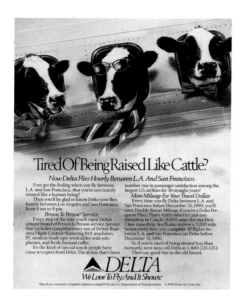

Tired Of Being Raised Like Cattle?

Now Delta Flies Hourly Between L.A. And San Francisco.

Ever get the feeling when you fly between L.A. and San Francisco, that you're not exactly treated like a human being?

Then you'll be glad to know Delta now flies hourly between Los Angeles and San Francisco, from 6 am to 9 pm.

Person To Person® Service.

Every step of the way, you'll enjoy Delta's unique brand of Person to Person service. Service that includes complimentary use of Delta's Business Flight Centers® featuring FAX machines, PC modem hook-ups, worktables with telephones, and fresh-brewed coffee.

It's the kind of special touch people have come to expect from Delta. The airline that's been

number one in passenger satisfaction among the largest U.S. airlines for 16 straight years.

More Mileage For Your Travel Dollar.

Every time you fly Delta between L.A. and San Francisco before December 31, 1990, you'll earn Double Bonus Mileage if you're a Delta Frequent Flyer. That's 4,000 miles for just one roundtrip in Coach—8,000 miles for one First Class roundtrip. You'll also receive a 5,000 mile bonus every time you complete 10 flights between L.A. and San Francisco on Delta before December 31, 1990.

So if you're tired of being treated less than humanly, next time call Delta at 1-800-221-1212. Then say good-bye to the old brand.

▲ DELTA

We Love To Fly And It Shows®

Based on consumer complaint statistics compiled by the U.S. Department of Transportation. © 1990 Delta Air Lines, Inc.

◄◄ Hyatt Hotels, 1990   Delta Air Lines, 1990

Doch die Reichen waren wie gewöhnlich schon wieder auf der Suche nach Neuem. Grandhotels wirkten irgendwie angestaubt und Boutiquehotels gekünstelt. Nun aber gab es höchst exklusive, ökobewusste Enklaven wie die Aman Resorts – kleine, luxuriöse Hotels, die sich gut in die natürliche Umgebung einfügten. Ihr Flaggschiff ist das 1988 auf der thailändischen Insel Phuket eröffnete Amanpuri.

Las Vegas reagierte damit, dass es familienfreundlicher wurde. Allein in den ersten elf Monaten des Jahres 1986 zählte die Hauptstadt des Glücksspiels über 14,2 Millionen Besucher. XXL lautete die neue Devise der Hotels. Der visionäre Kasinobetreiber Steve Wynn eröffnete 1989 das Mirage, mit 3303 Gästezimmern das größte private Hotel der Welt. Kostenpunkt: 0,5 Mrd. $. Und es war gleich ausgebucht.

Las Vegas präsentierte gewissermaßen ein All-inclusive-Angebot. Die Hotels erfüllten dem Gast jeden Wunsch, wie auf einer Kreuzfahrt. Da die Menschen im Alltag zunehmend gefordert waren, hatten sie hier ganz klar den Wunsch, dass man ihnen alles abnahm. Urlaub sollte schließlich Urlaub sein. Kein Wunder also, dass sich auch die Zahl der Passagiere einer Kreuzfahrt in die Karibik zwischen 1980 und 1990 von 3,8 Mio. auf 7,8 Mio. mehr als verdoppelte.

1985

1985

1986

Washington officially replaces Route 66, dubbed "The Mother Road" by John Steinbeck, with the Interstate Highway System

Route 66 offiziell aus dem U.S. Highway System entfernt, das durch das Interstate Highway System ersetzt wird

La Route 66 est officiellement retirée du système autoroutier américain et remplacée par l'Interstate Highway System

Eurailpass unofficial passport of young Americans traveling across Europe

Eurail-Pass als inoffizieller Reisepass für Europareisen junger US-Bürger

L'Eurail Pass devient le passeport officieux des jeunes Américains qui voyagent en Europe

Universal Studios' $6.5-million animatronic King Kong attraction ushers in new era in theme park design

Elektronisch gesteuerter, 6,5 Mio. $ teurer King Kong von Universal Studios läutet eine neue Ära der Themenparks ein

Le robot King Kong construit par Universal Studios pour 6,5 millions $ annonce une nouvelle ère dans le design des parcs d'attractions

424

Daneben war auch in den 1980er-Jahren Tempo gefragt. Der Boom bei den Flugreisen verdankte sich nicht allein den Billiglinien, denn es gab auch immer mehr Privatjets, eine Art Familienkutsche der Superreichen.

GEGEN ENDE DES JAHRHUNDERTS KAM IMMER WIEDER NOSTALGIE AUF. Daher hielten die Filmemacher ein Remake von *Sabrina* vermutlich für eine gute Idee, jene Kreation von 1954 mit Audrey Hepburn über eine bezaubernde Chauffeurstochter und zwei wohlhabende, doch sehr unterschiedliche Brüder. In der Fassung von 1995 wundert man sich, dass der eine Bruder, ein einflussreicher Geschäftsmann, um eine Reise nach Paris so viel Tamtam macht. Schließlich besitzt er doch einen Privatjet und lebt in New York, wo praktisch jede Stunde von den drei lokalen Flughäfen ein Linienflug nach Paris geht. Merkwürdig auch, dass er noch nie in Paris *war*.

In den 1990er-Jahren ein Flugzeug zu betreten war so, als würde man in einen Bus einsteigen – wenn auch weniger vergnüglich. Die eigentliche Beförderung verlief flott und äußerst bequem. Nach jahrzehntelanger Vorbereitung fuhren 1994 die ersten Hochgeschwindigkeitszüge durch den Eurotunnel. Mit 15 Mrd. Euro hatte man das Budget um 100 % überzogen, doch nun gelangte man in nur zweieinviertel Stunden mit dem Zug von Paris nach London.

Pauschalreisen förderten die Exklusivität des Topsegments, und Boutiquehotels waren umso gefragter. Ian Schrager eröffnete 1990 das Paramount in New York; dann zog er 1995 weiter gen Süden für einen 20 Mio. $ teuren Umbau des Delano in Miami Beach, eines Hotels der Streamline-Moderne von 1947; und 1996 hinaus nach Los Angeles, um das Mondrian am Sunset Strip aufzupolieren. Die Boutiquehotels fanden sogar in Paris Anklang. In der Stadt mit den erlesensten Hotels eröffneten die Costes-Brüder 1991 das Hôtel Costes, und es wurde zu einem der strahlendsten Orte in der „Stadt der Lichter". Doch auch die Pauschalreisen nahmen weiter zu. Preiswertere Ausführungen der Boutiquehotels erschienen 1999. Die Starwood-Kette, Eignerin der St.-Regis-Hotels, lancierte die W-Hotels. Andre Balasz, Eigentümer von Topherbergen wie dem Chateau Marmont am Sunset Strip, eröffnete das erste Standard. Die Billigfluglinie JetBlue Airways wurde noch im gleichen Jahr angekündigt.

1986	1988	1988

United buys Pan Am's Pacific Division for $715 million; expands service to Sydney, Australia, and 12 other Pacific cities

United erwirbt Pan Ams Pacific Division für 715 Mio. $ und bedient nun auch Sydney und zwölf weitere pazifische Städte

United rachète la division Pacifique de Pan Am pour 715 millions $ et étend le service jusqu'à Sydney et à 12 autres villes du Pacifique

Tunneling begins for "Chunnel" (English Channel tunnel) between Paris and London

Baubeginn des Kanaltunnels für die Verbindung Paris–London

Ouverture du Tunnel sous la Manche entre Paris et Londres

Roughly 7 million tourists visit Mexico; almost 50% increase over two years earlier

Fast sieben Millionen Touristen besuchen Mexiko, doppelt so viele wie zwei Jahre zuvor

Environ 7 millions de touristes visitent le Mexique, soit une hausse d'environ 50 % par rapport à 1986

Und das Reisen verwandelte Las Vegas, während die Bevölkerung immer jünger wurde. Las Vegas war die am schnellsten wachsende Stadt der Vereinigten Staaten. Vor allem Ruheständler ließen sich hier nieder, doch das Durchschnittsalter ging deutlich zurück, nachdem Peter Morton 1995 das Hard Rock Hotel & Casino eröffnet hatte, das für jüngere Besucher zur beliebten Anlaufstelle wurde.

Die moderne Kunst und Architektur beeinflusste auch das Reiseverhalten. Kunstkenner verwandelten das spanische San Sebastian in ein Reisemekka, nachdem Frank Gehrys faszinierendes Guggenheim-Museum 1997 im nahe gelegenen Bilbao eröffnet worden war. In dem verschlafenen Schweizer Örtchen Vals öffnete 1996 die Therme Vals ihre Pforten. Der Entwurf von Peter Zumthor, der 2009 mit dem Pritzker-Preis ausgezeichnet wurde, sorgte für Aufregung – und eine Warteliste. Bedeutende Kunstausstellungen etwa in Venedig oder Kassel sowie große Kunstmessen in Basel und Miami wurden zum Pflichtpensum wahrer Kunstliebhaber.

Und dann gab es ein Ereignis von besonderer Symbolkraft: der Tod von Pamela Harriman, US-Botschafterin in Frankreich, während ihrer morgendlichen Schwimmrunde 1997 im Pariser Hotel Ritz. Pamela Digby Churchill Hayward Harriman war viel herumgekommen. Die einstige Debütantin aus England heiratete Averell Harriman, jenen Multimillionär und Diplomaten, der die Union Pacific Railroad kontrollierte und ab 1936 mit Sun Valley das erste Skiresort der USA errichtet hatte. Pamela Harriman, einstige Königin zahlreicher Atlantikfahrten, hatte sich gekonnt in eine Größe des Jetsets verwandelt. Ihren Tod fand sie jedoch im Ritz, der Grande Dame der Grandhotels, das noch vor dem 20. Jahrhundert, nämlich 1898, eröffnet worden war. Dies war mehr als der Tod eines Menschen, denn Harrimans Dahinscheiden steht für den Abschied von einer bestimmten Art zu leben – und zu reisen.

► Hard Rock Hotel, 1999   ►► Cunard, 1998

1989	1990	1990
Steve Wynn builds Mirage in Las Vegas; largest private hotel in the world, with 3,303 guest rooms	Cruise passengers to Caribbean more than double since 1980 – to 7.8 million from 3.8 million	Ian Schrager adds 1928 Paramount hotel to boutique empire, hiring Philippe Starck to reinvent it to be "Hotel as Theater"
Steve Wynn baut das Mirage in Los Angeles, mit 3303 Gästezimmern das größte private Hotel der Welt	Zahl der Teilnehmer an Karibikkreuzfahrten seit 1980 mehr als verdoppelt – von 3,8 auf 7,8 Millionen	Ian Schrager bereichert sein Imperium um das Paramount Hotel von 1928, das Philippe Starck in ein „Hotel als Theater" verwandelt
Steve Wynn construit le Mirage à Las Vegas, le plus grand hôtel privé du monde avec 3303 chambres	Le nombre de croisiéristes aux Caraïbes a plus que doublé depuis 1980, passant de 3,8 à 7,8 millions	Ian Schrager ajoute l'hôtel Paramount de 1928 à son empire hôtelier et Philippe Starck le relooke en « théâtre »

LE TOURISME DE MASSES

*Le tourisme de masse encouragea plus
d'exclusivité sur le segment haut de gamme
du marché, et les « boutique hotels » firent d'autant
plus fureur.*

L'AIRLINE DEREGULATION ACT VOTÉ EN 1978 MIT UN TERME À TOUTES RESTRICTIONS SUR LES ITINÉRAIRES LE 1ER JANVIER 1982. Cette année-là marqua la déréglementation des transports aériens sur le territoire américain. Les compagnies aériennes établies de longue date firent face à la concurrence féroce de nouveaux rivaux plus agiles et aux syndicats moins puissants. La décennie s'ouvrit avec *Y a-t-il un pilote dans l'avion ?*, une parodie déjantée de tous les films jamais tournés sur les catastrophes aériennes. Parallèlement, People Express, un nouveau genre de compagnie aérienne sans chichi et à bas prix, commença à opérer à l'aéroport de Newark. À l'opposé du marché, la compagnie ultra luxe Virgin Atlantic Airways de Richard Branson se mit à assurer la liaison entre Newark et l'aéroport Gatwick de Londres en 1984, et devint rentable cette même année. C'étaient les transporteurs autrefois prospères qui rencontraient des problèmes. Par exemple, Braniff International Airways ferma en 1982. En fin de compte, neuf grandes compagnies jetèrent aussi l'éponge.

Au cours de cette période, un nouveau type d'établissement à l'ambiance intimiste mais élégante fit son apparition : le « boutique hotel ». Les clients pouvaient choisir leur marque d'eau minérale, et même le genre d'oreiller sur lequel ils souhaitaient dormir. Tout commença quand Ian Schrager et Steve Rubell, anciens propriétaires du Studio 54, ouvrirent le Morgans Hotel à New York en 1984. Il était si chic qu'il pouvait se passer d'apostrophe. Cet établissement décoré par Andrée Putman changea la donne dans l'industrie hôtelière. En 1988, le duo renouvela la performance avec un succès encore plus éclatant, le Royalton, dont le moindre détail fut conçu par Philippe Starck. Son hall froid et sombre devint le salon le plus couru de New York.

Comme d'habitude, les plus fortunés étaient déjà passés à autre chose. Puisqu'à leurs yeux, les grands hôtels sentaient le moisi et les «boutique hotels» faisaient trop de chichis, des chaînes ultra exclusives et sensibles aux questions d'environnement commencèrent à faire parler d'elles, comme Aman Resorts. Ses petits hôtels somptueux mettaient en valeur leur environnement naturel. Amanpuri, son fleuron, ouvrit à Phuket en Thaïlande en 1988.

Las Vegas réagit en devenant une destination familiale. Plus de 14,2 millions de visiteurs déferlèrent sur la capitale du jeu au cours des 11 premiers mois de l'année 1986. Les hôtels y étaient désormais gigantesques. En 1989, le propriétaire de casinos visionnaire Steve Wynn ouvrit le Mirage, le plus grand hôtel privé du monde avec ses 3303 chambres. Sa construction côuta un demi milliard de dollars. Et l'hôtel affichait complet. Las Vegas offrait plus ou moins des vacances «tout compris». Le personnel de ses établissements répondait aux moindres attentes des clients, comme sur un paquebot de croisières. Le quotidien des gens était toujours plus surchargé, et afin que leurs vacances en soient vraiment, ils avaient clairement besoin qu'on prenne en charge tous les détails à leur place. Rien d'étonnant, donc, à ce que le nombre de croisiéristes mettant cap sur les Caraïbes fit plus que doubler entre 1980 et 1990, passant de 3,8 à 7,8 millions de passagers.

En dehors de ça, la vitesse avait aussi son importance dans les années 1980. En plein boom du voyage aérien, les compagnies bon marché devaient partager la vedette. Le jet privé devenait un moyen de transport de plus en plus utilisé, comme une sorte de voiture familiale pour les personnes extrêmement riches.

QUAND UN SIÈCLE TOUCHE À SA FIN, LA NOSTALGIE EST SOUVENT À LA MODE. Voilà sans doute pourquoi des producteurs estimèrent qu'il serait avisé de tourner un remake de *Sabrina*, le film de 1954 avec Audrey Hepburn racontant l'histoire d'une charmante fille de chauffeur et de deux frères très différents. Dans la version de 1995, il est bizarre que le frère, un puissant homme d'affaires, fasse tout un foin à l'idée d'aller à Paris. Après tout, il possède un jet privé et vit à New York, où des avions de ligne décollent pour Paris presque toutes les heures depuis les trois aéroports de la ville. Il semble peu crédible qu'il ne *soit jamais* allé à Paris.

1991

1992

1993

Las Vegas theme hotels get "family friendly" with debut of Excalibur Hotel and Casino, world's largest hotel at opening

Das inzwischen „familienfreundliche" Las Vegas erhält Themenhotels wie das Excalibur Hotel and Casino

Désormais «familiale», la ville de Las Vegas accueille des hôtels thématiques tels que Excalibur Hotel and Casino

Donald Trump's shortlived airline, the Trump Shuttle, fails and stops flying

Trump Shuttle, die kurzlebige Fluglinie von Donald Trump, legt eine Bauchlandung hin und ist am Ende

Trump Shuttle, la compagnie aérienne de courte durée lancée par Donald Trump, fait faillite

Madame Tussaud's wax museum installs "Singapore Girl," the Singapore Airlines stewardess, its first commercial figure

Madame Tussaud's präsentiert mit dem „Singapore Girl", der Stewardess von Singapore Airlines, seine erste kommerzielle Figur

Le musée de cire de Madame Tussaud présente la «Singapore Girl», symbole des hôtesses de l'air de Singapore Airlines

Dans les années 1990, monter à bord d'un avion revenait à prendre le bus, en un peu moins agréable. On pouvait voyager rapidement et tout confort. En 1994, après des décennies de conception, les trains à grande vitesse finirent par rouler à travers le tunnel sous la Manche. Le projet subit un dépassement de budget de 100 %, coûtant au final 4650 millions de livres sterling. Cependant, les trains reliaient désormais Paris et Londres en deux heures 15 minutes.

Le tourisme de masse encouragea plus d'exclusivité sur le segment haut de gamme du marché, et les «boutique hotels» firent d'autant plus fureur. Ian Schrager ouvrit le Paramount à New York en 1990, mit cap sur le sud en 1995 afin de rénover le Delano – un hôtel moderne de Miami Beach datant de 1947 – pour un montant de 20 millions de dollars, puis partit à Los Angeles relooker le Mondrian sur Sunset Strip en 1996. La tendance des «boutique hotels» déferla même sur Paris, ville des grands hôtels par excellence. En 1991, les frères Costes inaugurèrent l'Hôtel Costes, aujourd'hui l'une des adresses qui a le plus d'éclat de la Ville Lumière.

Eastern Airlines, 1985

Le tourisme de masse poursuivit toutefois son développement. En 1999, des versions moins chères des «boutique hotels» firent leur apparition. La chaîne Starwood, propriété des hôtels St. Regis, lança son concept W, tandis qu'Andre Balazs, propriétaire d'établissements haut de gamme

1995

Hard Rock Hotel & Casino opens in Las Vegas, and demographics of Vegas visitors rapidly get younger

Eröffnung des Hard Rock Hotel & Casino in Las Vegas führt rasch zu einer demografischen Verjüngung der Vegas-Touristen

Avec l'ouverture du Hard Rock Hotel & Casino à Las Vegas, la moyenne d'âge des visiteurs de la ville chuta

1995

Club Med changes from nonprofit association to for-profit limited liability company

Umwandlung des Club Med vom gemeinnützigen Unternehmen in eine Aktiengesellschaft mit beschränkter Haftung

L'association à but non lucratif Club Med devient une entreprise commerciale

1995

Airlines begin tests of video-on-demand to personal monitors at each seat

Erprobung frei wählbarer Filme, die auf individuellen integrierten Bildschirmen betrachtet werden können

Les compagnies aériennes commencent à tester la vidéo à la demande sur des écrans personnels à chaque place comme le Chateau Marmont sur Sunset Strip, ouvrit le premier hôtel Standard. La compagnie JetBlue Airways, avec ses vols à prix discount, fut créée la même année.

Le marché du voyage transforma également Las Vegas quand sa moyenne d'âge se mit à baisser. Las Vegas était la ville qui connaissait la croissance la plus rapide d'Amérique, particulièrement pour les retraités. Néanmoins, l'âge moyen de la ville chuta quand Peter Morton ouvrit le Hard Rock Hotel & Casino en 1995. Des visiteurs plus jeunes en firent leur point de ralliement.

L'art moderne et l'architecture influencèrent également la façon de voyager. En 1997, les amateurs d'art transformèrent la ville espagnole de San Sebastian en Mecque du voyage dès l'ouverture de l'étonnant Musée Guggenheim de Frank Gehry près de Bilbao. En 1996, les Thermes de Vals s'installèrent dans un patelin suisse endormi. Le design de Peter Zumthor, qui remporta plus tard le prix d'architecture Pritzker, attira l'attention et généra une longue liste d'attente. Les grandes expositions comme celles de Venise en Italie et de Kassel en Allemagne, ainsi que les foires d'art contemporain de Bâle en Suisse et de Miami, devinrent des étapes incontournables sur le Chemin de Croix des pèlerins fanatiques d'art.

On peut presque considérer comme une métaphore le décès de Pamela Harriman, ambassadrice des États-Unis en France, qui mourut en nageant un matin dans la piscine du Ritz parisien en 1997. Pamela Digby Churchill Hayward Harriman avait roulé sa bosse. Cette Anglaise avait épousé Averell Harriman, diplomate multimillionaire qui contrôlait la compagnie Union Pacific Railroad et avait construit Sun Valley, la première station de sports d'hiver américaine, en 1936. Pamela Harriman, la plus belle femme de nombreuses croisières transatlantiques, s'était habilement reconvertie en membre éminent de la jet-set. Elle mourut néanmoins au Ritz, dans la « grande dame » des grands hôtels inaugurée avant le XXᵉ siècle, en 1898. Dans une certaine mesure, ce ne fut pas seulement la mort d'une personne. La disparition de Pamela Harriman marqua la fin de tout un art de vivre, et de voyager.

▶ Holiday Inn, 1998

1998

1999

1999

Starwood opens first W boutique hotel

Starwood präsentiert neue Boutiquehotels in Gestalt der W-Hotels

Starwood lance les « boutique hotels » W

Plans for JetBlue, hip budget airline, announced

Pläne für JetBlue, einen sich cool gebenden Billigflieger, bekannt gemacht

Annonce des plans de création de JetBlue, une compagnie branchée

Hyatt continues to favor towering, atrium-based design, developed by John Portman, with new Waikiki location

Hyatt favorisiert weiterhin das hoch aufragende Atriumhotel, wie es John Portman mit dem neuen Waikiki Hotel realisiert

Avec son nouvel hôtel à Waikiki, Hyatt continue à privilégier les tours construites autour d'un atrium, un design conçu par John Portman

HIGH PERFORMANCE

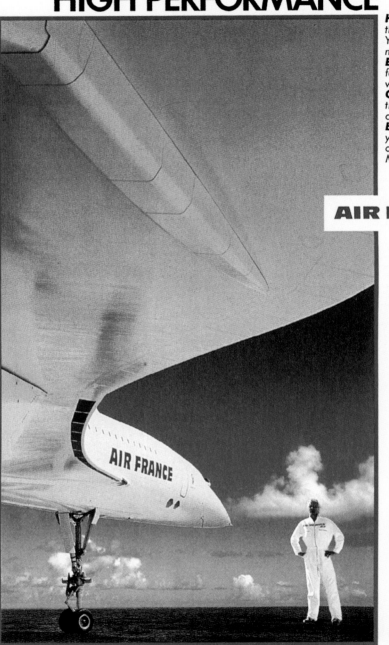

High Technology: We fl
the Concorde between Nev
York and Paris in just 22
minutes.

Efficiency: A leading recore
for on-time performance world
wide.

Cargo Leadership: One c
the world's 3 largest carge
carriers.

Business Sense: We make
your mileage count throug
our partnership in United'
Mileage Plus.

AIR FRANCE ///

Air France, 1985

The Concorde, a turbojet-powered supersonic transport, took three and a half hours to cross the Atlantic. You got there before you left. Britain and France subsidized the joint Air France-British Air effort. Air France commissioned the influential designer Raymond Loewy for the interiors. Regular, and expensive, service between the U.S. and Europe began in 1976.

Die Concorde, das Überschallverkehrsflug-zeug mit Turbojet-Triebwerken, überquerte den Atlantik in nur dreieinhalb Stunden. Kaum gestartet, war man schon angekommen. Das Gemeinschaftsprojekt von Air France und British Airways wurde von beiden Staaten subventioniert. Air France beauftragte den führenden Designer Raymond Loewy mit der Gestaltung des Interieurs. Regelmäßige – und teure – Flüge zwischen den USA und Europa begannen 1976.

Le Concorde, avion supersonique à turbo-réacteurs, traversait l'Atlantique en 3 heures 30. Avec le décalage horaire, on arrivait avant même d'être parti. L'Angleterre et la France subventionnèrent ce projet commun entre Air France et British Airways. La compagnie française confia l'aménagement intérieur de l'avion au designer en vue Raymond Loewy. Les liaisons régulières, et onéreuses, entre les États-Unis et l'Europe commencèrent en 1976.

▶ American Airlines, 1984

In a world of airlines, one airline has always been something special.

At first glance, all airlines may appear to be the same. But when you look closer, one airline offers you a special way to fly.

It's an airline so large it carries over 30 million people a year; yet so personalized, you can reserve your seat a year in advance.

It's an airline so committed to saving you time, you can get all your boarding passes for all your flights before you ever get to the airport.

It's an airline that's led the way by being innovative, not imitative. American Airlines. In a world of airlines, it's the one special airline that can make your trip something special.

AmericanAirlines
Something special in the air.

**KRISWORLD, THE BIGGEST SHOW IN THE SKY,
NOW IN EVERY SEAT IN EVERY CLASS.**

Singapore Airlines, 1998

The signature image of Singapore Airlines was its stewardess, the "Singapore Girl." Madame Tussaud's Wax Museum installed a figure depicting this Singapore Girl in 1991, the first commercial figure displayed there. The flight attendant uniform, a sarong kebaya, had originally been designed by the Parisian couturier Pierre Balmain.

Das Symbol von Singapore Airlines war ihre Stewardess, das „Singapore Girl"; es wurde sogar 1991 im Wachsfigurenmuseum der Madame Tussaud als erste kommerzielle Figur verewigt. Die Uniform der Flugbegleiterinnen, ein Sarong kebaya, wurde ursprünglich von dem Pariser Modeschöpfer Pierre Balmain entworfen.

L'image emblématique de Singapore Airlines était son hôtesse de l'air, la « fille de Singapour ». En 1991, le musée de Madame Tussaud en exposa même une statue de cire, tout premier personnage commercial présenté dans son enceinte. L'uniforme des hôtesses, le « sarong kebaya », avait été dessiné par le couturier parisien Pierre Balmain.

▶ Hawaiian Air, 1986

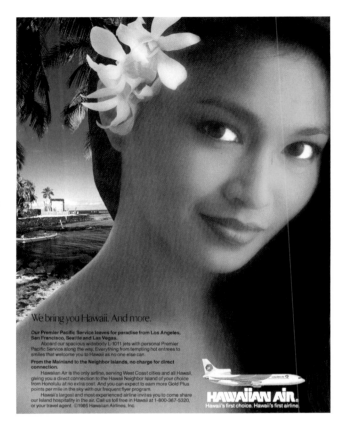

We bring you Hawaii. And more.

Our Premier Pacific Service leaves for paradise from Los Angeles, San Francisco, Seattle and Las Vegas.
Aboard our spacious widebody L-1011 jets with personal Premier Pacific Service along the way. Everything from tempting hot entrees to smiles that welcome you to Hawaii as no one else can.
From the Mainland to the Neighbor Islands, no charge for direct connection.
Hawaiian Air is the only airline, serving West Coast cities and all Hawaii, giving you a direct connection to the Hawaii Neighbor Island of your choice from Honolulu at no extra cost. And you can expect to earn more Gold Plus points per mile in the sky with our frequent flyer program.
Hawaii's largest and most experienced airline invites you to come share our Island hospitality in the air. Call us toll free in Hawaii at 1-800-367-5320, or your travel agent. ©1985 Hawaiian Airlines, Inc.

HAWAIIAN AIR.
Hawaii's first choice. Hawaii's first airline.

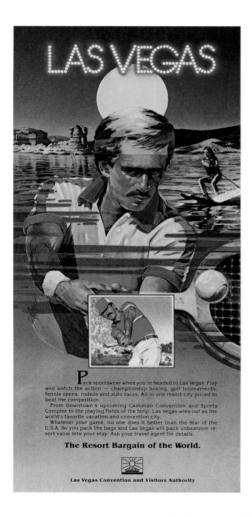

P ack sportswear when you're headed to Las Vegas. Play and watch the action — championship boxing, golf tournaments, tennis opens, rodeos and auto races. All in one resort city priced to beat the competition.

From Downtown's upcoming Cashman Convention and Sports Complex to the playing fields of the Strip, Las Vegas wins out as the world's favorite vacation and convention city.

Whatever your game, no one does it better than the Star of the U.S.A. So you pack the bags and Las Vegas will pack unbeatable resort value into your stay. Ask your travel agent for details.

The Resort Bargain of the World.

Las Vegas Convention and Visitors Authority

T he Star of the U.S.A., from dynamic Downtown to the scintillating Strip, Las Vegas glows with vitality and excitement.

Superstar entertainers, glittering showrooms, dazzling lights, gourmet restaurants, 24-hour action — no one does it better.

Star-studded nights and warm desert days beckon you to visit the world's premier vacation and convention city. Call your travel agent for reservations.

Las Vegas Convention and Visitors Authority

Las Vegas Convention and Visitors Authority, 1981   Las Vegas Convention and Visitors Authority, 1982

▶ Palm Springs Convention and Visitors Bureau, 1985

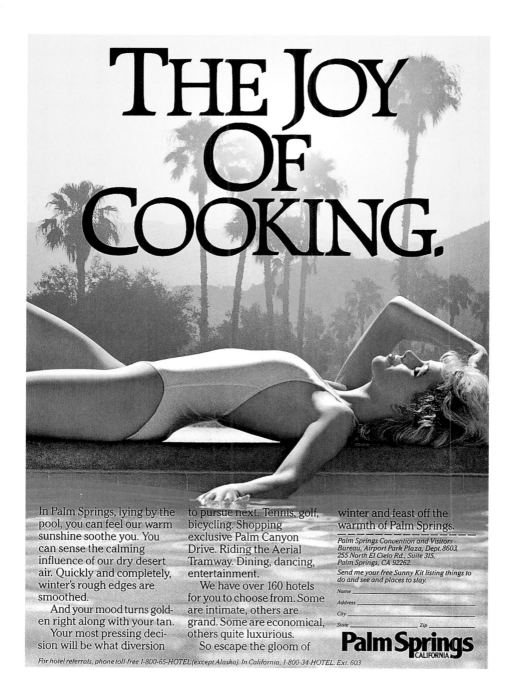

THE JOY OF COOKING.

In Palm Springs, lying by the pool, you can feel our warm sunshine soothe you. You can sense the calming influence of our dry desert air. Quickly and completely, winter's rough edges are smoothed.

And your mood turns golden right along with your tan.

Your most pressing decision will be what diversion to pursue next. Tennis, golf, bicycling. Shopping exclusive Palm Canyon Drive. Riding the Aerial Tramway. Dining, dancing, entertainment.

We have over 160 hotels for you to choose from. Some are intimate, others are grand. Some are economical, others quite luxurious.

So escape the gloom of winter and feast off the warmth of Palm Springs.

Palm Springs Convention and Visitors Bureau, Airport Park Plaza, Dept. 8603, 255 North El Cielo Rd., Suite 315, Palm Springs, CA 92262

Send me your free Sunny Kit listing things to do and see and places to stay.

Name _____

Address _____

City _____

State _____ Zip _____

Palm Springs
CALIFORNIA

For hotel referrals, phone toll-free 1-800-65-HOTEL (except Alaska). In California, 1-800-34-HOTEL. Ext. 603

L·I·F·E
ON · THE · BEACH

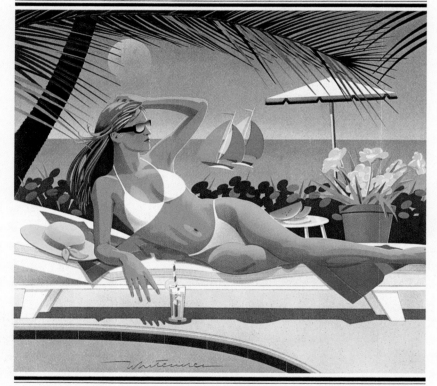

Life on the beach is ever so much better than life *at* the beach. The all-suite, all-luxury Alexander hotel is *on* Miami Beach. Recently, we have been transformed into one of the most tastefully exciting hotels in America. And when you dine, you'll dine at Dominique's, which is four-stars and for-gourmets. Or at Le Café for dining that's just as delicious, but more casual. When you add all our amenities, our service, our pool and our ocean, you'll know this. When you spend some small part of your life with us: you can do nothing. Gloriously.

For our free brochure or reservations, call 800 327-6121 or your travel planner.

THE
ALE✴ANDER
ALL-SUITE LUXURY HOTEL
Elegance with a splash.

5225 Collins Avenue,
Miami Beach, Florida 33140

IF WINSTON CHURCHILL WERE ALIVE TODAY
WHICH AIRLINE WOULD HE FLY TO LONDON

Virgin

VIRGIN ATLANTIC AIRWAYS. 747's MIAMI TO LONDON.
Take us for all we've got.

Virgin Atlantic Airways, 1986

Most airlines that took off after the Airline Deregulation Act of 1978 were no-frills bargains. But Richard Branson, with his Virgin Atlantic Airways, was aiming for the prestige passenger. First-class seating was booked as "Upper Class" and included a limousine pickup. It was profitable in its first year—1984. A brave new world.

Die meisten nach dem Airline Deregulation Act von 1978 entstandenen Fluggesellschaften waren Billigflieger ohne Schnickschnack. Mit Virgin Atlantic Airways zielte Richard Branson hingegen auf den anspruchsvollen Passagier. Wer ein Ticket der „Oberklasse" buchte, wurde sogar per Limousine abgeholt. Virgin war gleich im ersten Jahr – 1984 – profitabel. Schöne neue Welt.

La plupart des compagnies aériennes créées après le vote de l'Airline Deregulation Act de 1978 proposaient des tarifs bon marché et un service sans chichis, mais avec Virgin Atlantic Airways, Richard Branson ciblait la clientèle de prestige. Le billet de première classe était appelé « Upper Class » et incluait un trajet en limousine jusqu'à l'aéroport. La compagnie devint rentable dès la première année, en 1984. Le meilleur des mondes.

▶ Spain, 1989

The Duchess of Alba
by Francisco de Goya.
Courtesy of
The Hispanic Society
of America, New York.

For once,
view the works of
the Spanish masters
without flipping
pages.

Goya. El Greco. Velázquez. Miró. Picasso.

From the pages of art books, their paintings have fascinated and inspired you.

Yet the printed page does not really allow you to *see* them. For what makes each a masterpiece is what it demands of the viewer: a personal relationship in which the work reveals itself layer by layer. Until finally, standing before it, you come to experience the full emotional and spiritual power the artist intended you to feel.

At the Prado in Madrid—and in many other museums throughout Spain—you will find hundreds upon hundreds of the world's greatest works of art. And you will recognize many from reproductions you have seen.

But as you fix your gaze on them you will recognize something else.

That you are looking at them for the first time.

The Prado. An extraordinary destination along your journey of discovery.

Spain
Everything Under The Sun.

ESPAÑA

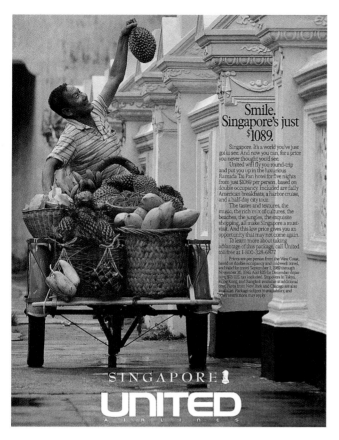

Smile. Singapore's just $1089.

Singapore. It's a world you've just got to see. And now you can, for a price you never thought you'd see.

United will fly you round-trip and put you up in the luxurious Ramada Tai Pan hotel for five nights from just $1089 per person, based on double occupancy. Included are daily American breakfasts, a harbor cruise, and a half-day city tour.

The tastes and textures, the music, the rich mix of cultures, the beaches, the jungles, the exquisite shopping, all make Singapore a must-visit. And this low price gives you an opportunity that may not come again.

To learn more about taking advantage of this package, call United toll free at 1-800-328-6877.

Prices are per person from the West Coast, based on double occupancy and midweek travel, and valid for travel September 1, 1989 through November 30, 1989. Add $35 for December departure. $13 U.S. tax included. Stopovers in Tokyo, Hong Kong, and Bangkok available at additional cost. Fares from New York and Chicago are also available. Package subject to availability and other restrictions may apply.

SINGAPORE

UNITED
A I R L I N E S

United Air Lines, 1989

The 747 jumbo jet set passenger-capacity records when it took off in 1970, and held them for the rest of the century. With so many seats, price per ticket could be far lower. Travelers could jet off to exotic locales on the other side of the globe for a reasonable cost.

In der 1970 eingeführten Boeing 747 fanden so viele Passagiere Platz wie auch später in diesem Jahrhundert in keiner anderen Maschine. Derart viele Sitzplätze ermöglichten drastisch reduzierte Ticketpreise. Nun konnte man zu vertretbaren Kosten auch exotische Ziele auf der anderen Seite des Globus ansteuern.

Quand il décolla en 1970, le Boeing 747 explosa tous les records de capacité d'accueil de passagers et en resta détenteur jusqu'à la fin du siècle. Avec autant de sièges, le prix du billet diminuait considérablement. Les voyageurs pouvaient enfin s'envoler vers des lieux exotiques à l'autre bout du monde à des tarifs raisonnables.

▶ United Air Lines, 1989

Imagine this: It's summer. You take off for two glorious, expense-paid weeks in Europe. You land in a fabulous continental city. And you're escorted to a first class home-away-from-home. With air conditioning, thick soft beds, a complete kitchen and bath—plus one very special feature.

Your home can travel wherever you do. Because it's an Airstream travel trailer! Off you'll go through land-marked streets and charming country roads. Seeing Europe the way very few do.

It all begins with your local Airstream dealer.

He can tell you how to enter the Airstream Caravan Sweepstakes. And give you a free booklet on "How to Buy A Travel Trailer." You might be one of 9 lucky couples who will wind up in Europe, Canada or Mexico. You might even discover that the Airstream way of life is the life for you.

WIN THE ULTIMATE FLY/DRIVE VACATION

FLY TO EUROPE AND JOIN THE AIRSTREAM CARAVAN

All entries must be submitted by June 30, 1979. Any licensed driver can enter. No purchase necessary. Void where prohibited by law.

CIRCLE # 1 ON READER SERVICE PAGE.

◄ Airstream Trailers, 1980

Eurailpass, 1986

Budget airlines and super-cheap fares after the 1978 Airline Deregulation Act enabled ever more travelers to get to Europe. Once there, students or others with limited means discovered that Eurailpass offered an inexpensive opportunity to explore the Continent. Amtrak seemed even less inviting after Americans had sampled the trains in Europe.

Die seit dem 1978 verabschiedeten Airline Deregulation Act entstandenen Billiglinien ermöglichten immer mehr US-Bürgern einen Flug nach Europa. Dort angekommen, entdeckten Studenten oder andere Reisende mit begrenzten Mitteln, dass der Eurail-Pass sich hervorragend eignete, um den Kontinent kostengünstig zu erkunden. Nachdem die Amerikaner die europäischen Züge kennengelernt hatten, erschien ihnen die heimische Amtrak noch weniger einladend.

Le vote de l'Airline Deregulation Act en 1978 autorisant les compagnies aériennes à proposer des prix cassés permit à encore plus de passagers d'aller en Europe. Une fois sur place, les étudiants et autres voyageurs à budget restreint découvrirent le forfait Eurailpass, un moyen abordable d'explorer le Vieux Continent. Après avoir goûté aux trains européens, les Américains ne firent que dénigrer davantage leur compagnie Amtrak.

Eurailpass admits there may still be a less expensive way to see Europe.

 Eurailpass gives you lots of ways to save money on European travel. With our Eurail Saverpass, for example, you get unlimited first-class rail travel in any or all of 16 European countries for only $199 per person.* That's less than $14 per day.

Of course, there is a way to travel around Europe that costs even less. If you like to pedal.

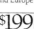 $199

*Applies to 15-day pass, when three or more travel together. Other inexpensive rates are available for one or two people.

EURAILPASS

Please rush me a *free* Eurailpass color brochure.

Name_____

Address_____

City_____ State_____ Zip_____

Mail today to Eurailpass, Box Q, Staten Island, New York, 10305.
G00586

**MEET THE BIGGEST
STARS IN HOLLYWOOD.**

When you visit L.A., be sure not to miss California's star attraction—Universal Studios.
No place else can you go behind the scenes
to see how and where we film hit movies
and TV shows like "Back to the Future" and
"Amazing Stories." Nowhere else can you cheer
on Conan® as he battles an 18-ft. fire-breathing
dragon. Or see the A-Team® swing into action. And
starting in June, only one place brings you eyeball-to-
eyeball with 30 feet of colossal fury that's unleashed
by our meanest, hairiest, terrifyingist star ever.
King Kong ™–live! So spend a day at Universal
Studios—where there's
always so much that's
new, you'll never have
the same fun twice.

**UNIVERSAL
STUDIOS**
AN MCA COMPANY

◄ Universal Studios Tour, 1986

Sea World, 1982

Sea World, like Disneyland, thrived as family
vacations became ever more focused on
amusing the children. Four UCLA graduates
founded the marine zoological park in 1964,
and it gradually evolved into a vast theme
park with whales, dolphins, penguins, and
amusement rides.

Wie Disneyland profitierte auch SeaWorld
davon, dass es beim Familienurlaub zunehmend
darum ging, die Kinder bei Laune zu halten.
Vier Absolventen der UCLA hatten 1964
einen Meereszoo gegründet, der sich nach
und nach zu einem riesigen Themenpark mit
Walen, Delfinen, Pinguinen und Fahrgeschäften
entwickelte.

Comme Disneyland, Sea World remporta un
immense succès car les vacances en famille se
concentraient toujours plus sur le divertissement des enfants. Fondé en 1964 par quatre
diplômés de UCLA, ce zoo marin se transforma
progressivement en un vaste parc à thème, avec
baleines, pingouins, spectacles de dauphins et
attractions.

San Diego's best just keeps getting better.

Sea World is a living, changing place—
alive with new animals to meet and new ways to have fun
every time you visit. Shamu™ and his trainers constantly give
you the world's newest, most thrilling animal show.
You'll flip over our new dolphin show and this summer
"Up With People," direct from their Super Bowl appearance,
will lift your spirits with their new show. Bring your family
back to Sea World. It's a whole different world every day.

A Five Star Grand-Luxe Hotel

Those Who Appreciate The Diffe

Beverly Wilshire

◄ Beverly Wilshire Hotel, 1981

Luxor Las Vegas, 1998

Travelers could go around the world without leaving Las Vegas. Theme hotels boomed. You could be in ancient Egypt at the Luxor, in France at the Paris, in Manhattan at New York New York, in Italy at the Venetian, in Brazil at the Rio, in the South Seas at Mandalay Bay, in ancient Rome at Caesar's Palace, even in Camelot at Excalibur.

Eine Weltreise war auch möglich, ohne Las Vegas zu verlassen, denn die Themenhotels verzeichneten einen wahren Boom. Im Luxor konnte man sich wie im alten Ägypten fühlen, im Paris wie in Frankreich, im New York New York wie in Manhattan, im Venetian wie in Italien, im Rio wie in Brasilien, in Mandalay Bay wie in der Südsee, in Caesar's Palace wie im alten Rom und im Excalibur gar wie in Camelot.

Les touristes pouvaient voyager dans le monde entier sans quitter Las Vegas. Les hôtels thématiques explosèrent. Le Luxor vous emmenait dans l'Égypte des pharaons, le Paris en France, le New York New York à Manhattan, le Venetian en Italie, le Rio au Brésil, le Mandalay Bay dans les mers du Sud, le Caesar's Palace dans la Rome antique, et l'Excalibur au château de Camelot.

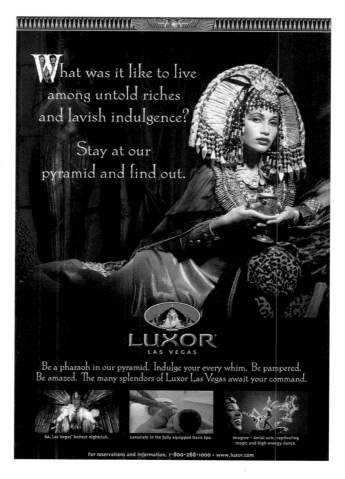

What was it like to live among untold riches and lavish indulgence? Stay at our pyramid and find out.

LUXOR
LAS VEGAS

Be a pharaoh in our pyramid. Indulge your every whim. Be pampered. Be amazed. The many splendors of Luxor Las Vegas await your command.

RA, Las Vegas' hottest nightclub.

Luxuriate in the fully equipped Oasis Spa.

Imagine - Aerial acts, captivating magic and high-energy dance.

For reservations and information, 1-800-288-1000 • www.luxor.com

the bonds of city life and unravel
your problems on a Windjammer
cruise. Surrender to the majestic
ocean and enchanting ports of
call. Let the currents guide you to
peace of spirit, mind and body.
Master the Windjammer knot
and untie yourself from everyday
hassles. Experience the real you.

Your share of the six day Windjammer
adventure can be as little as $400.

For reservations only call toll free
1-800-327-2600.

Loosen up

Cap'n Mike, please send me a free
Adventure Booklet in full color.

Windjammer Barefoot Cruises

◄ Windjammer Barefoot Cruises, 1983

Club Med, 1988

Club Med started as a sort of a seductive vacation mixer, largely aimed at singles or lithe young couples. Club Meds opened around the globe during the 1960s and '70s, thriving on their image as hedonistic escapes. But by the '80s, despite this ad families were increasingly checking in.

Der Club Med bot zunächst so etwas wie eine verlockende Ferienmixtur, die vor allem Singles oder sportliche junge Paare ansprach. Die in den Sechzigern und Siebzigern überall auf der Welt eröffneten Clubs profitierten vom Image eines sinnenfrohen Refugiums. Ab den 1980er-Jahren fand der Club Med trotz dieser Anzeige auch bei Familien zunehmend Anklang.

Club Med se présenta d'abord comme un mix de vacances séduisant largement destiné aux célibataires ou aux jeunes couples libérés. La marque ouvrit des clubs dans le monde entier pendant les années 1960 et 1970, prospérant sur son image de refuge hédoniste mais au début des années 1980, et malgré le message de cette publicité, elle remportait un succès croissant auprès des familles.

A CLUB MED VACATION BEGINS WHERE CIVILIZATION ENDS.

Imagine, for a moment, nothing. No clocks. No ringing phones. No traffic jams. No radios. No newspapers. No crowds.

Now imagine this. An island village where aqua seas brush dazzling white shores. Where lush green palms line wandering pathways. Where crystal blue skies change magically to golden sunsets.

Where you can indulge in everything from windsurfing, snorkeling and tennis, to afternoon classes in water aerobics or painting, to secluded moments on miles of sun-drenched beach.

Activities vary by village © 1988 Club Med Sales, Inc., 40 West 57th Street, New York, NY 10019.

Imagine not just three meals, but three gourmet banquets every single day. With freshly baked breads and pastries and free-flowing wine.

Where evenings are always filled with entertainment, dancing and a special atmosphere that turns new faces into old friends in moments.

If all this captures your imagination, drop by and see your travel agent or call 1-800-CLUB MED. It just may be the beginning of the end of civilization as you know it.

CLUB MED
The antidote for civilization.™

Stonehenge, 1985   ▶ United States Virgin Islands, 1989   ▶▶ Cunard, 1953

SELECTED INDEX

BIBLIOGRAPHY

Blume, Mary. Côte d'Azur: *Inventing the French Riviera*. New York: Thames and Hudson, 1992.

Denby, Elaine. *Grand Hotels: Illusion and Reality*. London: Reaktion Books, 1998.

Flinchum, Russell. *Henry Dreyfuss, Industrial Designer: The Man in the Brown Suit*. New York: Cooper-Hewitt National Design Museum, Smithsonian Institution, and Rizzoli, 1997.

Fox, Robert. *Liners: The Golden Age*. Cologne, Germany: Könemann Verlag, 1999.

Girard, Xavier. *French Riviera: Living Well Was the Best Revenge*. New York: Assouline, 2002.

Gygelman, Adele. *Palm Springs Modern: Houses in the California Desert*. New York: Rizzoli, 1999.

Hilton, Conrad. *Be My Guest*. Englewood Cliffs, New Jersey: Prentice-Hall, 1957.

Jodard, Paul. *Design Heroes: Raymond Loewy*. London: HarperCollins, 1994.

Krinsky, Carol Herselle. *Gordon Bunshaft of Skidmore, Owings & Merrill*. New York: The Architectural History Foundation and The MIT Press, 1988.

Lapidus, Morris. *Too Much Is Never Enough: An Autobiography*. New York: Rizzoli, 1996.

La Pietra, Ugo (ed.). *Gio Ponti*. New York: Rizzoli, 1996.

Loewy, Raymond. *Industrial Design*. New York: The Overlook Press, 1988.

Loos, Anita. *Gentlemen Prefer Blondes: The Illuminating Diary of a Professional Lady*. New York: Boni & Liveright, 1925.

Maddocks, Melvin, et al. *The Great Liners*. Alexandria, Virginia: Time-Life Books, 1978.

Melville, John H. *The Great White Fleet*. New York: Vantage Press, 1976.

Schönberger, Angela (ed.). *Raymond Loewy: Pioneer of American Industrial Design*. Munich: Prestel, 1990.

Sparke, Penny, and Felice Hodges, Emma Dent Coad, Anne Stone. *Design Source Book*. Secaucus, New Jersey: Chartwell Books, 1986.

Vaill, Amanda. *Everybody Was So Young: Gerald and Sara Murphy: A Lost Generation Love Story*. New York: Houghton Mifflin, 1998.

Varney, Carleton. *The Draper Touch: The High Life & High Style of Dorothy Draper*. New York: Prentice Hall Press, 1988.

Wharton, Annabel Jane. *Building the Cold War: Hilton International Hotels and Modern Architecture*. Chicago: University of Chicago Press, 2001.

Wilson, Richard Guy, Dianne H. Pilgrim and Dickran Tashjian. *The Machine Age in America 1918–1941*. New York: The Brooklyn Museum and Harry N. Abrams, 1986.

Zega, Michael E., and John E. Gruber. *Travel by Train: The American Railroad Poster 1870–1950*. Bloomington, Indiana: Indiana University Press, 2002.

IMPRINT

Frontispiece: The Airlines of the United States, 1945

▶ Braniff International, 1953

All images are from the Jim Heimann collection unless otherwise noted. Any omissions for copy or credit are unintentional and appropriate credit will be given in future editions if such copyright holders contact the publisher.

Text © 2010 Allison Silver

Images courtesy of: Amanresorts: Amanpuri (p. 34). Burton Holmes Historical Archive, www.burtonholmes.org: Burton Holmes (p. 11), Eiffel Tower (p. 12), Panama-Pacific International Exposition (p. 46). Charlie Brown, National Museum of History and Technology, Smithsonian Institution: RMS Mauretania (p. 45). Danubius Hotel Gellért (p. 52). Photograph by Ernest Lenart, courtesy Kathy Kohner: Gidget (p. 23). Georges Méliès: A Trip to the Moon (p. 41). Hard Rock Hotel (p. 427). Mandarin Oriental Hong Kong (p. 310). Nicholas Fasciano: RMS Titanic (p. 12), RMS Lusitania (p. 51). Parco dei Principi Grand Hotel & Spa (p. 29). The Queen Mary (p. 191). © Simon Fieldhouse: Peace Hotel (p. 22). Southwest Airlines (p. 382). Starwood Hotels & Resorts Waikiki: Royal Hawaiian Hotel (p. 15, 80), Moana Hotel (p. 80).

The publisher would like to thank Craig Gaines, Doug Adrianson, Teena Apeles, Nicole Greene, and Mia Chamasmany for their invaluable assistance in getting this book produced.

© 2016 TASCHEN GmbH
Hohenzollernring 53, D–50672 Köln
www.taschen.com

Original edition: © 2010 TASCHEN GmbH

Art direction: Josh Baker, Los Angeles
English-language editor & project management: Nina Wiener, Los Angeles
Design: John Yates, Alameda CA with J. Tyler Flatt, New York
Cover lettering: Michael Doret, Los Angeles
Production: Tina Ciborowius, Cologne
German translation: Helmut Roß, Krenglbach
French translation: Claire Le Breton, Paris
Collaboration: Isabelle Gioffredi, Los Angeles

Printed in Slovakia
ISBN 978-3-8365-5396-4